80 605760
WITHDRAWN

D1485808

A GRAPHEMIC-PHONEMIC STUDY OF A MIDDLE ENGLISH MANUSCRIPT

A GRAPHEMIC-PHONEMIC STUDY OF A MIDDLE ENGLISH MANUSCRIPT

BY

JOHN C. McLAUGHLIN
State University of Iowa

1963
MOUTON & CO . THE HAGUE

Printed in The Netherlands

TABLE OF CONTENTS

Preface 7

I. The Manuscript 11
1.1. Description 11
1.2. Relationship between extant manuscript and the original poems 12
1.3. The dialect 15
1.4. The author 16

II. Graphemic Theory 18
2.1. The nature of alphabetic writing 18
2.2. The graphemic-phonemic parallel 24
2.3. Graphemic terminology 29
2.4. Neutralization 33
2.5. Graphemic description and historical texts . . . 36
2.6. Conclusion 41

III. The Graphemic System 44
3.1. The allographs 44
3.2. The graphemes 48
3.3. Residues 48
3.4. Gemination 49
3.5. Predictable alternation of grapheme sequences with single graphemes 49
3.6. Privileges of occurrence 50
3.7. Neutralization 50

IV. THE PHONOLOGICAL SIGNIFICANCE OF THE GRAPHEMIC SYSTEM; Part I: THE VOCALIC NUCLEI 56
4.0. Introduction 56
4.1. The short vowels 56
4.2. Lengthened vowels 67

V. THE PHONOLOGICAL SIGNIFICANCE OF THE GRAPHEMIC SYSTEM; Part II: THE CONSONANTS 94
5.1. Allographic representation 94
5.2. The phonemic significance of graphemic neutralization 104

VI. THE GRAPHONEMIC SYSTEM 134
6.1. Vocalic system 134
6.2. Consonantal system 137

Appendix A: OE AND MnE PHONEMIC SYSTEMS 141
Appendix B: SAMPLE TRANSCRIPTION 144
Appendix C: INDEX OF CITATIONS FROM THE MANUSCRIPT . 147

List of Works Cited 159

PREFACE

0.1. The purpose. The aim of the present study is to present, first of all, a complete description of the writing system of a Middle English manuscript, the Cotton MS Nero A.x., as that system is an expression of the language in which the manuscript was written, independent of and distinct from the spoken system of that language; and, second, to reconstruct a phonemic system of the language basing critical assumptions on all available evidence from sound patterns, spelling, earlier and later expressions of the dialect in question, known scribal peculiarities of the period and locale, and on those linguistic principles which seem best to define the nature and development of language systems.

It is hoped that the description of the distribution of the graphemes here presented will provide a more accurate and detailed definition of the WRITTEN dialect of this text than has thus far been presented for any Middle English text; and that this information, when correlated with that of similar studies of other texts, will reveal something more than is now known about the provenience of Middle English written dialects.

Traditionally, the study of the spelling of Middle English documents (and perhaps this can be said of the historical documents of other periods and other languages as well) has been concerned almost exclusively with the distribution of those elements in the spelling system which correlate with the distinctive elements in the spoken system. The position taken in the following study is essentially that of Angus McIntosh who remarks that written texts '... also manifest other new distinctions of their own, distinctions which are in no sense a reflection of, or correlated with, anything in the spoken language.'[1] The study of non-correlating features in the writing system may yield information about the text in question as significant as that revealed by correlating features. The fact that there may be non-correlating features is in itself significant.

0.2. Symbols.

[ ]	enclose phones.
/ /	enclose phonemes.

Italics indicate graphs.

< >	enclose graphemes.
{ }	enclose morphemes.
§ §	enclose morphographemes.
/< >/	enclose graphonemes.
V	indicates any graph which represents a vowel.
C	indicates any graph which represents a consonant.
<V>	indicates any grapheme which represents a vowel.
<C>	indicates any grapheme which represents a consonant.
/V/	indicates any vowel phoneme.
/C/	indicates any consonant phoneme.
/<A>/	should be read 'archigraphoneme'.
<A>	should be read 'archigrapheme'.
/A/	should be read 'archiphoneme'.[2]
~	should be read 'is a variant of', 'alternating with', or 'in non-contrastive distribution with'.
-	should be read 'contrasting with,' or 'in contrastive distribution with.'
ø	should be read 'zero'.
:	should be read 'rhymes with' when it occurs between cited forms.

[1] The Analysis of written Middle English, *Transactions of the Philological Society* 1956.33.

[2] Confusion between, say, /V/ as 'any vowel phoneme' and /V/ as 'archiphoneme' is rarely possible; where the possibility exists the symbol is distinguished in context.

0.3. Abbreviations.

EOE	=	Early Old English.
OE	=	Old English.
LOE	=	Late Old English.
EME	=	Early Middle English.
ME	=	Middle English.
LME	=	Late Middle English.
EMnE	=	Early Modern English.
MnE	=	Modern English. (In Chapters IV and V the term 'modern English' should be understood to refer to the modern reflexes of the dialect of the text rather than to 'standard modern English'.)
ON	=	Old Norse.
AN	=	Anglo-Norman.
EOFr.	=	Early Old French.
OFr.	=	Old French.
CFr.	=	Central French.
ONFr.	=	Old Norman French.
MFr.	=	Middle French.

0.4. Acknowledgments. To my adviser, Professor Harold Whitehall, I owe a special debt for his guidance and encouragement of my studies in English language and linguistics. I am particularly grateful to Professor Fred W. Householder, Jr., who read parts of an early draft of the dissertation and pointed out to me several serious errors in linguistic theory. Thanks are due also to Professor Sol Saporta, to Professor Allan Orrick of Rutgers University, and to my colleague at the University of Iowa, John C. McGalliard, for reading parts of the manuscript and giving me valuable suggestions. The faults that remain are entirely my own. I should like to express my thanks to Mr. J. A. Lavin of the University of Iowa (formerly of Wigan, Lancashire) for valuable information on the middle-south speech variety of Lancashire. My debt to my wife, Mary Jane, is more considerable than can be appropriately expressed here.

CHAPTER I

THE MANUSCRIPT

1.1. Description. According to Sir Israel Gollancz, 'The manuscript now known as Cotton Nero A.x. came to Sir Robert Cotton from the library of Henry Savile of Bank, in Yorkshire (1568-1617), a great collector who secured rich spoils from the Northern monasteries and abbeys.'[1] The manuscript was bound by Cotton in a small quarto volume between two other unrelated manuscripts and is numbered F. 37 to F. 126. Ff. 37 and 38 contain four pictures illustrating Pearl, whose text begins on F. 39a. The last poem, Sir Gawain and the Green Knight, ends on F. 124b, and is followed by illustrations to that poem on Ff. 125, 125b, and 126. Between Pearl and Gawain stand the other two poems, Cleanness or Purity (by which name it will be referred to here), and Patience.[2]

[1] Facsimile Reproduction of Cotton Nero A.x., *EETS* 162.7 (London, 1923. repr. 1931). I am indebted to Gollancz for the description of the original MS.

[2] This order cannot be taken to indicate anything about the order of composition. In his edition of Pearl (London, 1891), Gollancz notes that 'The relation that they bear to one another, as regards time of composition, cannot be definitely determined, but judging by parallelism of expression in "Gawain" and "Pearl", it is clear that the poet passed at once from the former to the latter, or vice versa' (xlii). He refers to Gawain as the 'earliest of the four' (xlvii), and suggests that '"Cleanness" and "Patience" were probably written not long after the "Pearl"' (xlix). W. L. Savage appears to err when he remarks that 'Gollancz ... believed that Gawain was the last of the four poems of the Cotton Nero MS to issue from the poet's pen' (*The Gawain poet* 142, fn.4 [Chapel Hill, 1956]). For the order Pearl, Gawain, Purity, and Patience see Miss M.C. Thomas, *Gawain and The Green Knight* 33 (Zürich, 1883), and Friederich Knigge, *Die Sprache des Dichters von Sir Gawain and the Green Knight, der sogenannten Early English Alliterative Poems und De Erkenwalde* 117 (Marburg, 1886); B. Ten Brink, *History of English literature* 348 (New York, 1889), places Gawain before Pearl; C. G. Osgood, ed. *Pearl* xlix (Boston, 1906), thinks the order Purity and Patience, Pearl, Gawain more reasonable on stylistic

On F. 56a and 56b, following the text of Pearl, there are two illustrations relating to Purity, one of Noah's ark, and the other of Daniel expounding the writing on the wall to Belshazzar and his queen. Under the concluding lines of Purity, on F. 32a, there is a half-page picture of Jonah being cast from the ship into the waiting mouth of the whale. On F. 90a, preceding the text of Gawain, two scenes are represented, one presumably showing Gawain, Guinevere, King Arthur, and a bill-man, the other, the Green Knight on horseback, head in hand. The whole manuscript contains seven gatherings of twelve leaves, and an eighth of four leaves; the pictures at the beginning are separate.

The handwriting contains some Anglo-French scribal mannerisms and is generally considered to belong to about the end of the fourteenth century. No titles for the poems are given; those by which they are now known have been assigned by modern editors. Large letters of blue flourished with red together with the illustrations mark off the poems and their main divisions. In Pearl and Gawain, the scribe has used marks to divide stanzas; Purity and Patience are treated as consisting of quatrains, although the marks here are obliterated in many instances. The manuscript appears to be in one hand, but a corrector has been at work in some cases, and tracings by a third hand are visible.

1.2. Relationship between extant manuscript and the original poems. Little can be said with assurance regarding the remove at which the extant manuscript stands from the author or authors of the poems. 'It is difficult to theorize as to the relation of the MS. to the original script of the poet. It may be safely inferred that, after allowing for scribal errors, our MS. is not an exact transcript of the originals. Some years have evidently elapsed, and the scribe clearly belonged to a time and a district in which final *-e*'s sounded by the poet were dropped to the detriment of the metre–inside the line in

---

grounds; R.J. Menner, ed. *Purity* xxxviii (New Haven, 1920), argues for Patience, Purity, Pearl, and Gawain; H. Bateson, ed. *Patience* 5 (Manchester, 1912), proposes Patience, Purity, Gawain, and Pearl; Savage (op. cit. 142) places Gawain last. Arguments for the various orders are generally ingenious and all may be said to offer about the same degree of validity.

Pearl, and notably at the end of the line in the purely alliterative verse' (Gollancz, Facsimile 8).

Whether or not the dropping of final *-e* is detrimental to the meter depends, of course, on one's notion of what that meter should be. Within one tradition of English metrics, the meter of the four poems is perfectly acceptable without the final *-e*'s. Gollancz' view as to the passage of time between composition and the date of the manuscript seems, therefore, without valid foundation. It can be said, however, that scholars have generally been agreed on the following points: first, the extant manuscript does not contain the original version of the poems;[3] second, Gawain was probably composed late in the century, perhaps during the later 70's or early 80's;[4] third, the handwriting of the manuscript

[3] On the basis of a careful classification of scribal errors and a consideration of the proportion of these errors which each poem contains, J.P. Oakden, *Alliterative poetry in Middle English, the dialectal and metrical survey* (Manchester, 1930), argues that at least seven and possibly eight scribes were responsible for the poems as they now appear (263). W.W. Greg, in A Bibliographical paradox, *The Library* 4th ser., 13.188-91 (1933), objects to Oakden's 'elaborate and intrinsically improbable reconstruction.' He argues that no other copies or traces of copies of any of the poems have survived, a fact which may indicate lack of wide diffusion, and that it is unlikely that the works of an unknown author should be copied by several scribes of different localities, or that they should be reassembled by a single scribe in one volume. (But see Oakden's rebuttal, The Scribal errors of the MS. Cotton Nero A.x., *The Library* 4th ser., 14.356-8 [1933-4]). Briefly, Oakden's theory is this: some kinds of errors occur only in Pearl, thus scribe D; some only in Gawain, thus scribe C; some only in Purity, thus scribe B; no errors are unique in Patience, thus scribe A. Some kinds of errors occur only in Gawain and Pearl, thus scribe E; some occur only in Gawain, Pearl, and Purity, scribe F; some are common to all four poems, thus scribe G who copied A's copy of the original Patience and F's copy of copies of Gawain, Pearl, and Purity. This theory of copies, he thinks, is supported by the proportion of errors which occur in each poem: Patience, one error in eighteen lines; Purity, one in eleven lines; Gawain, one in thirteen lines; Pearl, one in five lines. 'This would seem to suggest that Pearl and Sir Gawayn and the Green Knight are relatively in a more corrupt state than the other two poems, and have therefore, passed through more hands' (262). Unless there is a printing error in Oakden's text, it appears to me that his proportions indicate that Pearl and Purity, not Gawain, are the more corrupt. At any rate, it is doubtful that proportions of this kind can tell us anything about the number of different scribes involved in the copying. It is not unreasonable to think that these proportions are the result of nothing more significant than chance.

[4] For example, J.R.R. Tolkien and E.V. Gordon, in their edition of *Sir Gawain and The Green Knight* xxi (Oxford, 1925), point out that 'The criteria,

is not later than the beginning of the fifteenth century. The implication is, then, that at the very most forty years may have elapsed between the date of composition of the last poem in the group and the date of the extant manuscript, and probably much less. One would not expect any very notable changes to take place in the phonology of the original dialect during this space of time.

There is no evidence to suggest that the dialect represented by the manuscript is not substantially that of the poet.[5] In the following

---

such as they are, point to a date in the last quarter of the fourteenth century, the latest possible date being determined by that of the manuscript, c. 1400. The most definite indication that the poem cannot be earlier than the last quarter of the century is in the *sabatounz* which Gawain wore. Even in the last quarter of the century they were not yet in ordinary use.' W. L. Savage, assuming a relationship between the writing of the poem and the English career of the Frenchman, Enguerrand de Coucy, speculates on a more precise date. If, as he thinks, the plight of Gawain parallels that of de Coucy, it does so only after 1377; further, the poem would have been written while popular interest in de Coucy's separation from his wife (Isabella, daughter of Edward III) and child ran high. He thinks, then, that a date between the final months of 1376 and the early months of 1380 is likely. (*Gawain poet* 141.)

[5] So Richard Morris in his edition of Early English alliterative poems, in the West-Midland dialect of the fourteenth century, *EETS* 1.viii (London, 1864): '... in the present poems, the uniformity and consistency of the grammatical forms is so entire, that there is indeed no internal evidence of subsequent transcriptions into any other dialect than that in which they were originally written'; and Menner (*Purity* lix): 'The evidence of the manuscript, to be sure, is not proof that the dialect of the original, as well as that of the scribe, was West Midland, but there is every likelihood that they were not very different. . . . most of the dialectal characteristics of the manuscript are undoubtedly those of the poet himself.' Oakden notes that all but a few minor dialectal points can be shown to be original on the basis of rhyme and alliteration (82), and that '... there is no indication of any dialectal differences in the four poems ...' (85). The one dialectal point on which there has been any major disagreement is that reflected by the alternate *qu*, *wh*, *w* spellings which occur throughout the text for the reflex of OE /xw/. Oakden, for example, states that 'The place names of the counties below Lancs and Yorks do not show *qu* spellings in local documents, but north of these two counties they are very plentiful. In Lancs *qu* forms were only written down north of the Ribble ...' (28). It is his opinion that the *qu* spellings are scribal. From this it follows that the poem was composed somewhere south of the Ribble-Aire valleys and later copied by a scribe from an area north of the Ribble. Savage, however, sees no reason why it could not have been the other way round; it may have been that the *qu* spellings were original and that the poems travelled south into a *wh* area. (*Gawain poet* 131.) Harold Whitehall, A Note on a North-West Midland Spelling, *PQ* 9.1-6 (January, 1930), has produced evidence to show that in

study it is so considered, although whether it is or not is largely irrelevant to our purpose.

1.3. The dialect. Almost without exception, scholars have considered the dialect of the poems to be that of the Northwest Midlands.[6] They have not, however, been generally agreed on a more specific provenience. In his study The Treatment of OE. *ȳ̆* in the dialects of the Midland and South Eastern counties in Middle English, *Englische Studien* 47.1-58 (1914), H. C. Wyld localizes the text in north Derbyshire, the Peak district (47), as does M. S. Serjeantson in her essay The Dialect of the West Midlands, *RES* 3.319-31 (July, 1927). Oakden considered the dialect to have been that of Rossendale, south of modern Burnley in Southeast Lan-

---

South Lancashire there existed a spelling convention which regularly used *qu* for *w*, and thus destroys the usefulness of the *qu* spellings as evidence of dialectal provenience.

[6] In supporting his choice of an Augustinian friar, John de Erghome of York, as author of the four poems, C.O.Chapman, Authorship of The Pearl, *PMLA* 47.346-53 (1932), attempts to show on the basis of the extensive Norse vocabulary in the text that the dialect was that of the East Riding of Yorkshire in the Northeast Midlands. His conclusions, either for author or for dialect, have not been generally accepted. The most telling arguments against definite assignment of the poems to the Northwest Midlands are presented by J.R. Hulbert in his article The 'West-Midland' of the Romances, *MP* 19.1-16 (August, 1921). It is his opinion that the language of the poems 'seems to correspond to no one dialect', and that the evidence thus far presented by scholars for a West Midlands provenience has been insufficient. The mixture of Northern and Midland forms to be found in the manuscript points, he thinks, to a border area between the Northern and Midland dialects. He cites the returns of the Norfolk Guilds, dated 1389, which are original uncopied documents, as exhibiting precisely the kind of variety of forms found in the poems. His conclusion is that '(1) There is no good evidence to connect alliterative romances with the West; their language should not be called West Midland; and (2) until new facts are found the only safe statement of the locations of these poems is that they were probably written in some place which possessed a mixed Northern and Midland dialect' (16). Hulbert's objections were answered in the following year by R.J.Menner in Sir Gawayn and the Green Knight and the West Midland, *PMLA* 37.503-26 (1922); Menner demonstrated that the East Midlands could be distinguished by the application of six dialect tests. His suggestions were elaborated upon somewhat later by Serjeantson (1927) and Oakden (1930). That the general dialect area of the manuscript is that of the Northwest Midlands is no longer seriously questioned.

cashire (*Alliterative poetry* 86); but he also suggests (261) that the Gawain poet may have had some connection with John of Gaunt and his castle at Clitheroe, which is situated to the north and west near the Ribble. R. Kaiser emphasizes the 'North' of Northwest Midlands in assigning the poems to the extreme Northeast section of Lancashire, or even Westmoreland or South Cumberland, primarily on the basis of vocabulary.[7] In the Introduction to his edition of Pearl (Oxford, 1953), E. V. Gordon states that '. . . the evidence of the topographical terms, as of the rhymes and vocabulary, places the Pearl group in the southern Pennine region, the area stretching from the southern edge of the Peak district northwest along the Pennine Chain as far as Clitheroe and upper Ribblesdale' (lii). As we have noted above, Professor Savage associates the Gawain poet with Enguerrand de Coucy, Knight of the Garter, who held lands at Wyresdale in Amounderness Hundred, which borders on and is north of the Ribble, and which is in the acceptable dialect area. He speculates, however, that the poem may have been written in a more northerly locality, perhaps within the Coucy manors of Ulverston or Moureholm, Comforth or Whittington. (*Gawain poet* 138.)

In the present study, the writer has thought it reasonable to suppose that the modern dialect areas which include the Peak district of Northwest Derbyshire, Southeast and middle South Lancashire, and the border area of the Ribble constitute the most likely reflexes of the dialect of the manuscript. In addition, the modern dialects of part of North Lancashire, the hill area of extreme West Yorkshire, and that area of West Lancashire which includes the Amounderness Hundred have been examined. These dialect areas are denoted on Alexander J. Ellis' map of the English dialect districts by D21, D22, D23, and D31 below the *hoose* line.[8]

1.4. The Author. Because the four poems in the manuscript show similarities in dialect, vocabulary, style, and phraseology, common

[7] Zur Geographie des mittelenglischen Wortschatzes, *Palaestra* 205.168 (1937).

[8] On Early English pronunciation, *EETS*, Extra S., 56.5 (London, 1889).

authorship has generally been assumed.[9] It may be remarked in passing that the evidence thus far adduced to support this conclusion has not always been convincing. Similarities in dialect, vocabulary, and phraseology prove nothing, and there is at present no adequate stylistic comparison of the four poems. As one might expect, there have been numerous attempts to identify the author, or authors; however, none has yet appeared which might be considered reasonably convincing, and there seems to be every likelihood that his name will never be known.[10] The whole question of authorship is beyond the scope of the present work and will be dealt with no further.

[9] See for example M. Trautmann, *Über Verfasser und Entstehungszeit einiger alliterierender Gedichte des Altenglischen* 25-33 (Halle, 1876); Morris, *Gawain*, title page; Thomas, *Gawayne* 1-12; Knigge, *Die Sprache* 1-14; Osgood, *Pearl* xlix; Oakden, *Alliterative poetry* 253; Tolkien and Gordon, *Gawain* xviii; Menner, *Purity* xix; Bateson, *Patience* 1; Savage, *Gawain poet* 5; et al.

[10] In his edition, *Syr Gawayn and the Grene Knyȝt*, published by the Bannatyne Club (1839), Sir Frederick Madden assigned the four poems to the supposed Scotch poet, Huchown, as did Edwin Guest, *History of English rhythms*, ed. W. W. Skeat, 460, 627 (London, 1882). (See George Neilson, '*Huchown of the Awle Ryale,' The Alliterative poet. A Historical criticism of the fourteenth century poems ascribed to Sir Hew of Eglintoun* [Glasgow, 1902]). Morris, Early English alliterative poems, discredits this theory. Gollancz, *Pearl*, argues for Chaucer's 'philosophical Strode.' Carleton F. Brown, The Author of the Pearl, considered in the light of theological opinions, *PMLA* 19.115-53 (1904), attempts to characterize rather than identify the poet. Brown's notions of the poem and of its author are refuted by W. H. Schofield, Nature and fabric of The Pearl, *PMLA* 19.154-215 (1904), who is in turn refuted by G. G. Coulton, In defence of 'Pearl', *MLR* 2.39-43 (1906). O. Cargill and M. Schlauch, The Pearl and its jeweller, *PMLA* 43.105-23 (1928), identify the 'Pearl' as Margaret Hastings, granddaughter of Edward III, and daughter of John Hastings, Earl of Pembroke, and Margaret, Countess of Pembroke, Edward's daughter. The 'Jeweller' is thought to be a John Donne, Pembroke's clerk and possibly Margaret's guardian. We have noted above (fn. 6) C. O. Chapman's choice of the Yorkshire friar, John de Erghome, and Oakden's suggestion that the author may have been a retainer of John of Gaunt. Savage, searching through parish and family records of the Northwest Midland counties, finds frequent mention of a Lancashire family named Hornby in the Register of John of Gaunt, the Calendars of Close, Patent, and Charter Rolls, and in the Public Record Office on the Duchy of Lancaster. He finds that members of this family were, throughout the fourteenth century, active in the business and government of the county, and that some appear to have been directly connected with the house and manors of Coucy (see fn. 4). Possibly, then, the last name of the Gawain poet was Hornby.

CHAPTER II

GRAPHEMIC THEORY

2.1. The nature of alphabetic writing. 'Writing,' according to Leonard Bloomfield, 'is a device for recording language by means of visible marks. By "recording" we mean that the beholder, if he knows the language of the writer and the system of writing, can repeat the speech which the writer uttered, audibly or internally when he set down the marks.'[1] And again, 'The important thing about writing is precisely this, that the characters represent not features of the practical world ("ideas"), but features of the writers' language...'[2] Bloomfield thus represents an attitude toward writing as dependent upon (and so secondary to) the spoken language which has had considerable support from American linguists during the past twenty-five years.

David Abercrombie's consideration of the fact that the term LETTER has in the past been frequently used in a sense very much like the term SPEECH-SOUND lends support to Bloomfield's view.[3] He points out that the meanings of the ambiguous Latin term LITERA were often distinguished by early English linguists who used the term LETTER in the spoken sense and CHARACTER in the written (although at times the term VOICE represented the spoken, and LETTER, the written). LITERA had three attributes: FIGURA, the letter as written; POTESTAS, the letter as pronounced; and NOMEN, the letter's identification. Abercrombie cites attempts to relate NOMEN

[1] Linguistic aspects of science, *International encyclopedia of unified science* 1.4.6 (Chicago, 1939).

[2] *Language* 285 (New York, 1933).

[3] What is a letter? *Lingua* 2.15–20 (August, 1949).

and POTESTAS and attempts to derive the FIGURA from the POTESTAS as evidence of the close relationship students of language seemed to feel existed between the letter and the sound it represented.

Implicit in Bloomfield's statement that 'writing is a device for recording language' is the notion that writing is not itself language. This notion is made explicit by W. Nelson Francis: 'Writing is not language and language is not writing. We have defined language as "an arbitrary system of articulated sounds", a definition which certainly does not include marks on paper, stone, and metal, or patterns of neon tubes, smoke in the sky, tracks in the snow, or any of the other fanciful or practical media we use for writing.'[4] And again, '... the linguist never forgets that in dealing with written material he is not dealing with language itself but with an arbitrary system of written symbols which more or less accurately represents the arbitrary system of sounds which is the language' (37).

This view of writing has given rise to two attitudes on the part of structural linguists toward the study of writing systems. Many American linguists have shown little interest in writing systems since they do not regard such systems as belonging to the proper domain of linguistic studies.[5] In their view, the term *language* means 'spoken language', and they confine their professional activities to the description of one or another aspect of one or another spoken language. On the other hand, some linguists consider that because writing is a means of recording language, a study of the written records of a language which cannot be directly observed will reveal something about the speech of the language in question which could not be known without such records, however inaccurate that 'something' might be.[6] The study of written records

[4] *The Structure of American English* 36 (New York, 1958).

[5] H. A. Gleason, *An Introduction to descriptive linguistics* 301 (New York, 1955).

[6] C. H. Borgström is more optimistic than this. 'These features (fixed number of letters, spaces between words and letters, and the more or less definite relations between letters and our phonemes) indicate that the invention, teaching, and learning of writing is a procedure of analysis of speech; therefore we must expect that a study of writing can give approximately the same results as a study of speech' (The Technique of linguistic descriptions, *Acta linguistica* 5.1–14 [1945-9]).

has, of course, provided the basis for historical linguistics; and some historical linguists, not wishing to be thought less exact and rigorous than their colleagues who describe spoken languages, have, in recent years, shown concern for the development of a graphemic theory which would parallel to some degree the rigorousness of phonemic and morphemic theory.

The rationale for such a theory is simply stated: the phonology of a language can be described in terms of the distinctive and non-distinctive character of the sounds of which it consists; the GRAPHONOMY[7] of a language can be described in terms of the distinctive and non-distinctive character of the graphs of which it consists. If the function of writing is to record language (speech) such that 'the beholder . . . can repeat the speech which the writer uttered, audibly or internally, when he set down the marks', it follows that the graphemic system, in order to make this possible, must reveal something about the phonemic system of the language it records. This view underlies Robert Hall's statement that 'Phonemic representation is the basic function of alphabetic writing'[8] and Gerald Kelley's remark that 'The purpose of this chapter [a description of graphemic structure] is to discover the system of graphemic contrasts which reflects the phonological structure of the dialect of this text.'[9]

The preceding views on the nature and function of writing are by no means shared by all linguists. According to W. F. Edgerton,

[7] A term proposed by C. F. Hockett in his review of John De Francis, *Nationalism and language reform in China* (Princeton, 1950), *Language* 27.445 (1951). Hockett's remarks concerning the study of writing systems are of interest here: 'Books like De Francis's—and reviews of them—will be easier to write when it is realized that the field of science primarily involved is not linguistics, but the yet unnamed scientific study of writing systems, and when at least some preliminary codification of the latter field has been done. Since the logical label for this sister-branch of anthropology, namely "graphology", is otherwise occupied, let us follow the students of celestial phenomena in a removal to the suffix *-onomy*, and speak of GRAPHONOMY. Like other branches of anthropology, graphonomy has a pure and an applied angle . . . Graphonomy can only progress on the basis of sound linguistics.'

[8] *A Theory of graphemics*, unpubl. paper 3 (Ithaca, 1957).

[9] *Graphemic theory and its application to a Middle English text: Sir Gawain and the Green Knight*, unpubl. diss. 21 (University of Wisconsin, 1956).

'... the received view, which restricts the function of writing to the recording and transmission of language, is erroneous ... Writing consists in the conventional use of visible symbols for the recording or transmission of ideas, or of ideas and sounds (as in most poetry and much prose), or of sounds unaccompanied by ideas (as in a phonetic recording of uncomprehended speech, and perhaps in some nonsense writing). The symbols used to record or transmit ideas may be either ideographic, suggesting the ideas directly, or phonetic, suggesting the ideas indirectly through the medium of speech sounds.'[10]

H. J. Uldall, taking his cue from Saussure's distinction between language as form, 'la langue', and speech as substance, 'la parole', suggests that neither speech nor writing is in itself 'language', but each is merely the substance in which language is manifested. '... it is only through the concept of a difference between form and substance that we can explain the possibility of speech and writing existing at the same time as expressions of one and the same language. If either of these two substances, the stream of air or the stream of ink, were an integral part of the language itself, it would not be possible to go from one to the other without changing the language.'[11] He notes the fact that 'something' remains constant when one substitutes or exchanges allophones, and this 'something' does not, apparently, lie either in meaning or in phonic substance. Since ink can be substituted for air without any consequent change in the language, Uldall suggests that '... the something, that which is common to sounds and letters alike, is a form—a form which is independent of the particular substance in which it is manifested, and which is defined only by its functions to other forms of the same order. The form ... will remain the same even if we change the substance, as long as we do not interfere with its functions' (12). He makes the further point that there is no question of the primacy of one manifestation of language over another; speech and writing are simply coexistent, 'mutually incongruent' systems which can

[10] Ideograms in English writing, *Language* 17.149 (1941).

[11] Speech and writing, *Acta linguistica* 4.11 (1944).

express the same language. This is possible because the orthographic units and the units of pronunciation are functions of the same units of context. So long as the units of context are kept constant, the language will be the same regardless of the system used to make up the corresponding units of expression (15).

This is not the place to argue the validity of the form-substance, content-expression dichotomies. Certainly, Uldall's article raises at least as many questions about the nature of speech and writing as it attempts to answer. The point is, however, that it makes a cogent case for writing as a system, independent of the speech system, of language expression.

Josef Vachek approaches the idea of writing as an independent expression of language from a psychological rather than a philosophical point of view. 'The function of the spoken utterance is to respond to the given stimulus (which, as a rule, is urgent) in a dynamic way, i.e. quickly, readily, and with equal attention to both the intellectual and the emotional factors of the situation that gave rise to the stimulus. On the other hand, the function of the written utterance is to respond to the given stimulus (which, as a rule, is not urgent) in a static way ... The response should be permanent (i.e. preservable), affording full comprehension as well as clear survey of the situation concerned, and stressing the intellectual factors of the situation.'[12] Vachek suggests an analogy between phonemic systems and graphemic systems. He defines the grapheme as 'a member of a complex "graphemic" opposition'; and he takes 'graphemic opposition' as the exact counterpart of phonemic opposition in spoken language: '... it denotes such an opposition of graphic facts as is capable of differentiating meanings in the given language' (88). Writing is not, he thinks, the inferior 'pseudo transcription' which many linguists have considered it to be: '... whereas a transcribed text is to be regarded as a sign of the second order (i.e. the sign of a sign of the outside world), the text recorded in writing is to be taken, at least in advanced cultural communities,

[12] Some remarks on writing and phonetic transcription, *Acta linguistica* 5.87 (1945-9).

as a sign of the first order (i.e. the sign of an outside world)' (89).

If it is true that writing and speaking are first order signs, it is clear that they must be independent systems which can be independently described. If the criterion for identifying graphemes is to be the capability of differentiating meanings in a given language, and if writing, as a first order sign, is something more than transcription, it must also be clear that graphemic oppositions will in no necessary way reflect the phonological structure of a given language. The words *hair-hare* are presumably distinguished by the grapheme sequences <ai> and <a e>; obviously, this opposition tells us nothing about the phonemic oppositions in the phonology.

There are, then, at least two quite contradictory views concerning the nature and function of writing. The first suggests that writing is not itself language, but is simply a device for transcribing speech, a function which it performs with varying degrees of efficiency. Whatever system is manifested in writing is in some way or other dependent upon the phonological system which it records, so that given only the writing system one can infer something significant about the nature of the phonological system. Opposed to this opinion is the notion that writing, like speech, is an independent manifestation of language; although its units may, like a transcription, at times represent phonological units, it is not their primary function to do so. As an independent 'substance' it deserves independent investigation by linguists, and such investigations will reveal something about the 'form' of a given language as significant as that revealed by investigations of the substance of speech.[13]

[13] In this connection it is informative to note Dwight L. Bolinger's case for visual morphemes, Visual morphemes, *Language* 22.333-40 (1946). Such units of language, he thinks, have not been adequately recognized because of the arguments over the primacy of the spoken versus the written language. He quotes behaviorist psychology to make the point that all thought is not necessarily laryngeal. Since tactile morphemes obviously exist for the deaf and dumb without relation to the vocal-auditory field, there is no valid reason for objecting to the concept of visual morphemes. His own experiments reveal a close indentification of distinctive spelling with distinctive meaning; concerning homonyms, for instance, his tests show that the more unlike their spellings are, the less likely are two homonyms to be identified as such.

2.2. The graphemic-phonemic parallel. The question now arises, in terms of which view of the nature and function of writing, if either, and to what extent, if any, can a theory of graphemics validly be said to parallel a theory of phonemics? Answers to the question may depend upon the way in which the term 'GRAPHEME' is defined.

According to Robert P. Stockwell, 'A grapheme is a class of written symbols in a given set of manuscripts, such that (1) all members of the class are in complementary distribution or free variation, and (2) the class belongs to a set of classes which are mutually contrasting.'[14] Now, what are the criteria for identifying such a class? How does one know when an allograph is in non-contrastive distribution with another allograph and so a member of the same grapheme? And on what basis does one decide that a set of classes are mutually contrasting? Stockwell's subsequent analysis makes it clear that the allographs of a given grapheme are allographs by virtue of the fact that they represent allophones of the same phoneme. Gleason states the criteria somewhat more directly: Greek ς and σ are to be considered allographs of the same grapheme because they are in complementary distribution and 'have a similar reference to the phonology of spoken Greek' (*Descriptive linguistics* 302). As a matter of fact, the criterion of complementary distribution plays almost no part in the graphemic studies of Stockwell and Kelley, and may as well be omitted. It is neither necessary nor sufficient. The condition that allographs of the same grapheme must represent allophones of the same phoneme is both necessary and sufficient, and no other is needed.

C. E. Bazell has pointed out that the preceding definition of the grapheme in no way parallels that of the phoneme. Whereas both the idea of similarity and of complementary distribution are necessary to the identification of phonemes, neither plays any part in the identification of graphemes as these are conceived by Hall, Stockwell, Kelley, Gleason, Francis, and others who emphasize the grapheme-phoneme correlation. Bazell thinks their use of the term

[14] *Chaucerian graphemics and phonemics: a study in historical methodology*, unpubl. diss. 14-5 (University of Virginia, 1952).

allograph more nearly parallels the term allomorph. The parallel would be exact '... if (1) the identification of allomorphs is held to be a semantic rather than a purely distributional procedure, and (2) phonemics is regarded as the "semantics" of graphemics.'[15]

Of those who consider writing an independent system, R. A. Crossland and Ernst Pulgram present the most detailed consideration of the parallel between phonemics and graphemics. Crossland states his attitude toward writing in this way:

> A script may be defined as a system of visual symbols whose purpose is to convey the thought of one individual or group to another. Writing is often treated as a means of representing a spoken utterance or utterances by visual symbols, but this is not its primary purpose, except where phonetic or phonemic transcription in linguistic work is concerned. Representation of actual, contemplated or imagined utterance is a particular mechanism for conveying meaning by graphic signals, one whose convenience lies in the small number of signs required. The adaptation of a particular form of it, alphabetic writing, in Western Europe, has led to its being highly regarded as the normal and natural mechanism, and some of those who have discussed the analysis of systems of writing have tended to write as if they were all more or less satisfactory systems of phonemic transcription of utterances. This attitude leads to and supports the view that the study of written documents should always be subsidiary to the study of spoken idioms, or as an extreme to the idea thac "texts" are not "language".[16]

He points out that graphic linguistics needs a set of terms parallel to SOUND or PHONE, SOUND CLASS or ALLOPHONE, and SOUND CLASS 'differentiated functionally from others', or PHONEME. He suggests GRAPH or SIGN as a term for 'a sign, modification of a sign or feature of arrangement in a particular segment of a particular document'; GRAPH-CLASS or SIGN-CLASS to designate 'a group of similar signs, modifications or features classed together, provisionally or permanently, in graphic analysis'; and GRAPHEME as a term for 'any such group which appears to contrast significantly with another or with zero' (15). *a*, then, is a graph; all such *a*'s a graph-class. *a*

[15] The Grapheme, *Litera* 3.43 (1956).

[16] Graphic linguistics and its terminology, *Proceedings of the University of Durham Philosophical Society* ser. B, 1.13 (1957).

and *a* belong to different graph-classes, but are not graphemically distinct; *A* is another graph and all similar *A*'s a graph-class graphemically distinct from a and *a* (e.g. *Archer* as a proper noun as distinct from archer or *archer* as a common noun).

The important difference between this notion of graphemics and the preceding is simply that the identification of the units of structure does not depend upon the sign behavior of those units (even though they may, and do, function as signs). The appeal of SAME-DIFFERENT can be made directly to written pairs of words without invoking phonemic structure at all. Whereas for Crossland the graph-class *A* is graphemically distinct from the non-distinctive graph-classes a and *a*, because it distinguishes the minimal written pairs *Archer* vs. archer or *archer*, for Stockwell, all three graph classes would be allographs of the same grapheme since they all have the same phonemic referent, whatever it may be. In this respect, Crossland's graphemics may be said to parallel more closely phonemics than does Stockwell's.[17]

In a series of correlative statements about the nature of graphemes and phonemes, Ernst Pulgram defines graphemes as 'the smallest distinctive visual units of an alphabet', a graph as the '*hic et nunc* written realization of a grapheme', and allographs as 'all graphs identifiable as members of one grapheme.' The graphic shape of an allograph is 'dependent upon its producer and on its graphic surroundings.'[18] Pulgram differs from Crossland in that he has no category similar to Crossland's non-distinctive graph-class. This omission may lead to some difficulty. Differences in the shape of allographs will be of two types: differences between graphs whose shapes are similar, and differences between those whose shapes are not. In other words there are two types of allographs. When Pulgram says that the graphic shape of an allograph depends on its

[17] One should note that although the criterion of similarity is applied by Crossland in establishing a graph-class, it is not a condition for establishing non-contrasting graph-classes, or allographs of the same grapheme; the two lower-case *a*'s are scarcely similar in shape. Nor does he make any use of complementary distribution. The parallel to phonemics, then, can hardly be considered close.

[18] Phoneme and grapheme: a parallel, *Word* 7.15-6 (1951).

producer and on its graphic surroundings one does not quite know whether he means that the differences between a and ɑ or the differences between a and *a* depend upon producer and/or environment, or both. It seems doubtful that the differences between a and *a* should depend upon environment.[19]

At this point, two matters should be clear. First, an alphabetic writing system is not necessarily just a method of phonemic transcription, and if it is not just such a method, its structure may be usefully investigated quite apart from any reference to the phonemic system of the language it expresses. Second, although the primary function of an alphabetic writing system may not be to represent phonemes, it is difficult to refute Abercrombie's point that the term LETTER has been traditionally associated with vocal sound. It is by no means a foregone conclusion that a native speaker and writer of English when asked to state the difference between *pate* and *Pete* will reply that the first refers to the top of the head and that the second is a proper name. It is just as likely that he will reply that the first is pronounced /peyt/, the second /piyt/; or, perhaps even more likely, he will ask, 'Do you mean what's the difference in sound or what's the difference in meaning?' The individual letters of the alphabet exhibit sign behavior; this being the case, no theory of graphemics can possibly parallel a theory of phonemics since phones are not signs. We may ask now whether or not it makes any difference that the notion of grapheme should be exactly, partially, or not at all parallel to the notion of phoneme. Apparently it does not, since the grapheme is another and a different thing from the phoneme. Descriptive statements about the nature and function of one kind of phenomenon are under no compulsion to parallel those about another kind of phenomenon.

The present study proceeds from the point of view that a complete investigation of a given 'living' language may involve three quite different operations. It will necessarily involve the analysis and description of the spoken system; if the language also has a

[19] Note that this situation is not paralleled in phonemics. There is phonetic similarity both between various manifestations of initial [p^{c}] and between various manifestations of final [p^{-}], and between [p^{c}] and [p^{-}].

writing system, this will be analyzed and described. To the extent that the linguist does not approach either manifestation of the language with a preconceived notion of what its structure is or ought to be, the method of investigation may be termed DESCRIPTIVE. Once these two systems have been described, the analyst may wish to investigate and describe the relationship between them. The study of such relationship is clearly, as McIntosh has pointed out, comparative and not descriptive. There should be no real question, it seems to me, of one kind of expression revealing something significant about the other. The analysis of the structures of the two systems will reveal something significant about the structure of the language of which each is an expression, and will enable the investigator to describe the FIT or relationship between the two. Any statement to the effect that a system of graphemic contrasts in a written text reflects the phonological structure of the language in which the text is written can only be meaningful if it is assumed that the phonological structure and the relationship between grapheme and phoneme have already been determined. No general theory of relationships between written and spoken expressions of a language is possible.

Since the term GRAPHEME has been defined in different ways by different linguists, it is not surprising that the term GRAPHEMIC THEORY should be equally ambiguous. For those who consider writing systems to be independent structures, graphemic theory pertains to the identification and description of distinctive graphic entities apart from any reference to a spoken system. For those who consider writing systems to be dependent upon spoken systems, it pertains to the relationship between these systems, since it is in terms of that relationship that distinctive graphic entities are identified. In this study the term will be used to denote BOTH the identification of graphemes as distinctive entities in an independent structure AND the description of the relationship which holds between the graphemes and the phonemes. It should be understood that these are separate operations and that the second cannot be performed until both the graphemic and the phonemic systems have been described.

2.3. Graphemic terminology. The term GRAPH will be used for a written character, modification of a character, or feature of arrangement in a particular segment of a particular document; the term ALLOGRAPH will be used for a group of similar characters, modifications, or features classed together, provisionally or permanently, in graphemic analysis.[20] The occurrence of a member of an allograph will be referred to as an INSTANCE OF AN ALLOGRAPH; a set of allographs which are in non-contrastive distribution will be called an ALLOGRAPHIC SET, regardless of their graphic similarity or lack of it; an allograph or allographic set which contrasts significantly with all other allographs or allographic sets or with zero will be called a GRAPHEME. By SIGNIFICANT CONTRAST is meant the fact that when one allograph or allographic set is substituted for another in a meaningful sequence of allographs a change in the meaning of the sequence occurs.

Thus in the text to be discussed, *s* is a graph; all such *s*'s are members of the same graph-class or allograph, and each occurrence of an *s* is an instance of the allograph *s*. *ſ* is another graph belonging to another allograph; each occurrence of *ſ* is an instance of the allograph *ſ*. The allographs *s* and *ſ* are in complementary distribution: *s* occurs only at the ends of words, *ſ* occurs elsewhere (e.g. *blys*, but *blyſful*). *s* and *ſ* therefore constitute an allographic set. Since as an allographic set they contrast significantly with all other allographs or allographic sets and with zero, *s* and *ſ* constitute a grapheme <s>.

Graphemes occur either singly or in combination with other graphemes to represent meaningful units in a written text. A meaningful group of graphs which cannot be subdivided into smaller meaningful units will be called a MORPHOGRAPH. A class of morphographs which are graphemically and semantically identical will be called an ALLOMORPHOGRAPH. A class of allomorphographs which are semantically similar and which are in non-contrastive distribution will be called a MORPHOGRAPHEME. Thus

[20] With slight modifications this wording has been borrowed from Crossland.

<-eʒ> is a noun plural morphograph; all instances of *-eʒ* constitute an allomorphograph; the morphographs *-eʒ*, *-es*, *-us*, *-ʒ*, *-s*, *-er*, *-ys*, *-ø* are allomorphographs of the same plural morphographeme. Any morphographeme bounded by space will be called a WORD.

It is frequently the case that in an alphabetic writing system NON-ALPHABETIC GRAPHS will occur in conjunction with ALPHABETIC GRAPHS. These tend to be of four main types: (1) PUNCTUATION GRAPHS frequently serve to indicate grammatical structure and to distinguish between morphographemes which have an identical alphabetic structure, as in *cats* vs. *cat's;* (2) GRAPHIC COMPONENTS occur in conjunction with other graphs, e.g. accent marks, cedillas, subscript hooks, dots, etc.; (3) TACHYGRAPHS occur only with an alphabetic graph, frequently joined to it, and are signs of one or more alphabetic graphs or sequences of alphabetic graphs, or of a morphograph; (4) WORD SIGNS are non-alphabetic graphs bounded by space.

Word signs apparently represent words rather than sequences of graphemes. A case in point is the non-alphabetic graph &. According to Gleason, 'The reference is typically to the morpheme {and}; not, it is important to note, a sequence of phonemes /ænd/' (*Descriptive linguistics* 304). He argues first that & may be read /ænd/, /ən/, /ɨŋ/, or as any of the other numerous allomorphs of {and}, but in no other way; and second, that 'if & represented a sequence of phonemes, then spellings such as **s&* for *sand*, **h&* for *hand* and **&rew* for *Andrew* would be possible. But no such spellings occur.'[21] It seems as reasonable to suppose that the sign & refers to the word *and* as that it refers to the morpheme {and}. Such signs are typically non-alphabetic substitutes for words, not morphemes. The fact that such hypothetical spellings as Gleason suggests do not occur is as easily explained by considering & a sign of *and*, not <and>, as by considering it a sign of {and}, not /ænd/.

Since one of the functions of an alphabetic writing system is to

[21] As a matter of fact, such spellings did occur in 16th and 17th century manuscripts. (See Samuel H. Tannenbaum, *The Handwriting of the Renaissance* 133 [New York, 1930]).

represent a segment of the spoken system, it is appropriate to consider the nature of the relationship which may exist between the spoken and written manifestations of a language. We repeat here that the nature of such a study is comparative; the structure of both systems must be known or at least, as in the case of those languages whose speech cannot be directly observed, guessed at.

The relationships which exist between the spoken and written systems of various languages appear to demonstrate no observable uniformity from one language to another; it is impossible, therefore, to develop a useful theory of FIT relationship. It is difficult to accept Kelley's assumption that '... the alphabet establishes the lower limit of phonemic distinctions in the language it records. There may be more phonemes than the alphabet accounts for, but there may not be less.'[22] These statements seem strange coming, as they do, immediately after the remark that an alphabet may record

[22] *Graphemic theory* 4. Kelley's statements here closely parallel Stockwell's: 'In a free spelling system (i.e. one not completely bound by scribal or typographical convention), by and large, phonemic distinctions and some subphonemic distinctions are maintained' (*Chaucerian graphemics* 6). Apparently, over-differentiation on the graphemic level is the product of a highly conventionalized system which has retained graphemic distinctions long after the phonemes once represented have fallen together. In a completely free spelling system this situation would not arise, but a completely free spelling system is a contradiction. A spelling system, in order to be a system at all, must be either completely or partially bound by some type of scribal or typographical convention. What kind of graphemic-phonemic correspondences exist in a completely bound system will depend upon the nature of the convention. If this should happen to be graphemic-phonemic correspondence, the relationship between the two will be one to one. If it happens to be something else, we may discover more graphemes than phonemes or more phonemes than graphemes. Presumably, a spelling system which is not completely bound by some convention or other, which is, therefore, 'free', is recognized as such because the writer is not compelled to use one and only one sequence of graphs in spelling a given linguistic item. I fail to see what possible use can be made of Stockwell's postulation. Certainly he does not mean to imply that a completely bound system does not maintain phonemic distinctions, since this would depend upon what the convention happened to be. Again, all spelling systems which are not completely bound exhibit varying degrees of freedom, and it is difficult to know to what extent a given system is free until one has identified the phonemic system. At some stages of its conventionalization a spelling system may permit allophonic representation; at other stages it may not. One cannot know *a priori* what stage in its development a system has reached.

allophonic distinctions. If the alphabet of a particular writing system records allophones, presumably the number of phonemes in the language will be less than the alphabet accounts for. In other words, it is no more likely that there be more phonemes than graphemes than that there be more graphemes than phonemes. One grapheme may represent one or more phonemes, e.g. ME <Þ> represents /θ/ and /ð/; several graphemes or combinations of graphemes may represent only one phoneme, e.g. MnE <e>, <ee>, <ie>, <ei>, <ea>, <i e>, <e e> may represent /iy/; some graphemes may represent non-distinctive variations in the phonology, e.g. in some cases of untutored writing; and some graphemes may represent sequences of phonemes, e.g. MnE <x> and Gk. <ψ>. At the same time, it should be kept in mind that the same writing system is often used by speakers of different dialects; as a result, a grapheme may have different referents in different dialects.

When one comes to define the relationship between the graphemes and phonemes of a given language, two additional terms are necessary: one for a class of signs each member of which represents the same phoneme, and one for each member of such a class. In MnE, for instance, the allograph *A* may contrast with the allographic set a and *a*. <A> and <a> are, then, distinct graphemes; however, the three graphs a, *a*, and *A* constitute a class of signs each one of which represents the same phoneme. Stockwell, Kelley, Hall, and others would call these three allographs of the same grapheme, but since in this study these terms have been preempted for a different level of analysis, we will say that on the level of the FIT a, *a*, and *A* are ALLOGRAPHONES of the same GRAPHONEME.[23]

On the graphonemic level it may happen that a sequence of graphemes will represent a single phoneme. According to Hall, 'A grapheme may be single (i.e., not further divisible into significant units), like the letters *a b c* etc., or compound, like the *ai* in French *faire*

[23] One hesitates to multiply terminology. If, however, he hopes to maintain a distinction between a writing system as an independent mode of language expression and as a system of signs representing segments in the spoken system, some such terms seem unavoidable.

or the *th*'s in English *thither*' (*A Theory of graphemics* 1). In a note, he further defines the term compound: 'We term *ai* in French *faire* or *th* in English *thither*, compound graphemes because they function as units in representing single phonemes, but are further divisible into units (*a, i, t, h*) which are significant within their respective graphemic systems' (9, n. 3). The difficulty with this notion lies in the fact that the same sequence of graphemes may represent in one context a single phoneme and in another context a sequence of phonemes, and when it represents one and when the other cannot be predicted. So, for example, one may identify the compound grapheme <ea> representing /iy/ in *beat, seat, feat, meat,* and *creature;* however, in *creator* the sequence *ea* represents not the phoneme /iy/, but the sequence of phonemes /iy/ (or /i/) plus /ey/. *ie* represents /iy/ in *belief, grief, relief, achieve, diesel, chief,* but /ay/ plus /e/, /ə/, or /ɨ/ in *diet.*

On the graphemic level, as we have defined it, the concept of a compound grapheme is of no particular value. However, on the graphonemic level, the level of sound representation (Hall's graphemic level), the idea is useful. In the present analysis, therefore, all sequences of simplex graphonemes which function IN ALL OF THEIR OCCURRENCES as symbols of single phonemes, within morphographeme boundaries, will be called COMPLEX GRAPHONEMES. Sequences of simplex graphonemes which sometimes represent single phonemes and sometimes sequences of phonemes will be listed as residues and referred to as HETEROGRAPHIC SEQUENCES.

2.4. Neutralization. It is sometimes the case in written texts that a graphemic or graphonemic contrast will either be suppressed or will be irrelevant in certain contexts. The occurrence of such phenomena will be termed NEUTRALIZATION.[24] On the graphemic

[24] Perhaps one of the best summaries of the linguistic position on neutralization is given by C. F. Hockett in his *A Manual of phonology*, Indiana University Publications in Anthropology and Linguistics, Memoir 11, for *IJAL* 21.4.164 (October, 1955): 'The American position has been that in English, for example, the stop after /s/ in *spill, still, skill* must be "the same" phonemically either as those of *pill, till, kill*, or as those of *bill, dill, gill*. On this assumption,

level a suppression of graphemic contrast occurs when a tachygraph is a sign of more than one alphabetic graph. The medieval TILDE, for example, is used over a vowel grapheme in some documents as a sign for an *m* or *n* before a consonant grapheme: *cāpo* for *campo*, *cāto* for *canto*.[25] Such a tachygraph will be called a NON-ALPHABETIC ARCHIGRAPHEME. In the manuscript under study here, the graphemic contrast between <a> and <o> is irrelevant before <m> or <n>), as in *man* ~ *mon*. (We may note here that this is both a graphemic and a graphonemic neutralization, reflecting a genuine phonemic neutralization of /a/ and /o/). This type of graphemic neutralization may be said to be mechanically regulated and is, therefore, predictable. We will say that in this environment the archigrapheme <A> occurs, and will write the form graphemically <mAn>. On the other hand, the neutralization of <u> and <i> represented by the alternates *gult* ~ *gylt* is NOT, either on the graphemic or graphonemic level, mechanically regulated. The

---

we showed [by recourse to pattern congruity] that the identification with the stops of *pill, till, kill* is neater. One result is that /b d g/ are somewhat defective phonemes: they occur for the most part in positions paralleling those of /p t k/, but do not occur in initial clusters after a spirant.

'The Praguian tradition affords greater flexibility in the treatment of such problems. In Prague terms, a pair of phonemes, say English /p/ and /b/, which differ in some one constituent feature but are otherwise identical and composed of features not all of which occur in any other phoneme, constitute an archiphoneme. In certain positions both phonemes of an archiphoneme occur, in contrast. In positions where the contrast is irrelevant, one does not say that what occurs is either one phoneme or the other; rather, one says that it represents the archiphoneme, the contrast in that position being neutralized.' We should note that neutralization occurs in situations of 'multiple complementation'; that is, the stops after /s/ are in complementary distribution with both /p b/ /t d/ /k g/. There is nothing parallel to this in graphemics. For further discussion of the concept of neutralization see, for instance, A. Martinet, Neutralisation et archiphonème, *TCLP* 6.46-57 (1936); C. E. Bazell, Three conceptions of phonological neutralisation, *For Roman Jakobson*, ed. Morris Halle a.o., 26-30 (The Hague, 1956); Sol Saporta, Morph, morpheme, archimorpheme, *Word* 12.9-14 (1956).

[25] See Hall, *A Theory of graphemics* 2. He points out that this practice led to a confusion in the use of alphabetic graphemes; *canpo* sometimes occurs for *campo* and *camto* for *canto*. Hall uses the term ARCHIGRAPHEME to refer to the resultant neutralization between *m* and *n* rather than to the tilde which is a sign of that neutralization.

variant spellings are the result either of a phonemic split, OE /y/ > LME /i/ or /u/ (in which case the two forms may represent variant pronunciations), or of the retention of an archaic spelling.

In some writing systems an allographone of one graphoneme will, in certain instances, represent the same phoneme as the allographones of a different graphoneme, as <o> in MnE *women* and *body*, or <u> in *full* and *busy*. It would be a violation of general linguistic theory to consider that <o> is an allographone of two different graphonemes, /<o>/ and /<i>/, or that <u> is an allographone of both /<u>/ and /<i>/. The criterion for assigning a given grapheme to a graphoneme can only be the frequency with which that grapheme occurs to represent a given phoneme. Since <o> and <i> generally represent different phonemes, they are assigned to different graphonemes. Where <o> represents /i/ rather than more frequent /a/, as in *women*, we will say that the contrast between /<o>/ = /a/ and /<i>/ = /i/ has been neutralized by the occurrence of <o> for both /a/ and /i/.[25a] Such neutralization is the result of the overlapping of the allographones of different graphonemes and will be called HETEROGRAPHIC NEUTRALIZATION. It is not mechanically regulated, and can only be predicted on historical grounds.

Just as a multi-valued tachygraph may suppress a graphemic contrast, so a multi-valued graphoneme may suppress a phonemic contrast. Such under-differentiation is illustrated by the use of /<Þ>/ for LME /θ/ and /ð/. This kind of graphonemic neutralization often occurs as the result of a phonemic split. After the split of OE /θ/, /<Þ>/ symbolized both /θ/ and /ð/. (The graph *ð*, which had been an allographone of /<Þ>/ in free variation, ceased to be used after the thirteenth century). When the complex allographone <th> came into use in the latter thirteenth or early fourteenth century, it was not as a separate graphoneme but as a free variant with <Þ>; <Þ> and <th> can be regarded, then, as allographones of the same archigraphoneme, /<þ>/.

[25a] One recognizes, of course, that within a given language the frequency with which an allographone represents a given phoneme and indeed the nature of the phonemic representation itself, may change from dialect to dialect.

2.5. Graphemic description and historical texts. One of the most interesting features of an alphabetic writing system is, of course, that as a system of signs it provides the basis for assumptions about the structure of the spoken system when that system is no longer available for direct observation. Obviously, it is only because there are writing systems and written texts that historical linguistics is possible. This fact should not prejudice our previously stated position that the relationship or FIT between the spoken and written systems of a language cannot be known until both of these systems have been described.

A writing system provides the starting point for a set of assumptions about the spoken system which, in one way or another, it represents; however, these assumptions are generally subject to a great variety of tests and subsequent revisions. It is frequently the case that once a beginning has been made, much of the evidence provided by the spelling system must be abandoned in favor of other types of evidence (e.g. one's knowledge of linguistic behavior in general and of the history of the language in question, rhymes, the structure of related languages, etc.). That this should happen is not at all surprising since we do not expect a writing system to be a transcription. Precisely HOW one 'discovers' the phonological structure underlying a historical document is difficult to state in any useful way. Apparently the procedure rests ultimately on a broad linguistic experience, on the ability to make intelligent guesses, on inspirations, and on a number of other factors which elude reduction to scientific methodology.

Once all available evidence relevant to the identification of phonological units has been assembled and the structure of the spoken language described in the most reasonable manner consistent with that evidence, initial assumptions about the relationship between the written and spoken systems can be revised and more precise statements made. It is important to emphasize the fact that the writing system is considered a point of departure only, and that the structure of that system is NOT assumed to represent the structure of the spoken system. Professor McIntosh has, it seems to me, suggested a valuable principle of the study of written documents in stating that '. . . only by understanding the limitations of the correlation [between the two systems] can we, for one thing, make proper use of the available written material as evidence about the spoken language.'[26]

It should be clear from what has been said thus far that a set of postulates which define the assumptions underlying any description of the phonology of a given language based on the written system must be particular rather than universal. Simple observation reveals the fact that the nature of the fit between spoken and written systems will vary markedly from one language to another and from one stage of a given language to another. One cannot, therefore, hope to provide a set of postulates for the analysis of the fit equal in rigor and usefulness to the postulates provided for the analysis of a phenomenon or set of phenomena which exhibit in their occurrence a constant conjunction of definable characteristics. All phonemic systems are, as Bazell points out, of essentially the same KIND of phenomena; fit systems, however, may be of many different kinds. For this reason, it seems that any such attempt as Stockwell's to construct a set of postulates for graphemic, or fit, analysis is doomed to frustration to the extent that the application of this set extends beyond the scope of the text for which it was provided. Stockwell's set appears to be modelled on Bernard Bloch's A Set of postulates for phonemic analysis, *Language* 24.3-46 (1948). The parallel, however, ends with the format. It is true that the majority of his postulates are presumably to be applied only to a ME text; but even this application seems too broad.

An objection has already been raised to one of Stockwell's postulates in fn. 22 (31). It may be appropriate to consider others in order to support the contention that such postulates would serve little purpose in the analysis with which the present discussion is concerned.[27]

[26] The Analysis of written Middle English, *Transactions of the Philological Society* 1956.28.

[27] The postulates here discussed occur in *Chaucerian graphemics* 6-11.

Postulate I. A recurrent spelling entity represents the same linguistic entity each time it recurs unless there is such other evidence as to demonstrate that there are differing forms for which spelling is identical.

This is true, but one cannot escape the feeling that it is also trivial.

Postulate II. Any two forms consistently spelled differently represent two distinct linguistic entities.

Precisely what is meant by 'distinct linguistic entities' is not clear. If the phrase refers to a sequence of phonemes, the statement is clearly not true since different words spelled differently often represent the same sequence of phonemes. If it refers to distinct morphemes, then I am not sure what use can be made of the postulate. *erþe* and *erthe* are two forms which are consistently spelled differently; i.e. *erþe* is consistently spelled *erþe*, and *erthe* is consistently spelled *erthe*. They do not represent, however, different morphemes.

Postulate III. Discussed in fn. 22 (31).

Postulate IV. It is impossible to know what exact phonetic value any alphabetic symbol represented. Phonetic interpretations of OE and ME vowel spellings are based on the following assumptions:

Postulate IV-A. The phonetic value represented by the spellings of SIMPLE vocalic nuclei is reasonably close to the phonetic value assigned the same spellings in most modern European languages.

Postulate IV-B. The phonetic value represented by the spellings of COMPLEX vocalic nuclei bears no necessarily exact one for one relation of the spelling components to the phonemic components of the nucleus.

Definition. A phonemic writing is a statement of structure within the language at the minimal level of sound distinction. It does not indicate exact phonetic quality, and the exact phonetic quality of any or all of the members of a given phoneme in a historical language is impossible to know or to describe, except in terms of approximation.

Postulates IV and IV-A present no problems. Postulate IV-B is implied by our position that an alphabetic writing system is under no obligation to be consistent in its representation of phonemes. The definition is an interesting and perhaps useful statement of a phonemic fact; however, it seems irrelevant in this context since writing systems and not transcription systems are under consideration.

Postulate V. All words which may be spelled with double vowels contain vocalic nuclei which are somehow different from the vocalic nuclei in words which cannot be spelled with double vowels, but spelling evidence alone is inadequate to define this difference.

It is not clear in what sense Stockwell is using the term WORD, whether to denote a written or spoken entity. Whatever it is, it cannot be 'spelled with double vowels'. It is difficult to know what words can or cannot be spelled with double graphs until the phonemic system of a text has been described.

Postulate VI. All end rhymes in Chaucer's verse are perfect sound rhymes, i.e. the phonetic repetition which constitutes the rhyme must be a repetition of identical phonemes.

In poems which exhibit end-rhyme this is a useful assumption to make. It is true, as Stockwell points out, that the history of English rhyme indicates an overwhelming preference on the part of poets for sets of identical phonemes in rhyme position. It is also true, however, that the exigencies of an extended and/or intricate rhyme scheme within a poem, even in an age when rhyming was comparatively easy, may often have compelled something less than identical phonemes in rhyme position.

Postulates VII-XII have to do with the status of final *-e* and the rhythmic conventions of Chaucer's verse and need not be considered here.

Postulate XIII. An analysis of ME which can show the same kind of structure points as are observed in NE is preferable to one which shows a different kind.

Aside from the matter of convenience in describing the history of English phonology, I fail to see why this is so. Such an assumption may lead one to overlook significant points of structure which are NOT of the same kind as those of MnE.

Postulate XIV. In order to provide a working basis for this analysis, the structure points of NE as set forth in *An Outline of English structure* are assumed to be correct.

Since the structure points of MnE as set forth in *An Outline of English structure*, by George L. Trager and Henry Lee Smith (*SIL*, Occasional Papers 3 [Norman, Okla., 1951]) are not accepted by all (perhaps even MOST) linguists, it seems unwise to assume that they are 'correct'.[28] Even though the Smith-Trager structure points should be acceptable for some dialects of MnE, it is not thereby a foregone conclusion that they are acceptable for ALL dialects of MnE.

Postulate XV. For the same reason, the structure points of OE as set forth in Chapter II are assumed to be correct.

It is not within our province to discuss the 'correctness' of Stockwell's OE phonology. It is perhaps sufficient to note here that the evidence for his system in all its particulars has been shown to be

[28] For a variety of views differing from those of Smith and Trager see the following: Einar Haugen and W. F. Twaddell, Facts and phonemics, *Language* 18.228-37 (1942); Morris Swadesh, On the analysis of English syllabics, *Language* 23.137-50 (1947); Kenneth L. Pike, On the phonemic status of English diphthongs, *Language* 23.151-9 (1947); Dwight L. Bolinger, Intonation levels versus configuration, *Word* 7.199-210 (1951); Raven I. McDavid, review of George L. Trager and Henry Lee Smith, *An Outline of English structure*, (*SIL*, Occasional Papers 3 [Norman, 1951]), *JEGP* 52.387-91 (1953); James Sledd, review of the same work, *Language* 31.312-35 (1955); Noam Chomsky, Morris Halle, and Fred Lukoff, On accent and juncture in English, *For Roman Jakobson*, ed. Morris Halle a.o., 65-80 (The Hague, 1956); Hans Kurath, The Binary interpretation of English vowels: a critique, *Language* 33.111-22 (1957); Fred W. Householder, Jr., Accent, juncture, intonation and my grandfather's reader, *Word* 13.234-45 (1957), and review of C. F. Hockett, *A Course in modern linguistics* (New York, 1958), *Language* 35.503-27 (1959); Noam Chomsky, review of C. F. Hockett, *A Manual of phonology*, *IJAL* 21.4 (October, 1955), *IJAL* 23.229, fn. 8 (1957).

somewhat less than adequate, and that his interpretation of the OE phonemes can lay little more claim to correctness than others which have been advanced.[29]

It is the feeling of the present writer that any attempt to establish postulates which will serve as a basis for defining the relationship between the spoken and written systems of a historical text must ultimately lead to a consideration and evaluation of the assumptions which underlie ALL historical linguistics. Although such an evaluation and consideration would undoubtedly be informative and useful, it is beyond the scope of our study.

2.6. Conclusion. It is the position of this study that a graphic linguistics, regarded as the identification and description of the segments of a written text in a systematic and economical way, is only possible AND useful when the writing of the text in question is considered to be an independent expression of a language. It may be, and frequently is, the case that the segments thus identified and described will provide a tentative basis for an investigation of the spoken system of the language in question, but this is not the primary function of graphic analysis. The purpose of such analysis, we think, should be to establish the WRITTEN idiolect of a text which when correlated with similar studies of other written expressions of the same language at approximately the same time will enable the

[29] The theories of Stockwell and his colleague C. W. Barritt regarding the nature of the OE phonemic system have been influenced to a greater or lesser degree by the following: Fernand Mossé, *Manuel de l'anglais du moyen âge des origines au XIVe siècle* (Paris, 1949); K. Brunner, The Old English vowel phonemes, *English studies* 34.247-51 (1953); M. L. Samuels, The Study of Old English phonology, *Transactions of the Philological Society* 1952.15-47 (London, 1953); Marjorie Daunt, Some notes on Old English phonology, *ibid.* 48-54. For objections to their theories, particularly those concerning the OE 'short diphthongs', see Sherman M. Kuhn and Randolph Quirk, Some recent interpretations of Old English digraph spellings, *Language* 29.143-56 (1953), and The Old English digraphs: a reply, *Language* 31.390-401 (1955); C. E. Bazell, review of Stockwell and Barritt, *Some Old English graphemic-phonemic correspondence, SIL*, Occasional Papers 4 (1951), *Litera* 1.75-7 (1954); and The Phonemic interpretation of the Old English diphthongs, *Litera* 3.115-20 (1956); C. F. Hockett, The Stressed syllabics of Old English, *Language* 35.575-97 (1959); and *A Course in modern linguistics*, 375-7 (New York, 1958).

analyst to define the WRITTEN dialect of a set of texts in terms of their COMMON CORE and OVERALL PATTERN.[30]

A written dialect thus defined may or may not be correlated with a particular spoken dialect; it is certainly under no compulsion to be so correlated. The written structure of texts issued from the same medieval scriptorium at approximately the same time may well exhibit a common core of shared features. It is not thereby to be assumed that the scribes who copied the texts all spoke the same dialect, although the possibility that they did may indeed be very good. On the other hand, major differences in the graphic structure of two or more texts which would serve to distinguish them dialectally do not necessarily imply phonologically distinct characteristics, although in fact they may. This conclusion stems in part at least from the fact that although a given letter seems in the majority of cases to have similar phonetic implications in all varieties of a particular writing system, one can cite instances in which it may not. ME *qu*, for example, may represent [hw], [kw], or [w], depending upon the spoken dialect and particular scribal practices. Conversely, different graphs or combinations of graphs may occur in different WRITTEN dialects to represent the same sound, as /š/ represented in some ME texts by *sc*, in others by *sch*, and in others by *ss*.

Differences between written dialects may show themselves in one or more of three ways. First, dialect A may differ from dialect B in its graphic realization of an identical graphemic system. Where *y* and *i* are members of an allographic set, for example, *y* may occur

[30] Again we borrow terms from phonology. According to Hockett, 'Effective communication in the face of divergence of idiolects is due to two factors. One is that the set of idiolects involved share certain features: the whole set of shared features we shall call the *common core* of the set of idiolects.

...What stands outside an individual's sphere of receptive control today may be within it tomorrow; what stands outside his productive idiolect today may be within it tomorrow. In these terms, it makes sense to speak of an overall pattern for any set of idiolects which are in direct or indirect contact with each other and which contain a common core. The overall pattern includes everything that is in the repertory of any one idiolect, productively or receptively. It includes, typically, if not by definition, more than any one idiolect, while any one idiolect includes, typically if not by definition, more than the common core' (*A Manual of phonology* 19, 21).

only in A, *i* only in B; or *i* and *y* may both occur in A, but *i* or *y* only in B, and vice versa. Second, the two texts may show a difference in the distribution and incidence of an identical set of graphemes. This is to say that text A may show the grapheme <e> in such forms as *begynne*, *beseche*, *behynde*, *beholde*, while text B may show only <i>, although both texts, as written idiolects, present contrasts between <i> and <e>.[31] Third, the graphemic system of text A may show differences in the number or kind of its graphemes from that of text B.

The significance of such differences to the study of ME texts is summarized by McIntosh:

> It is important here to stress the fact that there is a great deal to be learnt from a thorough examination of those numerous cases of orthographic variation which have no phonetic implications [e.g. *þ* ~ *th*, *i* ~ *y*, *ȝ* ~ *gh*, *u* ~ *v*] . . . They can be plotted on maps like any other variants, and many of them turn out to be demonstrably regional with a distribution in some cases of quite extraordinary interest . . . The very fact that such things cannot be correlated with anything in the spoken system gives them a special significance and importance.[32]

The value of a graphic linguistics applied in the way that has been suggested on the preceding pages remains hypothetical. To the best of my knowledge those who have written on the need for independent analyses of writing systems have not themselves performed such analyses nor demonstrated in specific terms precisely what can be learned from them. The description of the writing system of the Cotton Nero manuscript which follows does not in itself prove anything. One would wish to have several such descriptions with which to compare it; and perhaps these will eventually be forthcoming. In the meantime, it is felt that the description is of some interest in and for itself and that, beyond this, further justification is unnecessary.

31 The phonetic or phonemic value of <e> and <i> is irrelevant at this level of analysis.

32 The Analysis of written Middle English 35. The point is not that we lack studies of orthographic variations in ME, but that these studies have thus far been concerned almost exclusively with phonetically relevant variations.

CHAPTER III

THE GRAPHEMIC SYSTEM

3.1. The allographs.

3.11. Non-alphabetic allographs: tachygraphs.[1]

~ represents the alphabetic allograph *-e* in the environment *-l/gh(): ſogh~* ~ *ſoghe, hondel~* ~ *hondele*. In Pearl and Purity, ~ occurs only in *-gh();* it occurs in *-l()* once in Patience and twice in Gawain.

The following tachygraphs represent alphabetic, allographic sequences:

ꝰ represents *-us* in the environment *-(): vertuꝰ* ~ *vertuus.*

ꝭ represents *-es* in the environment *-(): þīgꝭ* ~ *þīges.*

ꝯ represents *con-* in the environment *()-: ꝯqueroR* ~ *conqueroR.*[2]

ˇ represents *-ui-* in *-q̆-: aq̆loū* ~ *aquiloun.*

— represents *-ro-* in the environment *p/P-: p̱phete* ~ *prophete.*

The following tachygraphic sets represent alphabetic allographs or allographic sets:

ʾ ~ ʺ represents *-r-* ~ *-ur-* in the environment *-ŏ: gou̓noʾ* ~ *gouernoR* ~ *gouernour, mőnez* ~ *mournez.*

∞ ~ ∞ represents *-re-* in the environment *p̊-: p̊cios* ~ *p̊cios* ~ *precios.*

[1] The manuscript does not show graphic components. The nearest thing to a PUNCTUATION GRAPH appears to be the marks which occur throughout the text in the left hand margin to indicate stanza divisions.

[2] Although the sequences *-us, -es, con-* may occur as bound allomorphographs, the instances of á, á, and **w** are not limited to the representation of such allomorphographs.

The following are non-alphabetic archigraphemes:

Tilde represents a following *m* or *n* in the environment (-)*a*/*A*/*e*/*E*/*i*/*y*/*j*/*I*/*o*/*O*/*u*/*V*/(-): *hē* ~ *hem*, *mȳde* ~ *mynde*, *dūt* ~ *dunt*, *Ī* ~ *In*, etc.[3]

" represents a following -*r*-, -*ra*-, or -*ru*- in the environment (-)*g*/*t*: *g̎ce* ~ *grace*, *t̎e* ~ *true*.

ꝑ represents a following -*er*-, -*re*-, or -*ar*- in the environment (-)*p*-: *ꝑil* ~ *peril*, *ꝑtermynable* ~ *pretermynable*, *deꝑted* ~ *departed*.

< ~ ≀ ~ / ~ ~ represents a following -*er*-, -*re*-, -*ri*- and may occur in all environments but those in which Tilde occurs (see above). It may also occur with *u* when that graph is preceded by one of the graphs in which Tilde occurs: *eu* ~ *euer*, *þ̃* ~ *þer*, *ṕde* ~ *pride*, *pſented* ~ *preſented*.

The following word signs occur:

ꝗ represents the word *quod*.
& represents the word *and*.
ſ represents the word *ſyre*.

The MS. shows these residues:

Am̋ represents *Adam*.
jhn̄ represents *john*.
jhc̄ represents *jeſus*.
jrlm̄ ~ *jhrm̄* ~ *jhrlm* represents *jeruſalem*.
ſc̄tā ſīoꝝ represents *ſancta ſanctorum*.

3.12. Alphabetic allographs. The following superscript allographs occur in abbreviations:

*w*ᵗ represents *wiþ* ~ *with* ~ *wyþ* ~ *wyth*.
*þ*ᵗ represents *þat* ~ *that*.
*þ*ᵘ represents *þou* ~ *þow*.

[3] Instances of tachygraphs with majuscules are rare.

In linear script the majuscules are these:[4] *A*, *B*, *C*, *D*, *Ė*, *ff*,[5] *G*, *H*, *I*, *K*, *L*, *M*, *N*, *O*, *P*, *R*, *S*, *T*, *V*, *W*, *Ʒ*, *Þ*; the minuscules are these: *a*, *b*, *c*, *d*, *e*, *f*, *g*, *h*, *i*, *j*, *k*, *l*, *m*, *n*, *o*, *p*, *q*, *r*, *ʀ*, *ſ*, *s*, *t*, *u*, *v*, *w*, *x*, *y*, *ʒ*, *þ*.

3.13. Alphabetic allographic sets.

3.131. Non-contrastive distribution between majuscules and minuscules. Majuscule and minuscule allographs are distributed in the following ways: (a) only majuscules occur in poem-initial and section-initial position; (b) both majuscules and minuscules occur in stanza-initial and line-initial position, and in proper names; (c) only minuscules occur elsewhere. The following alternations between majuscule and minuscule allographs occur:

A ~ *a* as in *Ande* ~ *ande*.
B ~ *b* as in *Bot* ~ *bot*.
C ~ *c* as in *Cortayſe* ~ *cortayſe*.
D ~ *d* as in *Dubbed* ~ *dubbet*.
E ~ *e* as in *Er* ~ *er*.
ff ~ *f* as in *ffor* ~ *for*.
G ~ *g* as in *Grace* ~ *grace*.
H ~ *h* as in *Hit* ~ *hit*.
I ~ *i* as in *In* ~ *in*.
K ~ *k* as in *Keſten* ~ *keſten*.
L ~ *l* as in *Lorde* ~ *lorde*.
M ~ *m* as in *Maſkelles* ~ *maſkelles*.
N ~ *n* as in *Now* ~ *now*.
O ~ *o* as in *Of* ~ *of*.
P ~ *p* as in *Pacience* ~ *pacience*.
R ~ *r* as in *Ryʒt* ~ *ryʒt*.
S ~ *s* as in *So* ~ *ſo*.

[4] The majuscule allographs in the manuscript vary in size and degree of ornamentation depending upon the position in which they occur. An allograph which stands, for example, at the head of a poem or a major section of a poem will be larger and more decorative than one which stands at the head of a stanza or a line. Such variations are ignored in this study.

[5] There is no majuscule *F*. The doubled minuscule allograph is used by the scribe in environments which would regularly require a majuscule.

T ~ *t* as in *Thys* ~ *thys*.
V ~ *v* as in *Vche* ~ *vche*.
W ~ *w* as in *When* ~ *when*.
Þ ~ *þ* as in *Þe* ~ *þe*.
Ȝ ~ *ȝ* as in *Ȝet* ~ *ȝet*.

3.132. Non-contrastive distribution between minuscules.

r ~ **ʀ**: *r* and *ʀ* are members of the same allographic set; *ʀ* is graphically similar to *R*, and is in complementary distribution with *r*: *ʀ* occurs only after *o*, *r* occurs elsewhere.

s ~ *ſ*. These two allographs may be identified as members of the same allographic set on the basis of such morphographemic changes as *blys* ~ *blyſful*, *choſe* (inf.) – *ches* (pt.), *deuiſe* ~ *deuys;* they are in complementary distribution: *s* occurs only in word-final position, *ſ* occurs elsewhere.

u ~ **v**. These two allographs may be identified as members of the same allographic set partially on the basis of graphic similarity and partially on the basis of non-contrastive distribution: *uyne* ~ *vyne*, *ueſture* ~ *veſture*. With the exception of the three words *uyne*, *ueſture*, and *uoched*, and the regular occurrence in Purity of *v* in *hov*, *nov*, *v* and *u* are in complementary distribution: *v* occurs after space, *u* elsewhere.[6]

i ~ **j** ~ **y**. The allographs *i* and *j* may be identified as members of the same allographic set on the basis of graphic similarity, which is considerably more marked in the handwriting of the manuscript than it is in typescript (*j* is little more than a lengthened *i*), and by the fact that they are in free variation: *in* ~ *jn*, *iugge* ~ *jugge*, *ioyles* ~ *joyles*, *ionas* ~ *jonas*. *i* and *y* are in free variation: *image* ~ *ymage*, *hit* ~ *hyt*, *knitte* ~ *knyt*, *lif* ~ *lyf*, etc.

[6] The practice in modern editions of the poems of printing such forms as *de vaye*, *a venture*, *a vowes* as *devaye*, *aventure*, *avowes* is certainly a reasonable one, but it confuses this distribution.

3.2. The graphemes.

<a> contains the allographic set *a* ~ *A*.
<b> contains the allographic set *b* ~ *B*.
<d> contains the allographic set *d* ~ *D*.
<e> contains the allographic set *e* ~ *E*.
<f> contains the allographic set *f* ~ *ff*.
<g> contains the allographic set *g* ~ *G*.
<h> contains the allographic set *h* ~ *H*.
<i> contains the allographic set *i* ~ *j* ~ *y* ~ *I*.
<k> contains the allographic set *k* ~ *K*.
<l> contains the allographic set *l* ~ *L*.
<m> contains the allographic set *m* ~ *M*.
<n> contains the allographic set *n* ~ *N*.
<o> contains the allographic set *o* ~ *O*.
<p> contains the allographic set *p* ~ *P*.
<r> contains the allographic set *r* ~ ʀ ~ *R*.
<s> contains the allographic set *s* ~ *ſ* ~ *S*.
<t> contains the allographic set *t* ~ *T*.
<v> contains the allographic set *v* ~ *u* ~ *V*.
<w> contains the allographic set *w* ~ *W*.
<x> contains the allograph, *x*.
<ȝ> contains the allographic set *ȝ* ~ *Ȝ*.
<þ> contains the allographic set *þ* ~ *Þ*.

3.3. Residues.

c ~ C. This allographic set is considered to have no graphemic status. In the environments *-()i/e-* and *-()aun-*, the set alternates with the allographs of <s>: *cience* ~ *ſyence*, *mercy* ~ *merſy*, *cheuicaunce* ~ *cheuiſaunce*. (Exception: in the words *ceuer*, *cerue*, and *ſcelt*, *c* alternates with the allographs of <k>). In all other environments but one, the set *c* ~ *C* alternates with allographs of <k>. All instances of *c* ~ *C* may be rewritten with <s> or <k> depending on the environment. Of the three allographs *ſ*, *k*, *c*, only *c* occurs in the environment *(-) ()h-*. It may be said that in this environment *c* substitutes for <s> or <k>, although we cannot specify which. Instances of *ch* will, therefore, be rewritten <Ch>, <C> being considered here an archigrapheme.

q. The allographs of *q* have a unique distribution, occurring only in the environment *(-)()va/e/i/o-*. The variants *venkquyſt* ~ *venkkyſt* suggest that the allographs *q* and *k* are in complementary distribution: *q* occurs in the environment specified above, *k* occurs elsewhere. All instances of *q* may be rewritten with an allograph of <k>: *venkquyſt* <venkkvist>.

3.4. Gemination.

3.41. Sequences of identical allographs. All minuscule allographs but *h*, *j*, *q*, *ȝ*, and *x* may be doubled. The sequences *aa*, *ee*, *ii*, *oo*, *uu*, contrast significantly with *aø*, *eø*, *iø*, *oø*, and *uø* respectively in all environments but *-( ): ſeet - ſet, moon - mon, iiſſe - is, buurne - burnyſt*. All other sequences of identical allographs occur in all but morphographeme-initial position, but contrast in the environment *-( )e* only; elsewhere this contrast is neutralized: *madde - made, robbe - robe, lokkeȝ - lokeȝ, melle - mele, marre - mare, mette - mete*, etc.

3.42. The doubling of allographic sequences. The allographic sequence *ch* may be doubled in all but morphographeme-initial position. <chch> contrasts with <chøø> only in the environment *-( )e: richche - riche.*

3.5. Predictable alternation of grapheme sequences with single graphemes. The following sequences vary freely in all of their occurrences with a single grapheme in the environment specified.

th ~ *þ* in the environments *()-*, *-()-*, *-()*: *Thys* ~ *þys*, *bothe* ~ *boþe*, *ſoth* ~ *ſoþ*. The sequence *th* is never doubled.

gh ~ *ȝ* in the environments *-()-* and *-()*: *wyȝe* ~ *wyghe*, *roȝ* ~ *rogh*, *boRȝe* ~ *buRghe*. *gh* rarely alternates with *ȝ* in *-()t*.

tȝ ~ *s* in the allomorphograph *-s* of the inflectional morphographeme {*-es*} of the following verbs only: *dotȝ* ~ *dos*, *gotȝ* ~ *gos*, *hatȝ* ~ *has*, *matȝ* ~ *mas*, *ſaytȝ* ~ *ſays*, *tatȝ* ~ *tas*, *watȝ* ~ *was*.

3.6. Privileges of occurrence. The chart on p. 51 presents the environments in which each grapheme is privileged to occur in both initial and non-initial positions, within morphographeme boundaries. Reading from left to right, the figure 1 indicates all graphemes which may FOLLOW the grapheme in question when that grapheme is in initial OR non-initial position. The figure 2 indicates all graphemes which may follow only when the grapheme in question is in non-initial position. Thus, in initial OR non-initial position, <b> may be followed by <a>, <e>, <i>, <l>, <o>, <r>, and <v>; it may be followed by <b> only in non-initial position. All graphemes may occur in final position.

3.7. Neutralization.

3.71. Archigraphemes.

3.711. We will say that the archigrapheme <∅> occurs in the following graphemic or morphographemic environments in which the alternation of <ø> with an alphabetic grapheme or graphemes is predictable:

When a sequence of two identical graphemes occurs in word-final or morphographeme-final position, one of the two may alternate with <ø>: *nee* ~ *ne* <ne∅>, *hoo* ~ *ho* <ho∅>, *knott* ~ *knot* <knot∅>, etc.

<b> ~ <ø> in morphographeme-final position after <m>: *klymb* ~ *clym* <klim∅>.

<d> ~ <ø> in morphographeme-final position after <n>: *monkynde* ~ *mankyn* <mankin∅>, *hondeſelle* ~ *hanſelle* <hAn∅-selle>.

<e> ~ <ø> in the environment *-():* *toRE* ~ *toR* <tor∅>, *made* ~ *mad* <mad∅>, *cloſe* ~ *clos* <klos∅>, etc.

<g> ~ <ø> in the environment *-i()n-:* *bretaygne* ~ *bretayn* <bretai∅n∅>.

<h> ~ <ø> in the environment *w()-:* *why* ~ *wy* <w∅i>.

<i> ~ <ø> in the environment *-i()e:* *byye* ~ *bye* <bi∅∅>.

<k> ~ <ø> in the environment *-n()þ-:* *lenkþe* ~ *lenþe* <len∅Þ∅>, *ſtrenkþe* ~ *ſtrenþe* <stren∅Þ∅>.

a	b	d	e	f	g	h	i	k	l	m	n	o	p	r	s	t	v	w	x	ʒ	þ
1	1	1		1	1		1	1	1	1	1		1	1	1	1	1	1	1	1	1
1	2		1				1		1			1		1			1				
1		2	1				1		2		2	1		1				1			
1	1	1	1	1	1		1	1	1	1	1		1	1	1	1	1	1	1	2	1
1		2	1	2			1		1			1		1	2	2	1				2
1			1		2	2	1		1		2	1		1			1				
1			1				1					1					1				
1	2	1	1	1	2		1	1	1	1	1	1	2	1	1	2	1	1		1	1
1			1				1	2	1		1	1		1			1				2
1	2	2	1	2	2		1	2	2	2	2	1	2	2	2	2	1	2		2	2
1	2		1	2			1	2	2	2	2	1	2		2	2	1				
1	2	2	1	2	2		1	2	2	2	2	1	2	2	2	2	1	2			2
	1	1	2	1	1		2	1	1	2	1	1	1	1	1	1	1	1	1	1	1
1			1			1	1		1			1	2	1		2	1				
1	2	2	1	2	2		1	2	2	2	2	1	2	2	2	2	1	2			2
1		2	1	2			1	1	1	1	1	1	1		2	1	1	1			
1			1			1	1	2				1		1	2	2	1	1			
1	2	2	1	2	1		1	2	2	1	1	1	1	1	1	1	1	2	2	2	2
1			1			1	1		1			1		1			1	2			
									2							2					
1			1				1					1				2	1				
1		2	1				1		2	2	2	1		1			1	1			2

<n> ~ <ø> in the environment *-()gn(-): rengne ~ regne* <reØgnØ>.

<p> ~ <ø> in the environment *-m()n(-): ſolempne ~ ſolemne* <solemØnØ>.

<v> ~ <ø> in the environment *-a()n-: graunte ~ grant* <ChaØngØ>.

<ʒ> ~ <ø> in the environment *-i()e: nyʒe ~ nye* <niØØ>, *lyʒe ~ lye* <liØØ>.

<bbe> ~ <ø> in the morphographemic alternation *habbes ~ has* <haØs>.

<Ch> ~ <ø> in the morphographemic alternation *-lych ~ -ly: luflych ~ lufly* <lvfliØ>, *frelich ~ frely* <freliØ>.

<ke> ~ <ø> in the morphographemic alternation in the preterite of *maked ~ made* <maØdØ>, and in the non-preterite plural of *taken ~ tan* <taØn>.

<ve> ~ <ø> in the morphographemic alternation of the non-preterite plural of *hauen ~ han* <haØn>.

3.712. Alphabetic archigraphemes.

<A> represents the neutralization of <a> ~ <o> in the environment *-()n/m(-): man ~ mon* <mAn>, *lambe ~ lombe* <lAmØØ>.

<B> represents the neutralization of <b> ~ <p> in the environment *-m()(e): lombe ~ lomp* <lAmBØ> or <lAmØØ>.

<D> represents the neutralization of <d> ~ <t> in the environments *-l/n/r()(e): bronde ~ bront* <brAnDØ> or <brAnØØ>, *gyld ~ gilt* <gilD>, *loʀde ~ loʀt* <lorD>.

<E> represents the neutralization of <e> ~ <i> in the environments *-()r-, -()ft(-), -()n(-): merþe ~ mirþe* <mErþØ>, *ſwefte ~ ſwifte* <swEft>, *renk ~ rynk* <rEnk>.

<G> represents the neutralization of <g> ~ <k> in the environment *-n()(-): þyng ~ þink* <þinG>.

<Ʒ> represents the neutralization of <ʒ> ~ <w> in the environments *(-)a/o/u()( )* and *-r/l()(-): ſaʒe ~ ſawe* <saƷØ>, *innoʒe ~ innowe* <innoƷØ>, *folʒande ~ folwande* <folƷAnDØ>,

ſoʀʒe ~ *ſoʀwe* <sorƷØ>.[7] In the environment *-e/i()(-)*, <Ʒ> represents the neutralization of <ʒ> ~ <i>: *ſweʒe* ~ *ſwey* <sweƷØ>.

<T> represents the neutralization of <t> ~ <d> in the morphographemic alternation of the preterite morphographeme *-ed* ~ *-et* {*eT*}: *fondet* ~ *founded* <fovndeT>.

<S> represents the neutralization of <s> ~ <ʒ> in the morphographemic alternation of the nominative plural morphographeme *-es* ~ *-eʒ* ~ *-s* ~ *-ʒ* {*-eS*}, and in that of the genitive singular, the present indicative 2d and 3d person singular, the present indicative plural, the imperative singular and plural, and in the derivational adjective suffix *-les* ~ *-leʒ* {*-leS*}.

3.72. Residues: capricious neutralization.[8]

3.721. Between graphemes and <ø>.

<a> ~ <ø> in *beaute* ~ *bewte*.

<e> ~ <ø> in *new* ~ *nw*, *hewe* ~ *hwe*, *endeured* ~ *endured*, *auenture* ~ *aunter*, *boerne* ~ *boʀne*, *feerſly* ~ *ferſly*, *leude* ~ *lude*.

<f> ~ <ø> in *maugref* ~ *maugre*, *iolyf* ~ *ioly*, *haſtyfly* ~ *haſtily*.

<h> ~ <ø> in *houreʒ* ~ *oure*, *habraham* ~ *abraham*, *herne* ~ *erne*, *ſchade* ~ *ſcade*, *throne* ~ *trone*, *theme* ~ *teme*.

<i> ~ <ø> in *meyny* ~ *meny*, *vilanye* ~ *vilaynye*, *reyſoun* ~ *reſoun*, *ſant* ~ *ſaynt*, *gawan* ~ *gawayn*, *niyʒt* ~ *nyʒt*, *fuyt* ~ *fute*, *buyrne* ~ *burne*, *miyry* ~ *miry*, *nieʒ* ~ *neʒ*.

<k> ~ <ø> in *ſclade* ~ *ſlade*, *ſclaʒte* ~ *ſlaʒt*.

<l> ~ <ø> in *clolde* ~ *colde*, *glolde* ~ *golde*.

<o> ~ <ø> in *aboute* ~ *abute*, *mouthe* ~ *muþe*, *bourne* ~ *burne*.

[7] The form *ſaʒ*, alternating with *ſays*~*ſaytʒ*, appears to be a unique exception to this rule. However, since the form *ſaʒ* consists of two morphographemes, a stem *ſaø* and the allomorphograph *-ʒ* of the bound morphographeme {*es*}, it does not constitute such an exception.

[8] By 'capricious neutralization' is meant graphemic overlapping which is not mechanically regulated and is therefore not predictable (see **2.4** above).

<s> ~ <ø> in *diſmayd* ~ *demay*, *woRſchyp* ~ *woRchip*, *ſchere* ~ *chere*, *cheriſch* ~ *cherych*.

<t> ~ <ø> in *ſaynt* ~ *ſayn*, *myʒt* ~ *myʒ*, *broʒt* ~ *broʒ*, *heſt* ~ *hes*.

<þ> ~ <ø> in *ſyþen* ~ *ſyn*.

<v> ~ <ø> in *flour* ~ *floR*, *court* ~ *coRt*, *pouer* ~ *poRe*, *nuye* ~ *nye*, *buurne* ~ *burne*, *leude* ~ *lede*.

<w> ~ <ø> in *flowre* ~ *floR*.

<ʒ> ~ <ø> in *ʒif* ~ *if*.

3.722. Between graphemes.

<a> ~ <e> in *arnde* ~ *ernde*, *warp* ~ *werp*, *caſt* ~ *keſt*, *waſchen* ~ *weſche*, *mayny* ~ *meyny*, *rayſoun* ~ *reyſoun*, *ſchawe* ~ *ſchewe*.

<a> ~ <o> in *fawre* ~ *fowre*, *aryʒt* ~ *oRyʒt*, *quaynt* ~ *quoynt*.

<b> ~ <p> in *cubites* ~ *cupydeʒ*, *babtem* ~ *baptem*.

<d> ~ <þ> in *foRde* ~ *foRþe*, *alder* ~ *alþer*.

<e> ~ <i> in *þeſe* ~ *þiſe*, *begynne* ~ *bygynne*, *geſerne* ~ *giſerne*, *pene* ~ *peny*, *hiʒe* ~ *heʒe*, *merþe* ~ *mirþe*, *gerdeʒ* ~ *gyrdeʒ*.

<e> ~ <o> in *ʒender* ~ *ʒonder*, *diſceuer* ~ *diſcouer*, *cheſe* ~ *choſe*, *wertes* ~ *woRt*.

<e> ~ <v> in *ſted* ~ *ſtud*, *reniſchche* ~ *runiſch*, *erþe* ~ *vrþe*, *lede* ~ *lude*, *meryly* ~ *muryly*, *ſeche* ~ *ſuche*.

<f> ~ <v> in *gafe* ~ *gaue*.

<f> ~ <w> in *þef* ~ *þewes*.

<f> ~ <ʒ> in *þof* ~ *þoʒ*.

<g> ~ <i> in *gentyle* ~ *ientyle*, *ſergaunteʒ* ~ *ſeriauntes*.

<g> ~ <ʒ> in *gate* ~ *ʒate*, *gef* ~ *ʒef*, *agayn* ~ *aʒayn*, *foRgat* ~ *foRʒate*.

<k> ~ <Ch> in *rocheʒ* ~ *rok*, *carle* ~ *choRle*, *woRch* ~ *woRk*.

<k> ~ <ʒ> in *ſtrenkþe* ~ *ſtrenghþe*.

<o> ~ <i> ~ <v> in *goRdel* ~ *girdel* ~ *gurdel*, *kyrtel* ~ *coRtel*, *gyrdeʒ* ~ *goRde* ~ *gurde*.

<o> ~ <v> in *ſonne* ~ *ſunne*, *blober* ~ *bluber*, *boRʒ* ~ *burʒ*, *doRſt* ~ *durſt*, *noye* ~ *nuye*, *bourne* ~ *buurne*, *bloſched* ~ *bluſched*.

<v> ~ <i> in *vche* ~ *iche*, *gult* ~ *gylt*, *buſyly* ~ *byſily*, *dunt* ~ *dynt*, *fuſt* ~ *fyſte*, *ſuſter* ~ *ſiſter*, *burþe* ~ *byrþe*, *bruny* ~ *bryne*, *rubie* ~ *rybe*.

<v> ~ <w> in *a vowes* ~ *a wow*, *deuoyde* ~ *dewoyde*, *vouche* ~ *wouche*, *vyf* ~ *wyf*, *flour* ~ *flowreȝ*, *nuye* ~ *nwy*, *truly* ~ *trwly*.

<ȝ> ~ <s> in *deȝyre* ~ *deſyre*.

<wh> ~ <kv> ~ <w> in *why* ~ *quy* ~ *wy*, *while* ~ *quyle* ~ *wyle*, *whene* ~ *quene*, *when* ~ *quen*.

<gw> ~ <g> ~ <w> in *gwenoRE* ~ *gaynour* ~ *wenoRE*, *gawayn* ~ *wawen*.

<m> ~ <n> in *blaunmer* ~ *blaunner*.

CHAPTER IV

THE PHONOLOGICAL SIGNIFICANCE OF THE GRAPHEMIC SYSTEM

PART I: THE VOCALIC NUCLEI

4.0. Introduction. The purpose of this and the following chapter will be to consider in some detail the value of the graphemic system as evidence for the phonemic system of the manuscript. Such evaluation will necessarily involve a careful weighing of the graphemic evidence against the stylistic evidence presented by the four poems, and against the historical evidence now available. In the process, we will present for the text that phonemic system which seems most consistent with the nature of the evidence adduced.

4.1. The short vowels.

4.11. Allographic representation.

/a/ < OE /æ/, /a/, and /ɑ/ is represented by the allograph *a* of <a>: *rande* < OE /rɑnd/ = /rand/, *laſt* < OE /lætest/ = /last/, *harme* < OE /harm/ = /harm/, MnE /a:m/.[1]

/e/ < OE /e/, /ə/, /e:/, /ə:/ is represented by the allograph *e* of <e>: *rent* < OE /rendɑn/ = /rent/, MnE /rent/; *heuen* < OE /həfon/ = /heven/, MnE /even/; *bleſſe* < OE /ble:tsiɑn/ = /bles/, MnE /bles/, /ble:s/; *frende* < OE /frə:nd/ = /frend/, MnE /frend/.

/i/ < OE /i/, /y/, /i:/, /y:/ (shortened before certain consonant

[1] The OE and MnE phonemic systems used in this study are presented in Appendix A.

clusters) is represented by the allographs *i*, *y*, *I*, *j* of <i>, and by the allograph *u* of <v>: *in* ~ *In* ~ *jn* < OE /inn/ = /in/, MnE /in/; *dyn* < OE /dyne/ = /din/, MnE /din/; *byſily* ~ *buſyly* < OE /bysig/ = biziliy/, MnE /bizili/; *fuſt* < OE /fy:st/ = /fist/, MnE /fist/.

/u/ < OE /u/, /u:/ (shortened before certain consonant clusters) is represented by the allographs *u* and *v* of <v>, and by the allograph *o* of <o>: *ful* < OE /ful/ = /ful/, MnE /ful/; *vp* < OE /up/ = /up/, MnE /up/; *duſt* < OE /du:st/ = /dust/, MnE /dust/; *ſonne* ~ *ſunne* < OE /sunu/ = /sun/, MnE /sun/.

/o/ < OE /o/ and /o:/ (shortened before certain consonant clusters) is represented by the allograph *o* of <o>: *ronk* < OE /ronk/ = /ronk/; *bloſſum* < OE /blo:smɑ/ = /blosum/, MnE /blozum/.

4.12. The phonemic significance of graphemic neutralization. The alternations of <e>, <o>, and <v> with <ø> in the environments *-e()*, *-o()*, *-u()*, and of <i> with <ø> in the environment *-i()e*, reflect the fact that short vowels do not occur in final position. The nuclei represented are either derived from original long vowels or have been lengthened in open syllables: *le* ~ *lee* < OE /lə:/ = /li:/; *fo* ~ *foo* < OE /jefɑ:/ = /fow/; *vertuu* ~ *vertu* < OFr. /vertu/ = /vertuw/; *bye* ~ *byye* < OE /byǰɑn/ = /biy/.

<a> ~ <e>. ME /e/ tended to become /a/ before /r/ during the fourteenth and fifteenth centuries: *arende* ~ *ernde* < OE /æ:rende/, ON /erendi/; *warp* ~ *werp* < OE /wərpɑn/ (perhaps influenced by ON /varpa/). It may be that the alternate spellings represent an attempt to indicate a wide allophonic range for either /a/ or /e/; however, it seems more likely that the occurrences of <e> in this environment represent no more than a traditional scribal retention, and that the phoneme indicated is /a/ as in MnE /arend/.[2]

[2] Cf. Joseph and Elizabeth Mary Wright, *An Elementary Middle English grammar*, 2nd ed. § 129 (Oxford, 1928).

/a/ was frequently raised to /e/ before /s/ and /š/: *caſt* ~ *keſt* < ON /kasta/; *waſchen* ~ *weſche* < OE wasčan/.[3] The fact that the modern dialect areas under consideration (chiefly Ellis' D21, D22, and D31) show similar alternations of /a/ and /e/ in this environment suggests that the graphemic neutralization in this MS. reflects a genuine phonemic neutralization of the contrast between /a/ and /e/. D21, for example, has /eš/ (the name of a tree) and /weš/, D22 has both /as/ and /es/, but only /weš/, D31 has both /waš/ and /weš/, /as/ and /es/.

<a> ~ <o>. The overlapping of the allographs of these two graphemes is generally considered to indicate the West Midland retention of the Anglian rounding of OE /ɑ/ before nasals (see Jordan, § 30; Wright, *EMEG*, § 42). It may be assumed either that /a/ plus nasal had a rounded allophone inconsistently represented by an allograph of <o>, that the spelling variation was by the date of this text simply capricious, i.e. had no phonemic significance, that the phonemic contrast between /a/ and /o/ was neutralized in this environment, or that for some OE forms doublets occurred. It is not easy to choose between these alternatives. Scribal practices in Pearl in both internal and external rhyme indicate that whatever sounds may have been represented by <a> and <o> spellings, these sounds were not distinctive. For example, line 407 has 'my loRde þe lamb loue ay ſuch chere,' while line 413 has, 'bot my loRde þe lombe þur his godhede.' The first half-line of the second is an obvious imitation of the first half-line of the first, and one is justified, I think, in assuming that the sound patterns are identical. Internal rhyme in line 775, 'o mony a comly on vnder cambe,' suggests rounding; however, in the same line *cambe* rhymes externally with *flambe* : *lambe* : *clamb*.[4] In line 13 *ſange* rhymes with *ſprange* : *wrange* : *þrange*, but its alternate *ſonge* occurs in line 882,

[3] Cf. Richard Jordan, *Handbuch der mittelenglischen Grammatik*, rev. H. Ch. Matthes § 29 (Heidelberg, 1934).

[4] It is not certain that the nucleus in these forms is short. A lengthened variety of the OE short vowel developed before the cluster /mb/ in uninflected forms; however, in the inflected plural, *lambru*, which contained a three member cluster, the phoneme was short. (Wright, *EMEG* § 72; Jordan, § 31). With the decay of the OE paradigm, one form or the other was adopted.

'þat nwe ſonge þay ſongen ful cler.' Evidence from the modern dialect is not conclusive. D21 and D31 generally have /a/, while F22 shows both the rounded and the unrounded vowel. Bolton, for instance, has /kom/, /lont/, /ont/ < OE /kɑmb/, /lɑnd/, /xɑnd/, but /lam/ < OE /lɑmb/; Blackburn has /kom/ and /mon/, but /lant/ and /ant/. Before velar allophones of /n/ Bolton has /u/ for the reflexes of OE /a/ or /o/: /lung/ 'long', /amung/ 'among', /strung/ 'strong', /sung/ 'song'. Blackburn, on the other hand, has /a/ or /o/: /long/, /amang/, /strong/, /song/. The forms in D31 are generally unrounded, those in D21 generally rounded.

Since both rounded and unrounded vowels occur in MnE, it is assumed that both occurred in the ME dialect. However, whether one is to assume a genuine neutralization of /a/ and /o/ before nasals or simply the occurrence of doublets in some instances is not clear. I have not been able to find in the modern dialect areas a contrast in this environment; but one cannot be sure that a contrast did not exist in some forms in the ME text. For example, *banne* /ban/ < OE /bɑnnɑn/ 'to curse' may have contrasted with *bone* /bon/ < OFr. /bon/ 'good'. The only conclusion seems to be that the whole matter of the neutralization of /a/ and /o/ before nasals is not clear.

<e> ∼ <i>. OE /y/ > /i/ in LOE in the Northumbrian dialect areas. In ME, this development is first apparent in the Northeast Midland and in the North, from whence it spread to the West Midland. In the dialect of the present MS. the reflex of OE /y/ appears to have been unstable before /r/, spelled either with <e> or <i>: *mery* ∼ *miry*, *merþe* ∼ *mirþe* < OE /myrge/, /myrgθ/. One cannot be certain whether the alternate spellings represent two current pronunciations, the neutralization of /e/ and /i/ before /r/, or the retention of an archaic spelling <i> to represent /e/. The D21 and D22 areas of the modern dialect have /e/ almost exclusively in such forms as /berθ/, /beri/, /merθ/. This fact does not, however, necessarily favor any one of the three suggested possibilities of interpreting the ME graphemic alternation.

The alternates *begynne* ∼ *bygynne* seem to be of no other phonemic significance than to suggest that the first syllable of the form was unstressed.

The pairs *renk* ~ *rynk* < OE /rink/ and *ſwefte* ~ *ſwyfte* < OE /swift/ illustrate the ME tendency to lower /i/ to /e/ in closed syllables before and after labials, liquids, and nasals, especially palatal nasals. (Wright, *EMEG*, § 131). It may be that the spelling *renk* has been influenced by ON /rekkr/. In any event, it appears that in these environments one may expect no phonemic contrast between /e/ and /i/.

/e/ tended to become /i/ during the thirteenth and fourteenth centuries in the North and in some parts of the Midlands before dentals '... besonders wenn dem Vokal *r* und *g*, *ȝ* vorhergehen, sonst auch vor *l* ...' (Jordan, § 34, 1). Thus, *geſerne* ~ *giſerne*, *ȝerne* ~ *ȝirneȝ*, *quel* ~ *quyl*. Again, it is impossible to say whether the phoneme represented was /i/ only, or whether at this stage of its development in this environment it could have been either /e/ or /i/.

The tendency for /e/ to become /i/ 'vor gedecktem *n*' and before palatals (Jordan, § 43,2,3; Wright, *EMEG*, § 132) is illustrated by the pairs *þenk* ~ *þynk* < OE /θenčɑn/, and *hende* ~ *hynde* < OE /jexende/. Although a graphemic contrast is generally maintained between the reflexes of OE /θenčɑn/ 'think', and /θynčɑn/ 'seem', the occasional appearance of *y* for *e* as in 'bot j haue bygonnen w^{t} my god and he hit gayn þynke' (Purity, 749) suggests phonemic neutralization in this environment.

<e> ~ <o> ~ <v>. OE /ə/, of whatever origin, became /ö/ in LOE and so remained in the West Midland and Southern dialects (except Kentish) until late in the fourteenth century when it was unrounded to /e/. Through the influence of AN orthography /ö/ was written *o*, *ue*, or *u*. (Wright, *EMEG*, 31; Jordan, 86). Evidence from the four poems in the MS. indicates that in some items unrounding had clearly been completed: *werk*, *hert*, *derk*, *ſeuen* < OE /wərk/, /hərt/, /dərk/, /səfon/. However, the forms *erþe* ~ *vrþe*, *ȝender* ~ *ȝonder*, *woRþe*, *choRle* < OE /ərθe/, /jənd/, /wərθ/, /čərl/, show that the reflex of the OE sound had split into a rounded and an unrounded phoneme. This split took place particularly in the palatal environments /y/, /č/, /š/, and under the influence of /w/. (Jordan, § 75.87.3).

<e> ~ <ø>. The alternates *feerſly* ~ *ferſly* reflect the fact that before /r/ plus /C/, AN /e/ was lengthened and fell together with LME /i:/. (Jordan, § 225). There is no question of phonemic neutralization; /e/ does not occur in this environment.

In the graphemic environment <(C)VC()>, <e> frequently functions as the second member of a discontinuous sequence of graphemes to represent a lengthened vocalic nucleus; thus, <made> = /ma:d/- <mad> = /mad/. The *-e* of the discontinuous sequence <a-e>, <e-e>, <i-e>, <o-e>, <v-e> may be omitted from words representing morphemes containing a lengthened nucleus, and may be added indiscriminately to words representing morphemes containing a short nucleus. As a result, graphemic contrasts between <a> and <a-e>, <e> and <e-e>, <i> and <i-e>, <o> and <o-e>, <v> and <v-e> are suppressed. In the environment <(C)VCC()>, *-e* has no phonemic significance.[5]

<e> ~ <i> ~ <o> ~ <v>. The traditional explanation of this overlapping is that OE /y/, spelled *y*, was retained in the West Midland dialects as *u* until the end of the fourteenth century at which time it was unrounded to /i/. However, unrounding did not take place in all environments. Before /š/, /č/, /ǰ/, /l/ plus /č/, /n/ plus /č/, before /r/, and after labials and /š/ the sound was frequently rounded to a high-back or mid-back vowel. Adding to the difficulties of interpreting the phonemic significance of spelling variations is the fact that from the end of the thirteenth century *o* often occurs for *u* in order to avoid orthographic confusion in the neighborhood of *n*, *m*, *u*, and *w* (see Wright, *EMEG* § 9, 49, 125, 126).

[5] It is the assumption in this study that all final *-e*'s except those representing an etymological /i/, /i:/ represent no phonetic material. This assumption appears to be supported by such spellings in rhyme position as the following: *ſertayn : in vayne* (Pearl, 685-7); *bryng : mynge : clynge : cnawyng*, *creſte : reſte : dreſt : : keſt : beſt* (Pearl, 853-64). Final *-e* sometimes occurs as a result of French scribal practice to represent /i:/, possibly /iy/. Although this practice is generally limited to words of French origin, final *-e* spellings may occur for *i* or *y* in some words of English or Scandinavian origin, e.g. *peny~pene*. The difference between the syllabic structure of *pene* /peni:/ and *mene* /meyn/ can only be determined on historical grounds; no rules of the graphemic system will account for it. For discussion of *nauel~naule*, *auenture~aunteres*, *haueke3~hawk*, see below p. 120.

The reflexes of OE /y/ in this text may be considered in four groups according to the nature of their graphic representation. First of all, there are those which show only *y*, *i* or *e: wynne, kynde, ſynne, hille, kyſſe, kyrf, lyttel, lyft, euel, wyſchande, brygge, rygge.* The consistent environment here appears to be apical, with the exceptions of *kyrf, wyſchande*, and *euel*. According to Wright, above, we might have expected to find *korf* or *kurf* and *wuſchande;* however, since each form occurs only once in the text (the verb *kerve* is from OE /kə:rfɑn/), one should, perhaps, avoid comment on the influence of environment here. The form *euel* occurs three times; we should not expect a rounded nucleus in this environment.

There are, secondly, those forms which show alternations between *i, y, e* on the one hand and *o* or *u/o* on the other. I take the *o* forms as conclusive evidence that a rounded nucleus occurs in this environment: *wyrkeȝ* ~ *worch, wertes* ~ *wort, gerdeȝ* ~ *gorde* ~ *gurde, girdel* ~ *gordel* ~ *gurdel, kyrtel* ~ *cortel.* Assonance in the line 'w^{t} al þe wonder of þe worlde what he worch ſchulde' (Gawain, 238) seems to suggest a rounded nucleus in *worch*, while the modern form /werč/ (Blackburn D22) points to a development from an unrounded nucleus. Again, assonance in the lines 'for quat gome ſo is gorde with þis grene lace and 'thenne gyrdeȝ he to gryngolet and gedereȝ þe rake' (Gawain, 1851, 2160) indicates that before /r/ reflexes of OE /y/ may be either rounded or unrounded. Lack of evidence prevents any clear understanding of the role of the preceding consonant although one may suspect that /w/ is a conditioning factor.

In the third place, there are a few forms which show only *u* or *o* for this reflex, as *bluſched* ~ *bloſched.* There is no reason to think that this graphemic overlapping does not indicate doublets.

Fouth, some forms occur in which *i, y*, or *e*, alternate with *u*: *buſyly* ~ *byſily, buſynes* ~ *biſineſſe, ſuche* ~ *ſeche, muche* ~ *mych, gult* ~ *gylt, munt* ~ *mynt, dunt* ~ *dynt, burþe* ~ *byrþe.* The last form clearly belongs in the second category. We expect rounding in the environment *b( )r-*, but modern dialectal /berθ/ points to an unrounded variant. Since the modern dialect has both /muč/ and /mič/, /suč/ and /sič/, we may assume doublets in the MS.

Now, one can by no means be certain that the spelling *u* for reflexes of OE /y/ always indicates a rounded vowel, either central or back. According to Zachrisson, 'Even if *u* is a survival of Southern ME SPELLINGS, where *u* was a symbol of (y), the original pronunciation of this *u* need not have survived, but can very well have been ousted by (i), (e), although *u* was orthographically kept.' His conclusion is that '... the spelling *u* for OE and French (y) in early English cannot be taken as a proof of the existence of an (y)-sound.'[6] There are two occurrences of the form *buſy(i)ly* in the text, one of *byſily*, one of *buſyeȝ*, one of *buſynes*, and one of *biſineſſe*. These do not occur in rhyme, nor is there anything in the assonantal pattern of the line environment of the *u* spellings to suggest a rounded nucleus. There is one spelling in Purity, however, that may be significant in this respect: *buſmar* < OE /bismer/, in the line 'þenne þe burde byhynde þe DOR FOR buſmar laȝed' (653). It must be pointed out that the *u* form is not unique with this manuscript. There are frequent occurrences throughout the fourteenth century so that a *u* convention may have been familiar to the writer of Purity.[7] This fact does not, however, argue against the significance of the form in our text. The earliest *u* spellings appear toward the beginning of the fourteenth century. These may have been reverse spellings influenced by the *buſy* ~ *biſy* variants, but the traditional explanation that the *u* forms represented a back vowel conditioned by a preceding labial seems more likely (e.g. *buſſchops*, Piers Plowman A (1) (Vrn), 8.13). If *buſmar* were a phonetic spelling, i.e. representing rounding following a labial, we would also expect to find *buſchop* rather than the spelling *biſchop* which actually occurs (Gawain, 112). Further, we would expect to find evidence of rounding in the modern dialect, but neither Wright (*The English Dialect grammar* [Oxford, 1905]) nor Ellis show such evidence. As we have noted above, in those environments in which *o* spellings

6 R. E. Zachrisson, *Pronunciation of English vowels 1400-1700* 87-8 (Göteborg, 1913).

7 See citations under **bī-smār (a** in *Middle English Dictionary*, ed. Hans Kurath and Sherman M. Kuhn, Pt. B.4 (Ann Arbor, 1958).

occur with *u*, thus arguing for a rounded vowel, a rounded vowel occurs in the modern dialect.

It is difficult to make a judgment regarding the word *gult*. *gylt* occurs once in Purity; *gylteȝ*, *gyltleȝ*, and *gyltyf* one each in Pearl; *gult(e)* occurs once in Pearl and once in Purity; *gulty*, twice in Patience. The only possible hint of the sound of the *u* forms seems to be in the phrase 'gulty of gyle' (Patience, 285) which in Gawain rhymes with *ſmyle* < OE /smi:le/ (1789). Nothing certain can be said about the variants *munt* ~ *mynt*, nor about *dunt* ~ *dynt*. In the case of both words, there is a small majority of *y* forms. While acknowledging the slimness of the evidence, we are disposed to the opinion that in this fourth category only *ſuche*, *muche*, and *burþe* contained a rounded mucleus; elsewhere *u* is taken to be a spelling convention representing /i/.

Finally, some reflexes of OE /y/ are represented only by *u: mulne*, *lur*, *ſturne*, *fuſt*, *bult*, *ſture*, *þurled*. Rounding has been assumed before /r/, and Wright cites a form [məl] for the east middle Lancashire dialect which may have developed from a rounded vowel. One would have expected to find *y* or *i* before *-ſt* rather than *u* (cf. apical environments of the first category and *lyſte* < OE /lystɑn/). It may be, however, that *u* in these words represents an allophonic centralization [ɨ] in the environments /-LC/, /-st/ as in some modern dialects.[8] In any event, the assumption is that the phoneme /i/ is represented. Little can be said about the preterit *bult* except that the present *bylde* also occurs, and that, as we have noted above, at this time and in this text the influence of a labial on a following vowel is uncertain.

Clearly, an account of the phonemic status of the late fourteenth century reflexes of OE /y/ is difficult, perhaps impossible, especially since the system in which they occur is an extremely unstable one. One thinks of no good reason why OE /hilt/ should be spelled *hult* in Gawain (1954) unless to represent a central allophone of /i/. In this environment, only *y* or *i* occur for OE /y/ (e.g. *hylle* ~ *hille* < OE /hyll/). If the environment *h()l-* were responsible for a form

[8] This was suggested to me by Professor Householder.

/hult/, one might justifiably expect a morpheme /hul/. So far as I have been able to determine, there seems to be no established convention for the writing of *hilt* as *hult;* the form in Gawain is the only one cited by the Stratmann-Bradley *Middle English Dictionary* (at this writing, *h* has not yet been published by Kurath and Kuhn). In this connection, an interesting rhyme occurs in Alisaunder (c. 1340: 'he ʃmot him on þe ʃcheld igult [< OE /gyldɑn/ 'gild'] þoruʒout þe bord þoruʒout þe hilte' (1270). There seems little doubt that the rhyming nucleus here is /i/ (OE /gyldɑn/ occurs only with *y* or *i* in the Cotton Nero A. x. MS.). It is difficult to avoid the conclusion that the spelling *hult* is a hyperurbanism.

Similarly, the form *ruchen* (Patience, 101) < OE /rečɑn/ is difficult to account for. It may have been influenced by the reflex of OE */ryčɑn/, ON /rykja/ for much the same reason that the meanings of *richche* ~ *ruchche* < OE */ryčɑn/ seem partly to be derived from OE /rečɑn/, namely, because the sounds of the two forms were identical, or nearly so. The nucleus must have been /i/; otherwise, one would not expect *i* spellings, and the Patience form *ruchen* is probably a reverse spelling. The forms *wruxled* (Gawain, 2191) 'wrapped', 'clad' (?) and *wruxeled* (Purity, 1381) 'raised' (?) are equally curious. According to the editors of these texts, the word is derived from OE /wri:kslɑn/ but related to /wrə:n/, one of a number of OE first class strong verbs which frequently formed their preterites and past participles by analogy with second class verbs (so /wruxon/ – /wroxen/ rather than /wrixon/ – /wrixen/). In this way, apparently, the *u* spelling is accounted for.

It is not precisely clear how or why the form *wruxled* is related to OE /wrə:n/. The strong preterite and past participle of this latter were retained at least as late as the early thirteenth century (see 'þet men wruʒen her and helen, 'Moral Ode, 160), and there is ample evidence for a weak form *wryed* (see Alisaunder, 2786) throughout the fourteenth century. The form *wruxled* can scarcely be thought to have taken over the past participial function of OE /wroxen/. Quite independently of /wrə:n/, the basic meaning of OE /wri:kslɑn/, which seems to be 'alternation', may easily have been specialized to 'wrapping by alternation' or perhaps 'decorating by alternation of colors' as, for instance, in 'Is him þæt heafod hindan grene wrætlice wrixleþ wurman geblonden.' (Codex Exoniensis, 218, 13; Ph. 294). The sense of 'covering by wrapping in alternate folds' may have been reenforced by a phonetic similarity of /wri:kslɑn/ to *wrigels* 'a covering'. The meaning 'enwrapped' seems quite clear from the context in which the form occurs in Gawain (2191): 'wel biſemeȝ þe wyȝe wruxled in grene' (2191).

The meaning 'raised' given by Morris for the word in the line, 'w^{t} a wonder wroȝt walle wruxeled ful hiȝe' (Purity, 1381) is not easily justified, and Morris makes no attempt to do so. The *NED* cites this occurrence but does not explain the usage; the Stratmann-Bradley dictionary refers only to the form in Gawain. I have found nothing in the semantic development of /wri:kslɑn/ to suggest even a marginal sense 'raise'. It seems to me that as part of the description of the city of Babylon the phrases 'wonder wroȝt walle' and 'w^{t} koynt carneles ['embrasures'] aboue coRuen ful clene' (1382) support the notion that the form *wruxeled* refers to some kind of interlacing ornamentation, perhaps even a mosaic pattern of a sort. This is conjecture; but it has the advantage over Morris' interpretation of at least being a logical extension of the core meaning of the term.

The point is this: *wruxled* is not in any necessary way indebted to OE /wrə:n/ for either its semantic or its phonemic content. Its relationship to the verb *wrixle* which the *NED* affirms 'is not clear' is perfectly clear if one accepts the hypothesis that in a number of environments *u* spellings were, by the last quarter of the fourteenth century, purely conventional representations of [i] or [ɨ] of /i/, and that the form *wruxled* is no more than additional evidence of this fact.

We conclude that where *u* occurs as a spelling of the reflex of OE /y/, we may expect /u/ in the following environments: before <r> /r/, <l> /l/, <Ch> /č/, and <sCh> /š/, especially when these environments are combined with a preceding labial. This statement is supported by the fact that in these environments *u* frequently alternates with *o*, and by the fact that rounding of the vowel frequently occurs in the modern dialect. Elsewhere, the graph *u* represents the phoneme /i/, a conclusion partially supported by the fact that *u* spellings infrequently occur for the reflex of OE /i/.

4.2. Lengthened vowels.

4.21. Allographic representations.

/a:/ < OE /æ/, /a/, /ɑ/, ON /a/, OFr. /a/, lengthened in open syllables; ON /a:/ and AN /a:/, is represented by the allograph *a* of <a>, the sequence of identical graphs <aa>, and by the discontinuous sequence <a-e>: *mane* < OE /mɑnu/ = /ma:n/, MnE /me:n/; *take* < ON /taka/ = /ta:k/, MnE /te:k/; *blame* < OFr. /blasmer/, AN /bla:mer/ = /bla:m/, MnE /ble:m/; *raas* < ON /ras/ = /ra:s/, MnE /re:s/.

/e:/ < OE /e/, lengthened in open syllables, is represented by the allograph *e* of <e> and by the discontinuous sequence <e-e>: *mete* < OE /metɑ/ = /me:t/, MnE /meyt/.

/i:/ < OE /æ:/, /e:/, /ə:/, and /ə/, lengthened in open syllables, /e:x/, /a:x/, /ə:x/, OFr. /e/ and /ie/ is represented by the allograph *e* of <e>, the continuous sequences <iʒ>, <eʒ>, <ie>, <ie>, <ee>, the allograph *y* of <i>, and the discontinuous sequence <e-e>: *yʒe* < OE /e:xe/ = /i:/, MnE /iy/; *dreʒe* ~ *dryʒe* < OE /drə:xɑn/ = /dri:/; *ſe* < OE /sə:n/ = /si:/, MnE /siy/; *grene* < OE /gre:ne/ = /gri:n/, MnE /griyn/; *menteene* ~ *maynteine* ~ *mayntyne* (rhyming with *quene* < OE /kwe:n/) < OFr. /mayntenen/ = /meynti:n/; *pece* ~ *pyeſe* < OFr. /pies/ = /pi:s/, MnE /piys/.

/u:/ < OE /o:/ is represented by the allograph *o* of <o>, the continuous sequences <oo>, <ov>, and the discontinuous sequence <o-e>: *god* ~ *good* ~ *goud* ~ *gode* < OE /go:d/ = /gu:d/, MnE /gud/.

/o:/ < OE /o/, lengthened in open syllables, is represented by the allograph *o* of <o> and by the discontinuous sequence <o-e>: *fol* ~ *fole* < OE /fol/ = /fo:l/, MnE /foyl/.

/ay/ < OE /æj/, /æ:j/, /ej/, e:j/, AN /ey/ is represented by the allograph *e* of <e>, and the sequences <ai>, <ei>, and <eʒ>: *day* < OE /dæj/ = /day/, MnE /de:/; *gray* < OE /græ:j/ = /gray/, MnE /gre:/; *play* < OE /plejɑn/ = /play/, MnE /ple:/; *ſwey* ~

ſweȝe < OE /swe:jɑn/ = /sway/; *fay* < AN /fey/ = /fay/, MnE /fe:/; *feye* < OE /fæ:je/ = /fay/.

/ey/ < OE /æ:/, /a:/, AN /ey/ (before liquids, dentals, and /s/) is represented by the allograph *e* of <e>, the continuous sequences <ai> and <ei>, and the discontinuous sequence <e-e> : *mene* < OE /mæ:nɑn/ = /meyn/, MnE /mi:n/; *ded* < OE /da:d/ = /deyd/, MnE /di:d/, /ded/; *rayſoun* ~ *reyſoun* < AN /reysoun/ = /rey-zuwn/, MnE /ri:zun/.

/iy/ < OE /i:/, /y:/, AN /i/, and /üy/ is represented by the allograph *i* of <i>, the continuous sequences <ii>, <ie>, <iȝ>, <vi>, and the discontinuous sequence <i-e> : *myn* ~ *myyn* ~ *myne* < OE /mi:n/ = /mi:n/, MnE /ma:n/; *hyde* ~ *huyde* < OE /hy:dɑn/ = /hi:d/, MnE /a:d/; *nye* ~ *nyȝe* < AN /anüy/ = /ni:/.

/uw/ < OE /u:/, /u:x/, /o:x/, /ɔ:/, AN /u/ is represented by the allograph *o* of <o>, the allograph *u* of <v>, the continuous sequences <ov>, <ow>, <oȝ>, <vv>, <vȝ>, and the discontinuous sequence <v-e>: *burne* ~ *buurne* ~ *bourne* < OE /bɔ:rnĕ/ = /buwrn/; *flor* ~ *flour* ~ *flowr* < AN /flur/ = /fluwr/, MnE /fla:r/; *muþe* < OE /mu:θ/ = /mu:θ/, MnE /ma:θ/; *roȝ* ~ *roȝe* ~ *ruȝe* < OE /ru:x/ = /ruw/, MnE /ruf/.

/ow/ < OE /a:/ is represented by the allograph *o* of <o>, and by the discontinuous sequence <o-e> : *ſton* ~ *ſtone* < OE /sta:n/= /stown/, MnE /stu:n/; *ſo* < OE /swa:/ = /sow/, MnE /sow/, /su:/.

/aw/ < OE /ɑ:w/, /o:w/, /ɑlV/, /ɑfV/, /ɑx/, /ɑ:x/, ON /a:g/ is represented by the sequences <av>, <aw>, <ow> : *ſnaw* < OE /snɑ:wɑn/ = /snaw/, MnE /snow/; *galle* ~ *gawle* < OE /gɑllɑ/ = /gawl/; *naule* < OE /nɑfel/ = /nawl/; *owen* ~ *awen* ~ *aune* ~ *auen* < OE /ɑ:xɑn/ = /awn/; *lawe* < OE /lɑxu/ = /law/; *lowe* < ON /la:gr/ = /law/.[9]

[9] The disposition of the reflex of OE /o:w/ is difficult since forms containing it do not occur in rhyme position in the MS. According to Wright (*EMEG* § 114) the reflex of OE /o:w/ fell together in some ME dialects with the reflexes of OE /ɑ:w/, /ɑx/, /ɑ:x/, etc. in the phoneme /aw/. He asserts, however, that in the North and Northwest Midlands these reflexes were kept apart. Now the only rhyme evidence in the text appears in Gawain (2234-8) in which the rhymes *ſnawe : lowe : trowe* occur. In EME, the reflex of OE /ɔ:w/ (*trowe*< /trɔ:wɑn/) split in some dialects into /ew/ and /ow/ (Wright, § 112), and this /ow/ fell

/ew/ < OE /a:w/ is represented by the sequence <ew> : *few* ~ *fewe* < OE /fa:w/ = /few/, MnE /fiw/, /few/.

/iw/ < OE /ə:w/, /i:w/, AN /üy/, /ew/ is represented by the allograph *w* of <w>, the continuous sequences <ew>, <ev>, <vi>, <eav>, and the discontinuous sequence <v-e> : *new* ~ *nw* < OE /nə:we/ = /niw/, MnE /niw/, /nyuw/; *endeure* ~ *endure* < AN /endürer/ = /endiwr/; *ſtewarde* < LOE /sti:wɑrd/ = /stiward/; *fruyt* < AN /früyt/ = /friwt/, MnE /frewt/, /friwt/, /fruwt/; *beaute* ~ *bewte* < AN /bewtey/ = /biwti:/, MnE /biwti/, /bi:ti/.

/oy/ < OFr. /ɔy/ < Lat. /aui/ and /oy/, /uy/ < Lat. /o:i/, /ui/ is represented by the sequence <oi>: *noyſe* < OFr. /nɔyse/ = = /noyz/, MnE /noyz/, /na:z/, /ne:z/; *poynt* < OFr. /poynt/ = /poynt/, MnE /poynt/, /pa:nt/.[10]

---

together in LME with /aw/. Because of the above rhyme and the alternate spellings *trowe~trawe*, and because modern Lancashire shows the same phoneme for the reflexes of both OE /ɑ:w/ and /o:w/ (e.g. /grow/ < OE /gro:wɑn/, /mow/ < OE /mɑ:wɑn/), it is assumed that in this MS the reflex of OE /o:w/ had become ME /aw/.

[10] The postulation of a single phoneme here is questionable. The traditional view has been that the reflexes of OFr. /ɔy/ and /oy/ (AN /uy/) remained separate throughout the ME period and for some centuries thereafter although both were spelled *oi, oy* (see Wright, *EMEG* § 206-7; *Elementary new English grammar* § 88; Jordan § 236-7). It is the opinion of H. C. Wyld (*A Short history of English* § 270.197-8 [London, 1927]), that ME [oi] < OFr. /ɔy/ remained in the standard dialect under the influence of spelling pronunciation and that ME [ui] fell together in LME or EMnE with LME /iy/ [əi], and developed in the non-standard dialects to [ai] [a:] along with the reflex of ME /iy/. Evidence for the coalescence of [əi] and [ui] is to be found in such spellings as *anynted* 'anointed', *dystryde* 'destroyed', *pyson* 'poison', *defoyling* 'defiling', *boyle* (sb.), a reverse spelling for *bile* (< OE /by:l/ 'boil'). There seems to be no evidence from sixteenth and seventeenth century phoneticians that the reflex of ME [oi] fell together with the reflex of ME /iy/ as did those of ME [ui]. However, in the non-standard dialects some such coalescence must have taken place since in many of those dialects the development of both the reflexes of ME [ui] and [oi] has followed that of ME /iy/ to /a:/ : ME [čois], [vois] > MnE /ča:s/, /če:s/, /va:s/, /ve:s/ in south, southeast, and middle south Lancashire along with occasional /voys/; ME [ǰuin] > MnE /ǰa:n/, /ǰe:n/, /ǰoyn/, ME [ǰuint] > MnE /ǰa:nt/, /ǰe:nt/, /ǰoynt/. Precisely when this coalescence took place is not clear, but one suspects that it could not have been later than the coalescense of the reflexes of OFr. /uy/ and ME /iy/, presumably at the stage [əi]. As far as the present text is concerned, the matter cannot be settled satisfactorily. A single phoneme /oy/ is postulated because there is no spelling or rhyme evidence to indicate a contrast between the reflexes of OFr. /ɔy/ and /oy/, and because the

4.22. The phonemic significance of graphemic neutralization.

<a> ~ <o>, <a–e> ~ <o–e>. This neutralization indicates the West Midland retention of Anglian rounding of OE /ɑ/, lengthened in open syllables. The phonemic interpretation of this rounding is somewhat more complex than that of the unlengthened nucleus because of the multiple phonemic value of the discontinuous sequence <o-e>.

To begin with, these spelling alternates appear to be open to at least four different interpretations. First, either the <a> <a-e> or the <o> <o-e> spellings may be archaic and may represent either a rounded or an unrounded vowel, but not both. If this were the case, however, explanation of the modern forms /še:m/ (Blackburn, D22), /šowm/ (Bolton, D22), /ša:m/ (D31) would be difficult. Second, the graphemic neutralization may represent a distinct phoneme; but if so, this phoneme has been lost in the modern dialect. Third, the spellings with <o> <o-e> may represent a rounded allophone of /a:/ before nasals; however, if this were the case, one would not expect a development to /e:/ in this dialect, and he would expect borrowed French forms such as *dame* (with which *ſchame*, *ſame*, and *grame* rhyme) to have had the same allophone and to have developed in the same way. But they have not—French forms show only a fronted development. Fourth, the graphemic neutralization suggests that both the rounded and unrounded variants of OE /ɑ/ plus nasal, lengthened in open syllables, developed independently in ME and MnE. That the allophone [ɑ] of OE /ɑ/ before nasals had the same development as the allophones of OE /ɑ/, lengthened, in other environments seems clear from the fact that they all appear as /e:/ in MnE: OE /sɑmu/ > MnE /se:m/, OE /bɑkɑn/ > MnE /be:k/. A more difficult question concerns the development of the lengthened reflex of the allophone [ɔ] of OE /ɑ/ before nasals.

---

historical evidence for separate phonemes is not, for this dialect, entirely convincing. The fact that some *ui*, *uy*, spellings occur in late fourteenth and early fifteenth century MSS. does not prove anything since it cannot be shown that forms containing these spellings are in contrast with forms containing *oi*, *oy* spellings.

OE /o/ in closed syllables remained unchanged, except in certain consonant environments, throughout the ME period and into MnE: OE /boks/ > MnE /boks/, OE /frost/ > MnE /frost/, OE /god/ > MnE /god/, OE /xoppiɑn/ > MnE /op/, etc. We assume that sometime after lengthening in open syllables took place, but before words borrowed from French could be affected, the allophone [ɔ] of OE /ɑ/ in closed syllables fell together with the reflex of OE /o/; thus, MnE /mon/ next to the unrounded /man/ in the same general dialect area. That this split occurred AFTER lengthening in open syllables seems clear from the fact that the development of the lengthened allophone [ɔ] of OE /ɑ/ did not follow that of OE /o/ lengthened.

OE /o/ was lengthened in open syllables along with /ɑ/ and /e/ before the end of the first half of the thirteenth century. The resultant vowel was presumably /o:/. In the standard dialect of the East Midlands this /o:/ fell together during the ME period with the phoneme /ow/ which arose from OE /ɑ:/. In the Northwest Midlands, however, /o:/ remained a distinct phoneme and became /oy/ sometime after the reflex of OFr. /oy/ had fallen together with the reflexes of OFr. /uy/ and ME /iy/ and moved to its present position in the vowel system, /a:/, /e:/ (see fn. 10). Thus, OE /kol/ 'coal' (with open syllable in the nom. plu. and oblique cases), /folɑ/ 'foal', /hol/ 'hole', > MnE /koyl/ in D22 and D31, /foyl/ in D22 and D21, /oyl/ in D22 and D31. The normal development of OE /ɑ:/, OE /o/ lengthened, and OFr. /oy/ is assumed to be this: /ɑ:/ > ME /ow/ > MnE /u:/, /o/ > ME /o:/ > MnE /oy/, /oy/ > ME /oy/ > MnE /a:/.

It should be pointed out that the modern dialects under consideration show a considerable amount of variation from this pattern. Where D21 and D22 have /foyl/, /koyl/, and /oyl/, D31 has /fu:l/ and /hu:l/; within the D22 area, Blackburn and Burnley have /loyn/ < OE /lɑne/ 'lane', Chorley has /lu:n/ (as does D31), and Ormskirk has /lown/ (as does D21). Similarly, OFr. /o/ lengthened has undergone different developments within the same dialect area. OFr. /broče/ appears consistently in D22 as /broyč/ 'brooch', while OFr. /koče/ has become /ku:č/ 'coach'. The difference may, of course, be the result of the consonantal environment; however, evidence on this point is lacking. At the same time, there is evidence that not all reflexes of OE /ɑ:/ became MnE /u:/. In D22, for example, Burnley has /tloyz/ 'clothes' < OE /klɑ:θ/ and /goyt/ 'goat' < /gɑ:t/; Ormskirk has /sto:n/ 'stone' < OE /stɑ:n/; Wigan has /to:d/ 'toad' < OE /tɑ:de/.

There is neither graphemic nor rhyme evidence in the Cotton Nero MS. for a phonemic distinction between the reflexes of OE /o/ lengthened and OE /ɑ:/. /o:/ and /ow/ as well as /u:/ < OE /o:/ are represented by <o> and <o-e>. The one distinguishing graphemic feature seems to be that /u:/ is infrequently represented by the sequence <ov>, as in *goud*. /u:/ and /ow/ are regularly distinguished in rhyme, but /o:/ may rhyme with either of the other two: *aros* /arowz/ (Pearl, 181): *clos* /klo:z/, *ſchore* /šo:r/ (Pearl, 230): *more* /mowr/; *mote* /mo:t/ (Pearl, 972) *fote* /fu:t/, *lone* /lo:n/ (Pearl, 1066): *mone* /mu:n/. Evidence, then, for the distinction between /o:/ and /ow/ in this MS. rests solely on the fact that they were derived from distinct phonemes in OE, and they have remained distinct in MnE.

To return now to the development of the lengthened reflex of the allophone [ɔ] of OE /ɑ/ before nasals. In the modern dialects the rounded nucleus is infrequent. In D22, Bolton and Wigan have /ow/, the sound having fallen together with the reflex of ME /aw/. I have found no instance in which the sound has fallen together with the reflexes of either ME /o:/ or ME /ow/.[11] The conclusion is that the spelling alternates in this text, *ſchame* ~ *ſchome* represent distinct phonemes, /a:/ and /aw/ respectively.

<aø> ~ <ai> ~ <eø> ~ <ei>. Before the phonemic significance of this neutralization is considered, it may be useful to review the front vowel system postulated for this text, to take note of the evidence, and lack of it, for the phoneme /e:/, and to suggest the stages in the Great Vowel Shift which the sounds in question

[11] The handbooks agree in writing the rounded nucleus before nasals with open *o* [ǭ]. Aside from the fact that the grapheme <o> occurs here (a convention derived from OE), there seems to be little justification for this interpretation.

may reasonably be thought to have reached, in order to explain the fairly considerable amount of graphic confusion that exists in the representation of these sounds.

We have assumed the following partial system for this MS.: ME /iy/ < OE /i:/, et al. > MnE /a:/, /miyn/ < /mi:n/ > /ma:n/ 'mine'; ME /i:/ < OE /e:/, et al. > MnE /iy/, /gri:n/ < /gre:ne/ > /griyn/ 'green'; ME /ey/ < OE /æ:/, et al. > MnE /i:/, /meyn/ < /mæ:nɑn/ > /mi:n/ 'mean' (vb.); ME /e:/ < OE /e/ lengthened > MnE /ey/, /me:t/ < /metɑ/ > /meyt/ 'meat'; ME /ay/ < OE /ɑj/, /ej/, et al. > MnE /e:/, /day/ < /dæj/ > /de:/ 'day'; /a:/ < OE /æ/, /a/, /ɑ/, lengthened > MnE /e:/, /ma:n/ < /mɑnu/ > /me:n/ 'mane'. This system receives some support from the following contrasts in the modern dialect areas: /we:v/ 'wave' (sb.) – /weyv/ 'weave', /breyd/ 'breadth' – /bri:d/ (sometimes /bred/) 'bread', /di:d/ 'dead' – /diyd/ 'deed', /me:n/ 'mane' – /mi:n/ 'mean' (vb.), /se:/ 'say', – /siy/ 'see', /heyd/ 'head' – /hiyd/ 'heed'.

No graphemic distinction is made in the MS. between /i:/, /ey/, and /e:/; all three may be spelled either with <e> or with <e-e>. /i:/ and /ey/, however, are consistently distinguished in rhyme.[12] /e:/ occurs most frequently in rhyme with /ey/ as in *mete* < OE /metɑ/: *hete* < OE /hæ:tu/ (Pearl, 641, 643), but occasionally with /i:/ as in *heue* < OE stem /hef-/: *leue* < OE /jele:fɑn/. The phonemic status of /e:/ is exactly parallel to that of /o:/, considered in the previous section. In the standard dialect the reflexes of OE /ɑ:/ and /e/ lengthened fell together in ME, and later these two fell together with the reflex of OE /e:/, so that the standard language now has 'meat', 'meet', 'mean', /miyt/, /miyt/, /miyn/. The decision to write OE /e/ lengthened as a separate phoneme in the ME of this text is based solely on the fact that all three sounds are distinct phonemes in the modern dialect.

As in the case of ME /o:/ and /ow/, there is some confusion in the development of forms which contained an original /e/ length-

[12] There are some exceptions. In several rhyme groups in Pearl *e* rhymes occur which appear not to be etymologically sound. Some of these can be explained; some have generally been regarded simply as inaccurate (see E. V. Gordon, ed. Pearl xlvii [Oxford, 1953]).

ened and of those which contained an original /æ:/. In the modern dialect areas considered in this study, some forms which contained an original /e/ lengthened have become /ey/, some have become /e:/, and some have become /i:/. The D22 area is the most consistent in having /ey/ in such forms: /breyk/ 'break', /weyv/ 'weave', /neyd/ 'knead', /meyt/ 'meat', but /fe:ver/ 'fever'. D21 has /e:/ in these forms. D31 has /bri:k/, /wi:v/, /ni:d/, /mi:t/, but /feyver/ and /speyk/ 'speak'. Similarly, some forms containing the reflex of OE /æ:/ may appear in the modern dialect as /ey/. OE /sæ:/ 'sea' occurs in D22 and D31 both as /sey/ and as /si:/; OE /læ:dɑn/ 'lead' occurs in D31 as /leyd/ and /li:d/; OE /klæ:ne/ 'clean' occurs as /kleyn/ in D22, as both /kleyn/ and /kli:n/ in D31; D22 has /sliyp/ 'sleep', < OE /sle:pɑn/, while D31 has /sleyp/ < OE /slæ:pɑn/ rather than the form /sli:p/ which one might expect.

Harold Orton has distinguished four patterns of development in the Northwest Midlands for the reflexes of OE /e/ lengthened, of OE /æ:/ (in traditional terminology ME $\bar{e}^2$, in this study /ey/), and of OE /e:/ (ME $\bar{e}^1$, in this study /i:/). (1) OE /e/ > [ɛi], ME $\bar{e}^2$ > [iə, ɪə], ME $\bar{e}^1$ > [i:, ɪi]; (2) OE /e/ > [e:, e:ɪ], ME $\bar{e}^2$ > [i:ə], ME $\bar{e}^1$ > [i:]; (3) OE /e/ > [ɪə], ME $\bar{e}^2$ > [i:], ME $\bar{e}^1$ > [ɛ:ɪ]; (4) OE /e/ > [i:], ME $\bar{e}^2$ > [i:], ME $\bar{e}^1$ > [ɛɪ].[13] The suggestion seems to be (although Orton does not make this point) that, with the exception of pattern 4, regardless of the particular development of each of these reflexes within a given speech variety, the over-all dialect pattern maintains a three-way contrast between the reflexes of OE /e/ lengthened, /æ:/, and /e:/. Lacking evidence for a phonemic split after the ME period, I find it more convenient to assume that a three-way contrast was present in the ME dialect of this MS.

The vocalic system presented in 4.21 assumes an earlier shift in the phonetic position of the phonemes than is characteristic of the majority of studies of fourteenth century English phonology. It is assumed, for example, that the reflex of OE /e:/ had become /i:/ before the date of this MS., and that the reflex of OE /æ:/ had

[13] The Isolative treatment in living North Midland dialects of OE *e* lengthened in open syllables in Middle English, *Leeds studies in English and kindred languages*, nos. 7-8.124-5 (1952).

shifted to /ey/. This analysis is in accord with Wyld's suggestion that '... it is quite possible ... that in some dialects, the raising of [e] to [i] was well on its way, if not completed, in the M. E. period.'[14] Evidence for this shift is of three kinds. There is, first of all, spelling. Reflexes of OE /ə:/, /e:x/, /yj/, and ON /ey/ are spelled *eʒe* or *yʒe*, most frequently the latter: Pearl has *yʒe* < OE /e:xe/ : *lyʒe* < OE /lyje/ : *dyʒe* < ON /deya/ : *ſyʒe* < OE /sə:n/; Gawayn has *yʒe* : *ſyʒe* : *dryʒe* < OE /drə:xɑn/ (Mn. Scot. 'dree'). That the sound indicated by these spellings was distinct from the reflex of OE /i:/ seems clear from the fact that the two are distinct inMnE. The first has become /iy/ as in /iy/ 'eye', /diy/ 'die', /θiy/ 'thigh', while the second has become /a:/ as in /a:d/ 'hide' and /ma:n/ 'mine'.[15] The OFr. form *maintenir* is spelled *menteene* in Pearl (where it rhymes with *quene* : *bene* : *ſene*), but *mayntyne* in Patience. OFr. *corbel* occurs in Gawain as *corbel*, but in Purity as *corbyal*. R. J. Menner notes that the latter spelling is not found elsewhere and suggests that it is possibly corrupt.[16] In exactly what way it is corrupt is not made clear. There is some likelihood that *corbyal* is simply a phonetic spelling of the phoneme /i:/.

Some rhymes in the text suggest that the shift in question had already occurred. These words are rhymed in Pearl: *ſene* : *bydene* :

14 *A Short history*, 170.

15 My position here is somewhat different from that of Wright who interprets the development of the reflex of OE /e:x/ in this way: 'When the *ēʒ* stood before a following vowel at the time of the formation of diphthongs it generally became *ei* in the North and Midlands, but *ī*, mostly written *y*, through the intermediate stage *īʒ* in some parts of the Midlands, especially the south Midlands including the dialect of Chaucer, and the South, but the modern dialects show that the *ī* did not occur in the north Midlands, otherwise it would have become *ai* whereas they have *ī* from older *ē* in words of this type.' (*EMEG* § 107). My point is that the *ī* did occur in the Northwest Midlands; however, it was /i:/ and not /iy/ < OE /i:/. This is borne out by the fact that these two phonemes remain distinct in the modern dialects. The double forms /iy/ and /ey/ 'high' in MnE and *hyʒe*~*heʒe* in the MS. reflect a double development of OE /e:x/. In final position and before another consonant /e:x/ > /ey/ in this dialect and so tended to remain; before vowels of inflectional morphemes /e:x/ > /ey/ > /i:/ > /iy/. An alternative explanation of MnE /ey/ and /iy/ is that LME *hyʒe* /hi:/ > /hiy/ (or /iy/) > /ey/, following the development of LME /iy/, while LME *heʒe* /hey/ > /hi:/ (or /i:/) > /iy/, following the normal development of LME /ey/.

16 *Purity* 136 (New Haven, 1920).

bene : yȝen : wene : ſchene; pyſe : grece : nece : ſpyce. Most editors of the poem emend the *y* spellings to *e* with no other justification than the fact that these spellings distort the eye rhyme. There is certainly some reason to think that the *y* spellings occurring in rhyme position with *e* spellings reflect a shift in the nature of the sound represented. In Gawain, *diſcrye* < OFr. /deskrier/ 'to behold' rhymes with *ſyȝes* < OE /sə:n/ 'see'; in Pearl, the related word *dyſcreuen* < OFr. /deskrivre/ rhymes with *cleuen, leuen* < OE /klə:fɑn/, /jele:fɑn/. The best explanation of the *e* in *dyſcreuen* seems to be that it is a reverse spelling to conform to the spelling of the other two words. The phoneme in all three is /i:/.

A third argument for the early shift of the reflex of OE /e:/ to /i:/ has to do with the lengthening of OE /i/ and /u/ in open syllables. The traditional view of this lengthening is stated by Wright:

> The result of the lengthening of *i, u* to *ē, ō* through the intermediate stage *ī, ū* was entirely different from that of *a, e, o* to *ā, ē, ō*. In the latter case there was only a change in quantity, but in the former case there was a change both in quantity and quality of the vowels. This change of *i, u,* to *ē, ō* took place in the dialects north of the Humber and in parts of the North Midland dialects in the latter half of the thirteenth century, and in the East Anglian dialects about a century later.[17]

The chief evidence for this change is to be found in spelling and rhyme. OE /wiku/ is spelled in ME *weke* and rhymes with the reflex of OE /e:/; OE /duru/ is spelled in ME *dore* and rhymes with the reflex of OE /o:/. However, in view of the history of English sound change which has emphasized the tendency of English vowels toward raising, fronting, and tensing, the lowering of /i/ and /u/ lengthened seems suspicious. It seems to me equally reasonable to suppose that OE /e:/, following what appears to be a fairly well-defined pattern, shifted to /ey/ early in the thirteenth century and then to /i:/ somewhat later where it fell together with /i/ lengthened before the fourteenth century in the North Midland dialects. OE /i:/ had shifted to /iy/ early in the ME period so that there was a clear contrast between this phoneme and the reflexes of OE /i/ lengthened

[17] *EMEG* § 84. Karl Luick first described this change in *Untersuchungen zur englischen Lautgeschichte* 209 ff. (Strassburg, 1896). See also Jordan, § 36.3.

and /e:/. The traditional grapheme <e> and the sequence <e-e> were retained after the shift of the reflex of OE /e:/ to /i:/, and since words containing the reflex of OE /i/ lengthened were relatively few in number, they occurred with the reverse spellings <e> and <e-e>, the most common spelling for /i:/ in the latter part of the thirteenth century.[18]

This hypothesis has at least two advantages over the traditional view. First, one is not obliged to explain a lowering tendency which appears to run counter to the general shift of English vowels. OE /i/ simply became what one would expect it to become, /i:/, and so remained until the beginning of the MnE period. In the second place, this theory may help us to explain the retention of the phonemic status of OE /e/ lengthened in the Northwest Midland and the loss of that status in the standard dialect. If Wright's chronology is correct, one can postulate the following sequences of vowel changes for the Northwest Midland and the East Midland dialects:

<table>
<tr><th></th><th>*OE*</th><th></th><th></th><th></th><th colspan="5">*ME*</th></tr>
<tr><th></th><th></th><th></th><th>*EME*</th><th></th><th>1st half *13th cent.*</th><th></th><th>2nd half *13th cent.*</th><th></th><th>*14th cent.*</th></tr>
<tr><td rowspan="5">Northwest Midland</td><td>/i:/</td><td>></td><td>/i:/</td><td>></td><td>/iy/</td><td>></td><td>/iy/</td><td>></td><td>/iy/</td></tr>
<tr><td>/e:/</td><td>></td><td>/e:/</td><td>></td><td>/ey/</td><td>></td><td rowspan="2">/i:/</td><td rowspan="2">></td><td rowspan="2">/i:/</td></tr>
<tr><td>/i/</td><td>></td><td>/i/</td><td>></td><td>/i/</td><td>></td></tr>
<tr><td>/æ:/</td><td>></td><td>/æ:/</td><td>></td><td>/e:/</td><td>></td><td>/ey/</td><td>></td><td>/ey/</td></tr>
<tr><td>/e/</td><td>></td><td>/e/</td><td>></td><td>/e/</td><td>></td><td>/e:/</td><td>></td><td>/e:/</td></tr>
<tr><td rowspan="5">East Midland</td><td>/i:/</td><td>></td><td>/i:/</td><td>></td><td>/iy/</td><td>></td><td>/iy/</td><td>></td><td>/iy/</td></tr>
<tr><td>/e:/</td><td>></td><td>/e:/</td><td>></td><td>/ey/</td><td>></td><td>/ey/</td><td>></td><td rowspan="2">/i:/</td></tr>
<tr><td>/i/</td><td>></td><td>/i/</td><td>></td><td>/i/</td><td>></td><td>/i:/</td><td>></td></tr>
<tr><td>/æ:/</td><td>></td><td>/æ:/</td><td>></td><td>/e:/</td><td>></td><td rowspan="2">/e:/</td><td rowspan="2">></td><td rowspan="2">/ey/</td></tr>
<tr><td>/e/</td><td>></td><td>/e/</td><td>></td><td>/e/</td><td>></td></tr>
</table>

[18] For a similar treatment of OE /i/ and /u/ lengthened see Robert P. Stockwell, *Chaucerian graphemics and phonemics: a study in historical methodology*, unpubl. diss. 121 ff. (University of Virginia, 1952). Professor Stockwell's article, The ME 'long close' and 'long open' vowels, *Texas studies in literature and language* 4.530-8 (1961), was not seen by the author in time for him to take proper account of it in this study.

The change of the reflex /ey/ of OE /e:/ to /i:/ was considerably earlier in the Northwest Midland than in the East Midland (converting, now, the traditional view that /i:/ became /ey/). This change left a gap in the system filled by the movement of the reflex of OE /æ:/ to /ey/, which in turn left a gap filled by the lengthened reflex of OE /e/. There was presumably sufficient phonetic contrast between /e:/ and /ey/ to preserve the phonemic contrast. In the East Midland dialects, since the change of OE /e:/ to /i:/ occurred much later, the reflex of OE /æ:/, thirteenth century /e:/, did not move until a considerable length of time after OE /e/ had been lengthened in open syllables. These two reflexes, then, fell together sometime during the second half of the thirteenth century.[19]

The neutralization **<ai>** ∼ **<ei>** ∼ **<eø>** reflects a spelling confusion which occurs as the result of the following phonological development. OFr. /ay/ and /ey/ fell together in AN /ey/, *ei*, which in England fell together with EME /ey/, the reflex of OE /ej/. This /ey/ then merged with EME /ay/, *ai*, *ay*, the reflex of OE /æj/, before the fourteenth century.[20] According to Wright, this nucleus in French loan words later split, /ay/ > /ey/ before liquids, dentals, and /s/ (§ 205). Forms which underwent this change are spelled in this MS. <ai>, <ei>, or <e>: *meny* ∼ *meyny* ∼ *mayny*, *counſel* ∼ *counſeyl*, *reſoun* ∼ *reyſoun* ∼ *rayſoun*, *ſeſoun*. That the nucleus in these forms was /ey/ is confirmed by the modern reflexes /ri:son/, /si:son/, /li:s/ < OFr. /layse/ 'leash'.

Since the sequence <ai> could occur for /ey/, the grapheme <e> and the sequence <e-e> could also occur for /ay/; thus *clem* (Pearl, 826) ∼ *clayme* (Gawain, 1490) < OFr. /klaymer/, MnE /kle:m/.[21] The graph *e* infrequently occurs in French loans

[19] The same hypothesis serves, of course, to explain the development of OE /o:/, /ɑ:/, and /o/ lengthened.

[20] M. K. Pope, *From Latin to modern French with especial consideration of Anglo-Norman* 444 (Manchester, 1934); also Wright, *EMEG* § 107.

[21] The word *clem* rhymes in Pearl with *drem : nem : bem : ſem* which contain the nucleus /ey/ < OE /a:/. Two explanations are possible. *e* is a reverse spelling of /ay/ which by the date of composition had shifted to [æi] and thus could appear in an imperfect rhyme with [ei]; or *clem* and *clayme* represent doublets either from a double root development in OFr. (see Pope, § 926) or

whose nucleus had fallen together with ME /ay/: *here* (Purity, 52) ~ *hayre* (Purity, 666) < OFr. /heyr/, MnE /e:r/; *gawen* (Gawain, 463) ~ *gawayn* (Gawain, 838), the ending /-wain/ presumably going back to primitive Celtic /-ganios/. The confusion between *ay*, *ey*, and *e* spellings which resulted from the disposition of French loan words in ME presumably accounts for the variants *contray* ~ *countre*, the final nucleus of which is a reflex of AN /eie/ which fell together in ME with the reflex of OE /e:/. In Pearl, *countre* rhymes with *be : þre : fle : ſe*, all containing /i:/ < OE /e:/. It may be, however, that the alternate forms indicate doublets, *ay* representing /ey/, *e* representing /i:/ (see Wright, *EMEG* § 197).

The spelling *etayn* (Gawain, 140) < OE /əten/ is explained by Tolkien and Gordon as being the result of accent shift in French loan words. The shift in the accent of polysyllabic French words to the first syllable resulted in the weakening of the vowel phonemes in succeeding syllables. Thus, for example, the syllable /-ayn/ was weakened to /-en/ but the spelling <ain> remained. Since the weakened form /-en/ now sounded like the /-en/ in native forms, reverse spellings occurred, <ain> spelling the /-en/ in native forms.[22] An alternative explanation of *etayn* is simply the fact that the symbolic function of <ai>, <ei>, and <e> had become completely confused by the date of this text for the reasons given in the previous paragraphs. It is not entirely clear that the spelling *gawen* indicates a weak stress on the second syllable in all of its occurrences. One might be tempted to think, for example, that the italicized syllables in the following line were intended to rhyme: 'he glent vpon & gaw*en* & g*ay*nly he ſ*ay*de' (476). It is quite likely the case that some occurrences of *e* spellings indicate unstressed /ay/, and that some reflect no more than the confusion between <ai>, <ey>, and <e> spellings.

---

as a result of the split of AN /ey/. Kurath and Kuhn do not cite this occurrence of *clem;* they do, however, show *cleme* rhyming with *bapteme* in Robert Mannyng's *Handlynge Synne* (9560), the rhyming nucleus presumably being ME $\bar{e}^2$, /ey/ in our notation.

22 J. R. R. Tolkien and E. V. Gordon, eds., *Sir Gawain and The Green Knight* 129 (Oxford, 1925). See also Pope, § 1159.

The question of stress shift in French loans brings us to a consideration of the **<i>** ~ **<ø>** neutralization indicated by the variants **<ai>** ~ **<aø>**. The following alternates occur in the MS.: *a* ~ *ay*, *aþer* ~ *ayþer*, *ſant* ~ *ſaynt*, *ſade* ~ *ſayde*, *halſed* ~ *haylſed*, *gawan* ~ *gawayn*, *ywan* ~ *ywayn*, *metalle* ~ *metail*, *vilanye* ~ *vilaynye*. Several possible explanations of these alternations present themselves. Perhaps the most facile is that they are due to nothing more significant than scribal error; the graph *y* was carelessly omitted. The second possibility has already been suggested, namely, that the shift in the position of the French accent resulted in the weakening of some nuclei in polysyllabic forms, and that this weakening is represented by the *a* spellings. This assumption serves well enough to explain the alternates *vilanye* ~ *vilaynye*, *gawan* ~ *gawayn*, *ywan* ~ *ywayn*, *metalle* ~ *metail*. It is necessary to add, however, that by the date of this text these alternate spellings were not in complementary distribution (if indeed they ever were), i.e. *a* occurring in unstressed positions, *ay* occurring in stressed positions. Both *gawan* and *gawayn* occur in rhyme position and in alliterative sequences of /g/ : *gawan* : *frayn* (487, 489), *gawayn* : *fayn* (838, 840); 'gawan & þe gay burde togeder þay ſeten' (1003), 'in god fayth & gawayn gayn hit me þynkke' (1241). The indication is that some instances of *gawan* occur with at least secondary stress on the rhyming syllable. As Gordon and Tolkien point out, the primary accent may very likely have been a floating accent, occurring on one or another syllable at the convenience of the poet. On the other hand, it may simply have been the case that with the shift in placement of the primary accent on French forms the superfix pattern became /ˈ + ^/. This would have entailed no weakening of the vowel nucleus in the syllable which lost the primary accent.

In his edition of Pearl, E. V. Gordon notes that the form *ſade* '. . . also occurs sporadically as the past tense or past participle in North-Western texts, as in the Stanzaic Life of Christ 8976 and Audelay's Poems (20.266). The writing of *a* for *ay* appears only in the verb "say" in this group of poems, and is therefore not likely to be connected with the northern simplification of diphthongs, which took place in all positions. *ſade* and *ſatȝ* more probably originated as unaccented forms, used together with *ſayt* and *ſayde* as stressed forms' (64. n. 532). Presumably, then, the unaccented forms were generalized in both accented and unaccented positions so that the spelling *ſade* was '... a genuine form in the copyist's usage, and possibly that of the original text.' If indeed it were the case that the spelling which arose from the occurrence of the word in unaccented positions had been generalized and was in fact characteristic usage in the original text, it seems curious that *ſade* occurs only twice in Pearl, once in Purity, and not at all in Gawain or Patience.

It is possible that the scribe who copied the present MS. revised all but three of the spellings in his source; or, alternatively, that the source, or sources, contained *ay* spellings throughout, contrary to the spelling habits of the last scribe who nevertheless remained faithful to his source in all but three instances. There are undoubtedly other possible explanations, not the least likely of which is simply the fact that the scribe made mistakes in his copying.

R. J. Menner suggests that the form *halſed* (Purity, 1621) next to *haylſed* (814) < ON /heylsa/ 'to greet' may have been influenced by OE /xæ:lsiɑn/ 'to conjure, adjure, predict', etc. The influence is possible, although there is no further evidence in the text to support it. The variants *a* ∼ *ay*, *aþer* ∼ *ayþer*, *ſant* ∼ *ſaynt* remain unexplained except by the assumption of scribal error.

One theory which would account for all instances of the <ai> <a> alternation has not, so far as I know, been considered by the students of this text. If in the dialect of the scribe ME [a:] and [aɪ] were no longer distinct phonemes, one might expect some confusion between <ai>, <a-e>, and <a> spellings although for the most part conventional spellings which had represented a phonemic distinction would have been retained. That such a coalescence had occurred in the dialect of the poet is hardly a tenable theory in view of the following set of rhymes in Pearl (1021-32): in the scheme abab abab bcbc, *þare* : *ſware* : *bare* : *ware* constitute the **a** rhymes; *ſtayre* : *fayre* : *glayre* : *repayre* : *manayre* : *cayre*, the **b** rhymes. For the poet, apparently, the phonetic distinction between ME [aɪ] and [a:] was obvious enough to permit him to use them in contrasting rhyme positions. It is not necessarily the case, however, that the same distinction obtained in the speech of the scribe who copied the extant MS.

The handbooks agree that the coalescence of /ay/ and /a:/ took place, at least in the north and north Midland counties, sometime during the fifteenth century (so Jordan, § 284; Wright, *EMEG* § 82; Wyld, § 268). According to R. E. Zachrisson, '... as early as the 15th cent. *ā* and *ai* had been levelled under the same sound or at least were pronounced very much alike. In the former case the sound given to both of them might have been [æ:] or [ɛ:], in the latter, at least the first element of *ai*, *ei* must have been identical with *ā* (possibly somewhat shorter), and the second component of the diphthong pronounced less distinctly than for instance German *ai*.'[23] Wyld notes that 'Evidence of the levelling of this M.E. *ai* under M.E. *ā*, the new sound being at first either [æ̅] or [ɛ̅], exists from the fifteenth century onwards.' His earliest citation of an *ai* spelling for ME /a:/ is dated 1421. If more or less conclusive evidence for such a shift is found in writing by the 1420's, one can reasonably assume that the change had been well established in the spoken dialects for some time. If our assumption that the speech of the Northwest Midland area was less conservative than that of the East Midland is correct, we should expect to find evidence of the coalescense of ME /ay/ and /a:/ in the writing of the late fourteenth century. The spelling *a* for *ay*, *aþer* for *ayþer*, and *ſant* for *ſaynt* may constitute such evidence.

Since the omission of a *y* is likely to be less conscious than its addition, a more convincing type of evidence is that in which *ay*, *ai* spellings occur for ME /a:/. In this MS. I have found only three forms that might be considered evidence of this kind: *daylyeden*, pt. plu. of *daly* 'to trifle, make love' < OFr. /dalier/; *vyſayge* 'countenance' < OFr. /visage/; *ſtayred* 'to gaze, look', < OE /starian/. Concerning *vyſayge*, the spellings *ay* and *ai* in French loans are not uncommon in ME before *ge* and may be attributed to palataliza-

[23] *English vowels* 65-6.

tion of /a:/ before /ǰ/. However, the other two forms are very difficult to account for unless they are indeed reverse spellings, *ay* for *a*, indicating that /ay/ and /a:/ had, in the dialect of the scribe, fallen together. That the movement in this direction was well under way by the date of composition of Gawain and Pearl is at least suggested by the word play in the following lines: 'þe mane of þat mayn HORS much to hit lyke' (Gawain, 187), 'and ʃyþen w^{t} frenkyʃch fare and fele fayre loteȝ' (Gawain, 1116), 'FOR if hit watȝ fayr þer j con fare' (Pearl, 147). The frequent occurrence of such formulaic phrases as 'date of daye', 'gracios gay', 'gay lady', 'fayr lady', 'fayr face', is suggestive but quite inconclusive.

Spelling evidence for the coalescence of ME /ay/ and /a:/ in the dialect of the scribe is certainly not strong, nor would one expect it to be. In a literary text even a small number of reverse spellings may be significant of a sound change since, unlike such spellings in private correspondence, they exist despite the strong scribal tradition which would certainly have inhibited attempts at phonetic spellings. That the two sounds in question were on the point of falling together can hardly be disputed in the light of early fifteenth century evidence; that they had already fallen together in the Northwest Midlands before the close of the fourteenth century seems at least a reasonable conclusion.

<aø> ~ <av>. The neutralization of <v> ~ <ø> indicated by such variants as *graunte* ~ *grant* occurs in words of AN origin before final *n*, before *n* plus *d, t, ʃ, c, g, ch*, and before *m* plus *p, b*. It reflects a phonological situation which developed in AN: 'vor einem derselben Silbe angehörigen Nasal erscheint wie in Anglonormannischen seit Anfang des 13. Jahrh. au als Reflex des franz. nasalierten a. ... Vor *ndž* und *mb* (*ntš*) erscheinen aber seit dem 14. Jahrh. Formen mit *ā*, das Ersatzdehnung für Schwund des *u* darstellt: *straange* (Trev.), *dānger, grānge, chāngen, chāmbre ...*' (Jordan, § 224.III; see also Wright, § 211). The spelling *ay* for the sound in question which appeared in some areas of the North and West, e.g. *raynge, straynge, braynche*, does not occur in this MS.

Wyld points out (§ 184) that the existence in the modern dialects of double types, e.g. /če:mber/ – /čo:mber/ (D22), indicates that the distinction in ME was not simply graphic. It is his opinion that the distinction was due to social causes. The upper classes who knew Norman-French were accustomed to the nasal vowel; to the lower classes, untutored in French, this sound was foreign and therefore ignored in their speech. 'Thus it seems probable that apart from court circles *dancen, ant*, 'aunt' were pronounced simply *dancen, ant*, etc., and these forms underwent no diphthongization.'

Again, several possibilities of interpretation present themselves. To begin with, the *a* spellings are too numerous to be set down merely as errors. Secondly, although an alternate pronunciation existed at the time the poems were written, it seems inconceivable that the poet, a thoroughly cultured individual who must have known French well, should have intended any but the reflex of the nasalized vowel. The scribe who wrote the final copy of the MS., however, may not have been so well schooled in French, so that the *a* spellings in the text may represent his own pronunciation. The rhyme *auinant : plesaunt : erraunt* (Gawain, 806 ff.) is the only one of five such rhymes in which *a* occurs with *au*. In the other four (three in Gawain, one in Pearl) the *au* spelling is consistent throughout. It may be significant that this is also the only rhyme-set in which all rhyme words are polysyllabic and in which, for that reason, the primary stress had shifted from the rhyme syllable. If the scribe were copying from dictation, the pronunciation of *auinant* may not have been clear to him, and the word itself strange. (It occurs only once in the MS.). As a result, he wrote what he thought he heard. Since the next word, *plesaunt*, is extremely common, the scribe would have known the traditional spelling, regardless of its pronunciation. The spelling of the third word, *erraunt*, would have presented no problems since it would already have been established by *plesaunt*. One can make no very valid assumptions, then, concerning the sound represented by *a* ~ *au* on the basis of this single occurrence of an *a* spelling in rhyme.

Thirdly, a few forms with *o* for *au*/*a* clearly suggest the presence of a rounded vowel: *braunch* ~ *bronch* (Purity, 487, 1461), *laumpe* ~ (Gawain, 2010) *lombe lyȝt* (Pearl, 1046). This last occurs in a passage in which there is an obvious pun on 'lamp' and 'lamb':

'þe ʃelf god watȝ her lombe lyȝt/þe lombe her lantyrne wythouten drede.' It is not clear whether the nucleus represented by <o> in *bronch* and *lombe* is short or long (see fn. 4). The modern dialects show both simple and complex reflexes of the sound in question as well as rounded and unrounded nuclei: /če:mber/ ~ /čo:mber/ 'chamber', /dons/ ~ /do:ns/ 'dance', /čo:ns/ ~ /čons/ 'chance', /čonǰ/ ~ če:nǰ/ 'change', /branč/ ~ /bro:nč/ 'branch', /donǰer/ ~ /do:nǰer/ in D22; D21 and D31 have chiefly /e:/ and occasional /a/ in these forms. To what extent shortening had already taken place in the dialect of the MS., and in what specific environments, cannot be determined. As has been suggested, there seems to be no good reason for assuming both rounded and unrounded nuclei in a literary text composed by a poet who obviously knew French. The *a* spellings are considered to indicate the pronunciation of the scribe. The modern dialect development seems to point to the fact that the reflex of AN [ã] fell together with the reflex of OE /ɑ/ rounded before nasals and lengthened in open syllables. It will therefore be written /aw/.

<e>~<e–e>~<v>~<v–e>~<o>~<o–e>~<oe>. The neutralization of these graphemes and grapheme sequences reflects a phonological problem similar to that discussed above. The reflexes of OE /ɔ:/ and AN /o:/ appear in ME variously spelled *eu, ue, eo, oe, o-e, e-e, u, u-e*.[24] Some reflexes of the OE phoneme had clearly fallen together and are rhymed with those of OE /e:/. Others split, falling together either with the reflexes of OE /e:/ or those of OE /o:/. As a result of this split, doublets often occur: *cheʃe* ~ *choʃe*, *ȝede* ~ *ȝode*, etc. This split is generally explained by an understandable assumption that OE /ɔ:/, spelled <eo>, had a diphthongal pronunciation and that double forms arose from a shift in stress from one element of the diphthong to the other.[25]

The alternates *lede* ~ *leude* ~ *lude* in Gawain offer some complications since it is not quite clear whether one has to do with two

[24] We are not concerned here with the phonemic status of EME [ö:]. There is no evidence for such a phoneme in LME in this dialect.

[25] This is a possible, but certainly not necessary, condition for the split of this phoneme (cf. the development of OE /y/, p. 61, and OE /y:/, pp. 87–8).

phonemes or one, and whether the spelling *leude* represents /i:/, /u:/, or a central allophone of one or the other. Friedrich Knigge, noting the rhyme *ȝede : leude* (Gawain, 1122-4), remarks that 'Was die Schreibung *eu, u* recht bedeuten soll, steht nicht ganz fest.' He goes on to conclude, however, that 'eu ist ohne Zweifel = *u*,' citing as evidence two forms from the Alexander Fragment, *beurd*, more frequently *burd* < OE /bry:d/, and *beurnes* < OE /bərn/. Further, 'Einen Anhaltspunkt bietet vielleicht Schreibung in den Alex.-Fr. wie *chused* (*cēosan*) 140. *hue* (hēo), *must* (mōst), so dass also *leud*, *lud* für *lod* stände, und dann hätten wir in *leud, lud* den schottischen *ö*-Laut.'[26]

Knigge's etymology for *burd* is doubtful. It seems more likely that, as Gordon and Tolkien suggest, the etymon is OE /byrde/ 'embroideress', cognate with ON /byrþa/, especially since both forms, *bryd* 'bride' and *burde* 'maiden' occur in the text. If Knigge is right and *eu* and *u* represent the same phoneme in William of Palerne and the Alexander Fragment, this fact considered together with the rhyme *leude : ȝede* in Gawain can only mean that the Gawain scribe had remembered only the spelling convention, not its significance. There seems to be no good reason for assuming that *leude* ∼ *lude* reflects the sound [ö:]. The form *leude* appears only in Gawain. Some thirty occurrences of the word in Purity show only <e>, <e-e>, and a single spelling <ee>. The fact that it rhymes with *ȝede* which in turn is rhymed with reflexes of OE /e:/ argues against a sound [ö].[27] *lud* may indeed 'stand for' *lōd*, but without the necessity to represent /lö:d/. Rounded forms which arose from OE /ə:/ fell together with reflexes of OE /o:/, *ȝod : gode* (Gawain, 1146), and presumably underwent the same development to LME /u:/. The form *lude* may simply reflect this development, or it may be an archaic spelling. Since it does not occur in rhyme, one cannot be sure.

26 *Die Sprache des Dichters von Sir Gawain and the Green Knight, der sogenannten Early English Alliterative Poems und De Erkenwalde* 50 (Marburg, 1886).

27 On this point see also Joyce Bazire, ME ẹ̄ and ę̄ in the rhymes of Sir Gawain and The Green Knight, *JEGP* 51.234-5 (1952).

When spellings once used to represent a given phoneme occur at a different time to represent a different phoneme, it may be assumed that the original significance of that spelling has been lost. Such appears to be the case with the *oe* spellings in this text. The variant *boerne* alternating with *borne* < OE /bu:rne/ (Gawain, 1570) is clearly a reverse spelling. There seems no reason to suspect either a phoneme /ö:/ or a phone [ö:].

Conversely, OE /bərn/, which one might reasonably expect to be spelled *boerne* ~ *beurne* ~ *beorne* ~ *buerne*, appears only as *burne* ~ *buurne* ~ *bourne*, presumably /buwrn/. The conclusion is that the reflexes of OE /ə:/ and AN /o:/ had fallen together in this text with /i:/, /u:/, or /uw/.

<i–e> ~ <v–e> ~ <vi> ~ <wi> ~ <ov> ~ <vv> ~ <v> ~ <oi>. A considerable amount of graphemic confusion arose in ME as the result of attempts to represent the reflexes of OE /y:/ and OFr. /oy/, /üy/, /ü/. OE /y:/ had much the same development in this dialect as did OE /y/; i.e. it remained a high central vowel until the fourteenth century (spelled *u*, *ui*, *uy* from about 1170) during which it was unrounded to /i:/. (Wright, *EMEG* § 57; Jordan, § 42; et al.). In this MS. the reflex is generally spelled *y* or *y-e*, although some examples of *uy* occur. Pearl has one instance of *hyde;* Gawain, two of *hyde*, and one of *hyden;* Purity, *hide* and *huyde*, < OE /hy:d/, /hy:dɑn/ 'hide'. Pearl has eight occurrences of *hyre;* Patience has one instance of *hyure*, for which there seems to be no precedent and which may be a metathesis for *huyre*, < OE /hy:r/, /hy:riɑn/ 'hire'. Purity has two instances of *druye* and two of *dryȝe;* Patience has only *drye*, < OE /dry:xe/ 'dry'.

According to Jordan, '$\bar{y}$ plus ȝ ergab wie die Kürze auf dem *ī*-Gebiet über *īj*, *ī*: *drīe* "trocken"; auf dem *ü*-Gebiet *ǖi*, das zu *ǖ* monophthongiert wurde (*drüie* R. Gl., Gaw., *drüe* Harl. 2253;)' (§ 92). The suggestion seems to be that the spelling *druye* in this MS. represents [dry:]. If this is the case, the spellings *drye* ~ *druye*, *hyde* ~ *huyde* presumably represent phonemic doublets. There is, however, little justification for establishing a phoneme /y:/. *pryde* < OE /pry:do/ rhymes in Gawain with *tyde* < /ti:d/ (587), and in Pearl with *byde* < /bi:dɑn/, *chyde* < /či:dɑn/ (401). *vnhyde* <

/on + hy:dɑn/ rhymes with *ſyde* < /si:de/ and *byde* in Pearl (973); *kyþe* < /ky:θɑn/ rhymes with /*ſwyþe*/ < /swi:θe/ and *myþe* < /mi:θɑn/ (356). The evidence suggests that the spelling *uy* in this MS. is a scribal convention retained in some forms in which reflexes of OE /y:/ had become either an allophone [i:] or, in some environments perhaps, an allophone [y:] of LME /iy/. It is the position of this study that the OE contrast between /ə:/ and /y:/, represented in LME by the forms dryȝe ~ dreȝ < OE /drə:xɑn/ and *druye* ~ *drye* ~ *dryȝe* < OE /dry:xe/, MnE /dra:/, became in this text a contrast between /i:/ and /iy/.

The alternates *burne* ~ *buurne* ~ *bourne* < OE /bərn/ (probably LOE /bə:rn/ with lengthening before /-rn/) have been discussed above. Perhaps the most one can say about the single occurrence of *buyrne* in the MS. (Patience, 340) is that it is no more than a scribal retention of a conventional grapheme sequence which was used at an earlier date to represent the sound [y:].

It is difficult to say whether the variants *rybe* (Pearl, 1007) ~ *rubies* (Purity, 1471), *kyryous* ~ *curious* (Purity, 1109, 1452) represent two phonemes or one. The development of the nucleus in these forms, < OFr. /ü/, is explained by Jordan in this way:

In den Gebieten aber, welche ae. *y* zu *i* entrundeten (vor allem dem östlichen Mittelland), hatte die volkstümliche Aussprache die Fähigkeit zur Aussprache des *ü* verloren, und hier wurde frz. *ü:* durch den Diphthong *eu* ersetzt, fiel also mit *eu* aus ae. *ēo* plus *w* zusammen.

. . . .

Dass der *eu*-Diphthong, mit dem frz. *ü* in der volkstümlichen Hauptentwicklung zusammenfiel, in unserer Periode, d.h. bis gegen 1400, nur diesen Laut hatte, wurde unter *ēo* plus *w* gezeigt. Der Übergang von *eu* > *iu* hing wohl organisch mit dem Vorrücken von *ē* > *ī* zusammen.

Eine Stütze für Luicks Ansicht, dass *eu* schon früher, d.h. Ende des 13. Jahrhs., zu *iu* wurde, bieten ihm Fälle mit *i*, das er auf *iu* mit Reduktion durch Labial zurückführt: *rīby* 'Rubin', *trīfle* 'Kleinigkeit', *limenour*, ne. *limner* 'illuminator'. *Tryfle* und *rybi* begegnen aber beim Gawain-Dichter, wozu *kyrious* für *cürious* ohne Labial, und andere Belege erweisen die *i*-Formen als vorwiegend westmittelländisch . . . Im Westen konnte *ü* in die einheimische Entwicklung von *ü* > *i* einmünden (204, 205).

The forms *fryte* < OFr. /früyt/, *difſtrye* < OFr. /destrüyre/, and *nye* < OFr. /anüyer/ are explained by the fact that OFr. /üy/ vacillated in AN between a rising and a falling diphthong, variants with rising stress frequently yielding /iy/, those with falling stress undergoing the same development to /iw/ as OFR. /ü/ above. Since *ui*, *uy* were characteristic spellings of this latter development, along with *u*, *eu*, *ew*, *iu*, *iw*, it is assumed that the alternates *fryte* ∼ *fruyt*, *nye* ∼ *nuye* represent doublets, /friyt/ ∼ /friwt/, /niy/ ∼ /niw/ (cf. Wright, *EMEG* § 202).[28]

The variants *fute* ∼ *fuyt* < OFr. /füyte/ 'track' indicate no phonemic variation; the phoneme represented is probably /iw/.

In addition to the alternates *nye* ∼ *nuye*, the form *noye* also occurs in the MS. The variation between *nuye* and *noye* is explained by the fact that OFr. verb forms had /üy/ in the first person singular, but /oy/ in the first person plural. According to Wright, 'In ME. the strong form of the singular generally became the type for the whole of the inflexion, but sometimes the weak form of the plural became the type, hence in ME. we have side by side forms like *anuien* and *anoien*, *destruien* and *destroien*, *vuiden* and *voiden*.' (*EMEG*, § 99). The underlying principle seems to be that OFr. /oy/ tended to become /üy/ depending upon whether or not the stem syllable received the stress; this new /üy/ fell together with OFr. /üy/ and developed in ME to /iy/ or /iw/ as noted in the preceding paragraphs. Thus, three phonemic variants may have occurred: *noye* /noy/, *nuye* ∼ *nwy* /niw/, and *nye* /niy/.

The variants *boyled* ∼ *byled* < OFr. /boyll-/ - /buyll-/ are probably to be explained in the same way. It is tempting, in view of our previous arguments for an early vowel shift in the Northwest Midlands, to consider *byle* a reverse spelling suggesting the coalescence, or near coalescence, of LME /iy/ and /oy/. And, indeed, some <i-e> spellings of OFr. /oy/ in the fourteenth century have so been considered.[29] However, any clear evidence for this interpretation is lacking until well into the fifteenth century. (Zachrisson, 73, 89). Had the shift actually been accomplished by the date of this

[28] Pope (§ 1227) notes the fact that 'When the diphthongs *üi* and *iü* were levelled to *ü*, the symbols *u*, *ui*, and *iu* became interchangeable . . .'

[29] e.g. W. Horn in *Untersuchungen zur neuenglischen Lautgeschichte* 92 (Strassburg, 1905) thus interprets *fyson*.

MS., one would reasonably expect to find some *ai*, *ay*, *ei*, *ey*, *oi*, *oy* spellings for LME /iy/, but I have found none. These alternates, then, presumably represent two pronunciations, /boyl/ and /biyl/.

<ai> ∼ <oi>. The variants *koynt* ∼ *quoynt* ∼ *quaynt* reflect the vowel change /oy/ > /ey/ (ME /ay/) which took place in OFr. during the latter part of the twelfth and thirteenth centuries. According to Pope, '. . . the less stressed high element . . . under the influence of the lower first element, was lowered to *ę*, stress shifted and the first element, become the less stressed, consonantalised to *u̯* (> *w*): thus *ọi* > *oę* > *u̯e* > *we* and *ọi* (ui) > *u̯e* > *wę*' (§ 519). EOFr. /oy/ developed an allophone [uy] before nasals which followed the line of development indicated above for /oy/, but which apparently did not develop quite so rapidly (Pope, § 474). *koynt*, then, is from EOFr. /koynt/, while *quaynt* is from later /kweynt/. The spelling *quoynt* is interesting. The pronunciation /kwoynt/ is etymologically impossible; however, it is fairly clear from the alliteration in the following line that such a pronunciation is intended: '& by queſt of her *quoyntyſe* enquylen on mede.' (Patience, 39). There are three possible explanations of *quoynt*. First, after the change of /oy/ to /wey/, the spelling *oi*, *oy* was frequently retained with the value /ey/ (see Pope, § 1223). Second, when in OFr. initial /gw/ and /kw/ were simplified to /g/ and /k/, the sequences *gu* and *qu* could be used to represent /g/ and /k/, especially, though not exclusively, before /i/ and /e/ (see Pope, § 701). Third, it is quite likely that both the spelling *quoynt* and the pronunciation /kwoynt/ were developed in ME on the analogy with *quaynt* /kwaynt/. The alliteration in the line quoted above seems to demand the initial cluster /kw/, while the rhyme *quoynt : poynt* (Pearl, 889) clearly demands a nucleus /oy/. In view of these two circumstances, the third explanation appears the most likely; nevertheless, one cannot quite rule out the possibility of interpreting the alliterating *quoynt* as /kwaynt/, the rhyming *quoynt* as /koynt/.

<v–e> ∼ <vv> ∼ <v> ∼ <ov> ∼ <ow> ∼ <oy>. The grapheme sequences <ov> and <ow> frequently represented ME /uw/ in the second half of the thirteenth century and became general during the course of the fourteenth. (Wright, *EMEG* § 9).

However, in the North, <v> and the sequence <v-e> were retained for this sound somewhat longer. (Jordan, § 55). The unique spellings in this MS. *abute* (Patience, 290) and *muthe* (Gawain, 447) may reflect the influence of Northern spelling practice, or may simply indicate a retention of the <v-e> <v> spelling convention longer in the Northwest Midlands than is generally thought to have been the case. The variants *ennourned* ~ *ennurned* < OFr. /aorner/ show that these spellings were not limited to OE forms in which the nucleus had originally been represented by the grapheme <v>. In any event, the alternation appears to have no phonological significance.

The alternation between <ov> and <oø> frequently occurs before <r>, especially in words of French origin as in *errour* : *honour* : *flour* : *fauour* : *douſour* : *faſor* (Pearl, 421-32) and *flor* : *tor* : *fauor* : *cloyſtor* : *vygour* (Pearl, 961-72). It is difficult to know what, if any, phonological significance this alternation has. In his edition of Pearl (97), Gordon suggests that the *o* spellings may indicate a lowering of [u] to [o], but it is not clear from his notation whether he means that in this environment /uw/ > /ow/, or simply that the *o* spellings indicate a lowered allophone of /uw/. The former hardly seems likely since *flor*, for example, shows the normal development in this dialect of LME /uw/ to MnE /a:/. The *o* spellings in the pronominal forms *yor* and *horſeluen* occur for the most part under weak stress and probably represent an unstressed allophone of /uw/.

Before certain consonant combinations AN /u:/ became short in ME (see Wyld, § 190); the variation between <ov> and <o> before <rt> in this text may suggest such shortening, e.g. *court* ~ *cort*. In addition, the environment /-()rC/ appears to have had a more marked effect on the quality of the nucleus than the environment /-()r/. The development of the latter has generally been to MnE /a:/, while that of the former has been to /ow/ or /u:/: ME *cource* ~ *cors* < OFr. /kors/ > MnE /ku:rs/. The spelling in *cors* may indicate a lowering to or in the direction of /ow/; the spelling *cort* may indicate a change in either the quantity or the quality of the nucleus, or both. For lack of more precise evidence, the two forms are written phonemically /kuwrs/ and /kuwrt/.

<i-e> ~ <e-e>. Of the variants *þyſe* ~ *þeſe*, the first is probably derived from the OE neuter, nominative and accusative *þis*, the second from the masculine, nominative singular *þes*. According to Wright, '*þēs*, *þēse* seem to occur earliest in the Midland dialects and then to have spread to the northern dialects, and by about 1500 to all the dialects . . . *þis*, *þise* (Orm, etc., *þise*) were special Midland forms, and remained in these dialects until about 1500, by which time they had been supplanted by *þēse*' (§ 383). In a note to this passage he continues, 'The precise quality of the *ē* in ME. *þēse* is uncertain. The ordinary ME. spelling may represent ẹ̄ or ę̄. In the sixteenth century it was often spelt *þeis* which points to ę̄, and the pronunciation of the various forms for these in many of the modern dialects also presupposes a late OE form *þǣs* which according to the NED did exist.'

In this MS., <i-e> spellings far outnumber <e-e> spellings, and the phonological status of the former seems clearly defined by the rhyme *ryſe* < OE /ɑ:ri:sɑn/: *þyſe* (Gawain, 1101). The question to be raised here is whether the <e-e> spellings in this MS. represent an innovation in both spelling and pronunciation, or in spelling only. Since <e-e> spellings do not occur in rhyme, any conclusion will be dubious. Only one tenuous bit of evidence for the pronunciation of *þeſe* occurs. In Gawain, the line 'and pite þat paſſeȝ alle poynteȝ þyſe pure fyue' (654) is followed two lines later by 'now alle þeſe fyue ſyþeȝ for ſoþe were fetled on þis knyȝt.' In the first there is internal rhyme between *þyſe* and *fyue*, in the second between *fyue* and *ſyþeȝ*. On the basis of the repetition, which seems to be quite conscious, one can make a case for considering the nucleus in *þyſe* and *þeſe* to be the same. It may be that the <e-e> spellings were not original with the poet but were an innovation by a scribe at a later date. Whether this spelling was a hyper-urbanism or actually represented the pronunciation of the scribe, /ðeyz/ or /ði:z/, cannot, obviously, be determined. Reflexes of both OE *þis* and *þes* occur in the modern dialects: /ði:z/, for example, can be found in middle, east middle, and south Lancashire; /ðiyz/ in north, southeast, southwest, and middle south Lancashire.

Since <i-e> spellings are the more numerous, and since they seem best to represent the sound intended by the poet, the morpheme {these} will be considered to be /ðiyz/ regardless of spelling. However, the <e-e> spellings would appear to indicate a gradual encroachment of the reflex of OE *þes* during the latter part of the fourteenth century.

<aw> ~ <ew> ~ <ve> ~ <w> ~ <v> ~ <ev>. The handbooks are generally agreed that the sound [iu], which arose from OE /i:w/, /ɨ:w/, /ə:w/, OFr. /ü/, /üy/, AN /ew/, and [eu], which arose from OE /æ:w/ and /a:w/, remained distinct throughout the ME period. Zachrisson points out that '*ẹ̄u* and *u*' were pronounced with the same sound in the fifteenth century, and goes on to say that '*ẹ̄w* must have been kept apart from *ę̄w*, for ... I have found no instance of *u* written for *ę̄u*' (84). The spelling distinction obtains in this MS.: [iu] is spelled *ew, eu, w, u, u-e;* [eu] is spelled *ew* only.

The variants *ſchawe* ~ *ſchewe* represent phonemic doublets, the result of a shift in stress from one element of the OE nuclei /a:w/ (*eaw*) and /ə:w/ (*eow*) to another.

The variant spellings *eau* ~ *ew* occur for reflexes of OFr. /eaw/. Originally a falling triphthong, /eaw/ was simplified to /ew/ following a stress shift in the later twelfth century and this /ew/ fell together with ME /iw/. (Pope, § 539). Before labials, /š/ and /č/, the second element of the nucleus was lost and the sound fell together with LME /ey/; thus the form *reme* /reym/ < OFr. /reawme/.

CHAPTER V

THE PHONOLOGICAL SIGNIFICANCE OF THE GRAPHEMIC SYSTEM

PART II: THE CONSONANTS

5.1. Allographic representation.

5.11. Obstruents.

/p/ < OE /p/ and /pp/ is represented by the allograph *p* of <p>, and by the graphemic sequence <pp>: *pipe* < OE /pi:pe/ = /piyp/, *cuppe* < OE /kuppɑ/ = /kup/.

/t/ < OE /t/ and /tt/ is represented by the allograph *t* of <t>, and by the graphemic sequence <tt>: *telle* < OE /tellɑn/ = /tel/, *lette* < OE /lettɑn/ = /let/.

/č/ < OE /č/ and /čč/[1] is represented by the sequences <Ch>, <ChCh>, and <CCh>: *chaffer* < OE /ča:p + fɑru/ = /čafer/, *hachche* < OE /hæč/ = /hač/, *ricchis* < OE /klyččɑn/ = /klič/.

/k/ < OE /k/ and /kk/ is represented by the allographs *k* and *q* of <k>, the allograph *c* of <C>, and the graphemic sequences <kk> and <Ck>: *clyffe* ~ *klyffe* < OE /klif/ = /klif/, *quene* < OE /kwe:n/ = /kwi:n/, *mokke* < OE /mok/ = /mok/, *muckel* = /mukel/.

/b/ < OE /b/ and /bb/ is represented by the allograph *b* of <b>, and the graphemic sequence <bb>: *bed* < OE /bedd/ = /bed/, *habbeʒ* < OE /hɑbbɑn/ = /habez/.

/d/ < OE /d/ and /dd/ is represented by the allograph *d* of <d>,

[1] The OE phonemes written here /č/ and /ǰ/ were probably the palatalized stops [k] and [g] until assibilation took place in LOE or EME.

and the graphemic sequence <dd>: dede < OE /de:d/ = /di:d/, wedde < OE /weddiɑn/ = /wed/.

/ǰ/ < OE /ǰ/ and /ǰǰ/ and AN /ǰ/ is represented by the allographs *i* and *j* of <i>, the allograph *g* of <g> and the graphemic sequence <gg>: *iugge* < AN /ǰuǰier/ = /ǰuǰ/, *gentyle* ∼ *jentyle* < AN /ǰentil/ = /ǰentil/, *egge* < OE /eǰ/ = /eǰ/, *ſwangeande* < OE /swenǰɑn/ = /swanǰand/.

/g/ < OE /g/ and /gg/ is represented by the allograph *g* of <g>, and by the graphemic sequence <gg>: *glad* < OE /glæd/ = /glad/, *doggeȝ* < OE /doggɑ/ = /dogez/.

/f/ < initial and final allophones of OE /f/ and medial /ff/ is represented by the allograph *f* of <f>, and by the graphemic sequences <ff> and <ph>: *fare* < OE /fɑru/ = /fa:r/, *clyffe* < OE /klif/ = /klif/, *offre* < OE /offriɑn/ (or OFr. /offrir/) = /ofre ∼ ofer/, *cofer* < OFr. /kofre/ = /kofer/, *prophete* < OFr. /profete/ = /profi:t/.

/θ/ < initial and final allophones of OE /θ/, and medial /θθ/ is represented by the allograph *þ* of <þ>, the graphic sequence *th*, the graphemic sequence <þþ>, and the graphic sequence *thþ*: *þider* < OE /θider/ = /θider/, *ſiþen* < OE /siθθɑn/ = /siθen/, wrathþe < OE /wræθθu/ = /wraθ/.

/s/ < initial and final allophones of OE /s/, and medial /ss/ is represented by the allographs *ſ* and *s* of <s>, and the graphemic sequence <ss>: *ſlepe* < OE /sle:pæn/ = /sli:p/, *myſſe* < OE /missɑn/ = /mis/, *mas* < OE /messe/ = /mas/.

/š/ < OE /sč/[2] is represented by the graphemic sequences <Ch>, <sC>, <ssCh>, <sChCh>, <sCh>: *fleſch* < OE /flæ:sč/ = /fleš/, *fiſſche* < OE /fisč/ = /fiš/, *worchip* < OE /wərθ + sčipe/ = /woršip/, *ſcade* < OE /sčɑ:dɑn/ = /ša:d/.

Voiced spirants became phonemic in ME as a result of a split between the voiced and voiceless allophones of the OE spirants /f/, /θ/, and /s/. Hans Kurath explains this split in the following way:

The older English short fricative phonemes /f, þ, s/ had voiced allophones [v, ð, z] between vowels, and contrasted in this position

[2] Probably /š/ in LOE.

with the voiceless long fricatives /ff, þþ, ss/ both in quantity and in vocalization. Since quantity was the sole distinctive feature between the short and the long sonorants and stops, the quantitative difference between short and long fricatives of OE must be regarded, from the point of view of the system, as their primary distinctive feature, and the difference in vocalization as a secondary concomitant feature. With the loss of quantity as a distinctive feature in the stops and the sonorants, and hence also in the fricatives, voicing becomes the distinctive feature of the fricatives in intervocalic position. Thus, although between vowels the phonemes /f, þ, s/ and /ff, þþ, ss/ of older English continue to be pronounced as [v, ð, z] and [ff, þþ, ss] respectively, undergoing no phonic change, they now contrast phonemically as /v, ð, z/ vs. /f, þ, s/.

The shift from length to vocalization as the distinctive feature entailed a regrouping of the allophones of the fricatives. Intervocalic [ff, þþ, ss], derived from the older phonemes /ff, þþ, ss/, join the initial and final allophones [f, þ, s] of the older phonemes /f, þ, s/ to constitute the new phonemes /f, þ, s/, while the intervocalic allophones [v, ð, z] of the phonemes /f, þ, s/ of older English come to function as the separate phonemes /v, ð, z/.

At this stage in the development of the English consonant system the voiced fricatives /v, ð, z/ occurred only between vowels, as in *liven*, *bathen*, *risen*. Initial /v/ became established later through the adoption of French words ... initial /z/, through the slow adoption of such words as *zele* 'zeal', *zodiac* (usually *sodiac* and always *senith*, *cenith* 'zenith'). Initial /ð/ arises at a later date from a native development in such normally (or frequently) unstressed words as *the*, *there*, *than*, starting as a prosodic allophone.

Not until final /ə/ was lost, beginning circa 1300 in the North Midland and the North, did the voiced fricatives /v, ð, z/ also occur in final position, e.g. *live*, *bathe*, *rise*.[3]

[3] Kurath, The Loss of long consonants and the rise of voiced fricatives in Middle English, *Language* 32.438-9 (1956). In those areas in the North and Midlands in which Scandinavian influence was most notable OFr. initial /v/ was reinforced by ON initial /v/, the result of the North Germanic change /w/ > /β/ > /v/ (cf. OE /wi:f/, ON /vi:f/).

The lengthening of all short nuclei in open syllables in EME caused a change in syllabic structure which resulted in the loss of phonemically long consonants. As Kurath points out, these structures were in contrast as late as the beginning of the eleventh century:

/VCCV/
/VCV/
/VVCV/

With the lengthening of all short nuclei in open syllables, /VCV/ falls together with /VVCV/ ([VVCə]) so that now either the vocalic length feature or the consonantal length feature is redundant. Kurath selects the vocalic length feature as phonemic since vocalic length is already phonemic in the structures /VVC/ and /VC/. Since /CC/ and /C/ are no longer distinguished, the two contrasting structures are /VCV/ and /VVCV/. Now if /C/ is a spirant, it will be voiceless in /VCV/ and voiced in /VVCV/, i.e. voiced and voiceless spirants will still appear to be in complementary distribution in medial position in ME. There were, however, some conditions which inhibited the lengthening of short vowels in open syllables, and where these conditions were operating one may look for contrasts between voiced and voiceless spirants in native words.

One such condition was the fact that disyllabic forms which could become trisyllabic by the addition of a suffix did not lengthen the stem vowel in the inflected form and frequently generalized the short vowel to the uninflected form as well. A case in point is the form *wyþer* (Pearl, 230) < OE /wiθer/ 'against' inflected to *wyþerly* (Purity, 198). The derived form contrasts in analogous environments with, for example, such forms as *ſyþen* < OE /siθθɑn/. Intervocalic /s/ and /z/ are contrasted in *bloſſumeȝ* < OE /blo:stmɑ/ (Gawain, 512) and *boſum* < OE /bo:sme/ (Patience, 107), with shortening of the stem vowel before the consonant cluster. Intervocalic /f/ and /v/ are contrasted in *offre* < OE /offriɑn/ (with vocalic [r̩]) and *ouer* < OE /ofer/.

With the weakening of inflections in EME and the eventual loss of final [ə], intervocalic consonants in a number of items become final so that previously disyllabic structures become monosyllabic: /VCV/[VCə] > /VC/, /VVCV/ [VVCə] > /VVC/. One may now expect the voiced allophones of original intervocalic spirants to contrast in final position with the voiceless allophones of original final spirants; thus *lyf* /liyf/ < an uninflected OE /li:f/ contrasts with *on lyue* 'alive' < an original inflected dative singular. However, two additional types of changes occur in ME which make the identification of contrasts between final voiced and voiceless spirants difficult. From the beginning of the thirteenth century there was a tendency in some dialects to shorten long vowels in monosyllables. And furthermore, the early loss of final [ə] in the northern dialects led to the unvoicing of the voiced spirants which now stood in final position. As a result, the voice-voiceless contrast tended to be dissipated between final spirants (and between final stops as well).

The interpretation of the double graphemic forms which occur in this MS. as a result of the phonological situation is difficult; e.g. *rys* ~ *ryſe*, *ryf* ~ *ryue*, *lof* ~ *loue* < OE /ri:sɑn/, /ri:f/, /lufu/. One wonders whether the first set of variants suggests /ris/, /riys/, /riz/, /riyz/ or some combination of these. The rhyme *rys : wyſe : enpreſſe : gyſe* occurs in Pearl (1093-9). If one accepts the form *enpreſſe* < OFr. /enpres/ as being correct, he may assume that the spirants are voiceless and the nuclei probably short. However, most editors have accepted Gollancz' emendation of the form to *enpryſe* < OFr. /enprise/ 'glory', 'renown' (with probable voicing of the spirant in intervocalic position). Considering the context of the line, 'þis noble cite of ryche enpreſſe,' the emendation seems eminently suitable. One may wonder, nevertheless, how the error happened to occur since it scarcely seems to be a mistake in copying. Perhaps it occurred as the result of a similarity in sound between the two words; i.e. the spirant in *enpryſe* may have been voiceless in this dialect and/or the preceding nucleus short (cf. Lydgate's spelling *enprices* in The Serpent of Division 63.27). If this were the case, it is very probable that the spirants in the whole series were voiceless. On the other hand, there is always the possibility that the rhymes were not identical.

Again, the forms in the rhyme *ryf : vyf : lyf : ſtryf : dryf : ſtyf*

(Pearl, 770-9) < OE /ri:fe/, /wi:f/, /li:f/, /dri:fɑn/, /sti:f/, and OFr. /estrif/ are subject to more than one interpretation. By the date of this MS. OE /sti:f/ had become /stif/, a new formation modelled on the inflectional form /stiffer/ with short stem nucleus. This fact, together with the spelling, suggests that the nucleus in each item in the sequence was short. The spelling and rhyme in the sequences *knyffe : bilyue : ryue* (cf. *ryf* above) and *hafe : ſtaue : ſaue* (Gawain, 2042-6, 2135-9) seem to indicate a neutralization of the voice-voiceless feature in final position.

Before the end of the thirteenth century, final [s] > [z] after vowels of unstressed syllables, and this [z] was then retained under stress. That the pronunciation of *hys* was regularly /hiz/ seems to be indicated by the rhyme sequence *þyſſe : blyſſe : myſſe : iwyſſe : hyſſe* (Pearl, fit VII) in which the unique spelling *hyſſe* induces an artificial pronunciation /his/. Presumably, the unique spelling *wace* (regularly *watȝ*) serves the same purpose in the sequence *ſpace : grace : wace : face* (Pearl, 61-7). That the spirant in *hys* was not voiceless even in stressed positions seems clear from the rhyme *deuiſe : pryſe : hys : wyſe* (Pearl, 1129-35), 'devise', 'prize', 'his', 'wise'.

The graphic representation of /s/, /z/, /θ/, and /ð/ is confusing. The allographs *s* and *ſ* may both represent /s/ and /z/, *ſſ* regularly represents /s/. *ȝ* generally occurs for /z/, but appears to represent /s/ in the bound morpheme {-les} (OE /la:s/) in the rhyme sequence *pres : pes : deſe : depres : maſkelleȝ*. According to E. V. Gordon, the sequence *tȝ* :. . . . is used only for voiceless *s*, as in *watȝ*, *hatȝ*, *gotȝ*, *ſaytȝ*, etc. and is restricted to the end of stressed monosyllables, while simple *ȝ* occurs most frequently in unstressed syllables.'[4] Gordon is not altogether accurate here. The items cited frequently occur in unstressed positions, but so far as I have been able to determine no difference in spelling is occasioned by a difference of position. Of 87 occurrences of *watȝ* in Pearl, 19 are clearly stressed, 17 are ambiguous as to stress, and 51 are unstressed. Since there is general agreement among the handbooks

4 *Pearl* 93 (Oxford, 1953).

that final [s] in the unstressed allomorphs of these items had become [z] prior to the date of this MS., Gordon's interpretation does not seem justified. F. Knigge remarks that 'doch findet sich in *was*, *watȝ* .... schon eine Annäherung an den ne. *z*-Laut, der durch Reime freilich nicht sicher gestellt ist'[5]; and Richard Jordan, 'Reime wie *is : amis*, *was : allas* bei Ch. (Wild 246) sprechen nicht dagegen [i.e. do not contradict the fact that the spirant in *is*, *was*, *his*, etc. was voiced in unstressed morphemes], da bei Worten wie *is*, *was*, *has* je nach dem Satz-rhythmus schwächere oder stärkere Betonung, also Wechsel von *z* und *s* möglich war.'[6]

It is not clear how one should interpret *tȝ* in the rhyme sequence *ros : porpos : gotȝ : clos : totȝ : þos* (Pearl, 506-15); the spirants in each of the forms may be voiced or voiceless. One may make the point, however, that in rhyme sequences in which the spirant is unquestionably voiceless, the writer does not use the graphic sequence *tȝ*, but *c* or *ſſ* : *ſpace : grace : wace : face* (Pearl, 61-7), *glaſſe : waſſe : paſſe : waſſe* (Pearl, 1106-12), *hyſſe : blyſſe* (Pearl, 418-20), *þyſſe : blyſſe* (Pearl, 370-2), etc. The two instances of *ȝ* in *ſayȝ* (Pearl, 615) and *ſaȝ* (Pearl, 689) in stressed positions, beside the more frequent *ſaytȝ*, suggest that [z] occurs not only in the unstressed allomorphs of *is*, *his*, *was*, *does*, *goes*, etc. but in the stressed allomorphs as well. Our conclusion is that the graphic sequence *tȝ* is not used 'only for voiceless s,' that nothing can be determined from its two occurrences in rhyme, and that the weight of the evidence seems to favor its interpretation as [z].

There is some attempt in ME to distinguish /θ/ and /ð/ by the use of *th* and *þ* respectively; for example, these lines from Cursor Mundi:

storis als o sere kin *th*inges
o princes prelates and o kynges
sanges sere of selcu*th* rime
inglis frankys and latine

[5] *Die Sprache des Dichters von Sir Gawain and the Green Knight, der sogenannten Early English Alliterative Poems und De Erkenwalde* 59 (Marburg, 1886).

[6] *Handbuch der mittelenglischen Grammatik*, rev. H. Ch. Matthes § 208 (Heidelberg, 1934).

to rede and here ilk on i prest
*þ*e *th*ynges *þ*at *þ*am likes best
*þ*e wis man wil o wisdom here
*þ*e foul hym drawe to foly nere
*þ*e wrang to here o right is la*th*
and pride wy*th* buxsumnes is wra*th*
o chastite has lichur le*th*
on charite ai werrais wre*th*. (3-14.)

That some effort has been made by the copyist of this MS. to distinguish graphically between /θ/ and /ð/ is indicated by the distribution of *th* and *þ*. In Purity, for example, in the environment *V()V*, there are 131 occurrences of *þ*, 7 of *th*, and these seven only before a bound morpheme; in *V()e*, 136 occurrences of *þ*, 13 of *th;* in *V()*, 2 occurrences of *þ*, 59 of *th*. One would expect to find a voice-voiceless contrast between *V()e* and *V()* respectively, e.g. between *kyþe* /kiyð/ < OE /ky:θɑn/ 'to make known', and *kyth* /kiyθ/ < OE /ky:θ/ 'country', 'region', and very likely there is. However, the fact that *th* occurs sporadically in *V()e* (and the *e* is not in every case non-etymological), coupled with the tendency to neutralize the voice-voiceless feature in final position, leaves the whole matter uncertain.

In *()V*, *þ* is almost universal. *th* does not occur in Gawain, and in the other three poems all but 6 of 39 instances are majuscules. Since majuscule Þ is rare in the MS., it may be that it was simply a matter of scribal practice to write *Th* for Þ in environments requiring a majuscule, and that no other significance ought to be attached to such occurrences. Knigge, however, finds some significance in the fact that *Th*, and *þ* alternate only in those items in which the spirant had regularly become voiced: *Then* ~ *þenne*, *Thus* ~ *þus*, *Thow* ~ *þou*, *Thys* ~ *þys*, *That* ~ *þat*, *Thaȝ* ~ *þaȝ*, *The* ~ *þe* (58). It may be that the scribe used *th*, the less common of the two, in an attempt to distinguish between the voiced spirant in these few forms and the voiceless spirant elsewhere, even though in final position it represented /θ/.

There is little doubt that the initial spirant was voiced in these items by the date of this text. According to Wright, 'There is no indication either in ME. or NE. to show when the *þ* became voiced in such words, but the dialects of Sus., Ken., and s. Pem. show that it must have taken place pretty early, because in these dialects the *þ*- has become *d*-, although the forms with *d*- are now obsolescent in the latter two counties. Examples are: *deə*, 'their', 'there', *dem*, *den*, *di* 'the', *dis*. These forms with *d*- show that the voicing of the *þ*- in pronominal and adverbial forms was older than the voicing of it in the other OE. words beginning with *þ*.'[7] The change [θ] > [ð] apparently took place at about the same time that [č] > [ǰ] in unstressed syllables, and evidence for the latter is accepted as evidence for the former. Jordan cites *ostrige* < OFr. *autruche*, in Wyclif, for the fourteenth century, *cabage* < *caboche*, *sausige* < *sausiche*, *Burbage* < *Burbache* for the fifteenth. The form *brutage* (Purity, 1190) < OFr. *bretesche*, AN *brutesche*, indicates that in this dialect voicing was already well established in this environment before the end of the fourteenth century (cf. William of Palerne, 3001, *bretages;* Piers Plowman A (1), 6.79, *brutaget*). Whether [ð] had been extended to items other than those cited above, for instance to *Thaȝ* 'though', cannot be determined.

Loan words in the MS. establish contrasts which are sometimes difficult to find in native words. /z/ is established in initial position, and intervocalic /f/, by *ȝeferus* /zeferus/ – *ſeuen* /seven/, *cofer* /kofer/ < OFr. /kofre/ – *couer* /kover/ < OFr. /kovrir/; initial /v/ by *vyne* /viyn/ < OFr. /viñe/ – *fyin* /fiyn/ < OFr. /fin/; medial /s/ by *taſſel* /tasel/ < OFr. /tasel/ – *haſel* /hazel/ < OE /hæsel/. Final /s/ and /z/ contrast in unstressed syllables in *pryncece* /prinses/ < OFr. /prinses/ (the first syllable falls under metrical stress) – *prynceȝ* /prinses/ < OFr. /prins/, and in stressed syllables in *kneȝ* /kni:z/ < OE /knə:/ – *nece* /ni:s/ < OFr. /niese/ or /nyese/.

/v/ < intervocalic allophone of OE /f/ and OFr. /v/ is represented by the allograph *v* of <v> in the environment <()V(-)>, by the allograph *u* of <v> in the environment <(-) V()V(-)>, and per-

[7] Joseph and Elizabeth Mary Wright, *An Elementary Middle English grammar*, 2nd ed. § 236 (Oxford, 1928).

haps by the allograph *f* of <f>: *vyne* = /viyn/, *leuen* = /li:ven/, *hafe* = /ha:v/.

/ð/ < the intervocalic allophones of OE /θ/ seem most frequently to be represented by the allograph *þ* of <þ>, although the sequence *th* may occur for this sound, especially in initial position: *Then* = /ðen/, *kyþe* = /kiyð/.

/z/ < the intervocalic allophones of OE /s/ and OFr. /z/ is represented by the allograph *ʒ* of <ʒ>, the allographs *ſ* and *s* of <s>, and by the sequence *tʒ* : *deſyre* ~ *deʒyre* /deziyr/, *ſays* ~ *ſaytʒ* /sayz/, *ʒeferus* /zeferus/.

5.12. Sonorants.

/m/ < OE /m/ and /mm/ is represented by the allograph *m* of <m>, and by the graphemic sequence <mm>: *merþe* < OE /myrgθ/ = /merθ/, *ſum* ~ *ſumme* < OE /sum/ = /sum/.

/n/ < OE /n/ and /nn/, is represented by the allograph *n* of <n>, and by the graphemic sequence <nn>: *neuer* < OE /næ:fre/ = /never/, *ſunne* < OE /sunne/ = /sun/.

/l/ < OE /l/ and /ll/ is represented by the allograph *l* of <l>, and by the graphemic sequence <ll>: *lyf* < OE /li:f/ = /liyf/ (perhaps with shortened nucleus /lif/), *falle* < OE /fɑllɑn/ = /fal/.

/r/ < OE /r/ and /rr/ is represented by the allographs *r* and *ʀ* of <r>, and by the graphemic sequence <rr>: *rot* < OE /rot/ = /rot/, *foʀ* < OE /for/ = /for/, *marreʒ* < OE /mærrɑn/ = /marez/.

/w/ < OE /w/, /ww/, and /x/ when preceded by /a/, /o/, /u/, /l/, /r/, is represented by the allograph *w* of <w>, the allograph *ʒ* of <ʒ>, the graphic sequence *gh*, the graphemic sequence <ww>, the allographs *u* and *v* of <v>: *wyte* < OE /wi:tɑn/ = /wiyt/, *wlonk* < OE /wlonk/ = /wlonk/, *wrake* < OE /wrɑku/ = /wra:k/, *ſaghe* ~ *ſaweʒ* < OE /saxu/ = /saw/, *folwande* ~ *folʒande* < OE /folxiɑn/ = /folwand/, *rowwe* < OE /ro:wwɑn/ = /row/, *aboute* ~ *abowte* < OE /ɑ:bu:tɑn/ = /abuwt/, *hov* ~ *how* < OE /xu:/ = /huw/.

/y/ < OE /j/, /x/ when this was preceded by palatal vowels, and from an initial, stressed, palatal vowel when this occurs as the first element of a complex nucleus is represented by the allograph *ʒ* of

<ȝ,> the allograph *y* of <i>, and graphic sequence *gh: ȝef* < OE /jefɑn/ = /yef/, *ȝed* < OE /ə:de/ [e:ode] = /yi:d/, *yowre* ~ *ȝowre* < OE /ə:wer/ [e:ower] = /yuwr/, *day* < OE /dæj/ = /day/, *waye* < OE /wej/ = /way/, *heȝe* < OE /he:x/ = /hey/, *neghe* < OE /ne:x/ = /ney/.

5.13. Residues.

[h] < OE initial /x/ is represented by the allograph *h* of <h>: *help* < OE /xelp/ may = [help]. The phonemic status of [h] is not clear in this dialect and will be discussed below.

[x] < OE /x/ in the environment /-()t(-)/ and /-r-1()/ is represented by the allograph *ȝ* of <ȝ>, and the graphic sequence *gh: nyȝt* < OE /nixt/ may = /nixt/, *hawbrgh* < OE /xalsbərx/ (or OFr. /hawberk/) may = [hawberx]. Like [h], the phonemic status of [x] is questionable.

5.2. The phonemic significance of graphemic neutralization.

<p> ~ <b>. The variants *lombe* ~ *lomp* 'lamb' attest to the unvoicing of final stops under stress especially after nasals. Apparently some unvoicing of voiced stops also occurred intervocalically as a result of a stress shift: *cubites* ~ *cupydeȝ* < Lat. *cubitum.* The alternates *babtem* ~ *baptem* < OFr. /baptesme/ present an instance of apparent dissimilation similar, perhaps, to that in *lobster* < OE /lopestre/ (also influenced by OE /lobbe/ 'spider'). Kurath and Khun cite no other instance of *babtem* in ME.[8] Professor Householder has pointed out to me that the spelling may represent an early instance of a pronunciation which is now quite common in many parts of the United States.

<p> ~ <ø>. Long before the date of this MS. French scribes had begun to represent the /p/ which intruded as the second stage of a transition from /m/ to a following dental (i.e. a denasalization of /m/). Both the spellings *damner* ~ *dampner, solemne* ~ *solempne*

[8] *Middle English Dictionary*, ed. Hans Kurath and Sherman M. Kuhn, pt. B 1.636-7 (Ann Arbor, 1956).

can be found in EOFr.[9] In native English words this /p/ was being represented in the spelling system as early as the beginning of the thirteenth century: OE /æ:mtij/ appears in St. Katherine (c1225) as *empti* (392). Of the alternates *ſolempne* ~ *ſolemne* in this text, the latter would appear to be an older archaic spelling, the former, a more recent attempt to represent the phonetic situation. In view of the date of the MS., however, this does not seem likely. With the loss of final [ə], /n/ no longer functions as an onset in this position, and one suspects that it has been lost.

There is little in the two lines in Purity in which the word occurs to indicate its pronunciation: 'he ſete on Salamones ſolie on ſolemne wyſe' (1171) and 'in þe ſolempne ſacrefyce þat goud ſavor hade' (1447). Whether or not /p/ was retained after the loss of the final unstressed syllable, and for how long, is uncertain. At any rate, the pronunciation /solempne/ is quite unlikely. The slightly earlier York play Harrowing of Hell, the meter of which is regularly iambic, contains the line, 'now ſe j be þis ſolempne ſight' (355). One would not, I think, be inclined to consider /solempne/ a possibility here.[10]

Regarding the alternates *ſolempnete* ~ *ſolemnete* the situation is somewhat different. /n/ is retained as an onset to the inflectional syllable, and since the second syllable retains the major stress, /p/ is perhaps more likely to occur here than in the form *ſolempne* in

[9] M. K. Pope, *From Latin to modern French with especial consideration of Anglo-Norman* § 369 (Manchester, 1934).

[10] The spelling *ſolempne* is quite consistent in Chaucer's verse, and the meter of the lines in which it occurs indicates that it represented both /sólem/ or /sólemp/ and /solémpne/: 'a lýmytóur a fúl solémpne mán' (Canterbury Tales, I [A] 209 [Robinson's edition]); 'and hált his féeste so sólempne ànd so rýche' (Canterbury Tales, V [F] 61). The meter of the second line clearly indicates that at least in casual speech the major stress had shifted to the first syllable and that the form contained two syllables, not three. One cannot be sure, of course, whether *solempne* in the first line represents a pronunciation which was still current in the East Midlands, or whether it is a deliberate archaism. In view of Chaucer's use of what must have been an archaic pronunciation of final [ə] for metrical purposes, I suspect the latter.

which the stress is at least in the process of shifting to the first syllable—if, indeed, the shift had not already occurred.

<b> ~ <ø>. The variants *clym* ~ *klymbe* < OE /klimbɑn/ and *wame* ~ *wombe* < OE /wɑmb/ indicate the complete assimilation of final /b/ to a preceding /m/ (see Jordan, § 211). The forms *ſloumbe* < OE /slu:mɑ/ (Mdn. dial. *sloom*) 'slumber', *ſlomeryng* < OE /slumeriɑn/ 'slumber' are somewhat puzzling in that one would expect to find **ſlomberyng* and **ſloume* rather than *ſlomeryng* and *ſloumbe* since the tendency was for /b/ to intrude between /m/ and a following /l/ or /r/ (e.g. OE /θy:mel/ > /θy:mle/ > ME /θimbl/). There is no evidence of such intrusion in this MS. (which does not mean, of course, that it did not occur). It is quite possible that *ſloumbe* is a hyper-urbanized spelling patterned after such forms as *klymbe* and *wombe* in which final /b/ had been lost.

<t> ~ <d>. The alternate spellings *bront* ~ *bronde*, *loʀt* ~ *loʀde*, reflect the West Midland unvoicing of /d/ in certain stressed monosyllables in original /-Vn-l-r()/ and in reflexes of /-VVn-l-r()/ where /VV/ became /V/ in ME.

During the OE period short vocalic nuclei were lengthened before certain consonants, especially /l/, /r/, /m/, /n/ plus homorganic voiced stop; however, all lengthened nuclei before /rd/ and all but /i:/ and /u:/ before /nd/ were regularly shortened again during the ME period with, in the West Midlands, an attendant unvoicing of the final stop. The forms /blint/ 'blind' and /wint/ 'wind' in Mn. Bolton (D 22) suggest that at some time and in some areas the shortening of lengthened nuclei before /nd/ with subsequent unvoicing of the stop was extended to forms containing the reflex of LOE /i:/. Clearly, this must have taken place before LME /iy/ had shifted to /əy/ early in the fifteenth century. Certainly, /blint/ must date from a period not much later than that of this MS., and possibly before. /wint/ may, as Wright points out, be a back-formation from forms like *windy* and *windmill*.[11] A similar explanation of /blint/, however, is more difficult to find evidence for. Since no such

[11] See *An Elementary historical new English grammar* § 73.6 (Oxford, 1924).

alteration appears in the Mn. dialect in *bind*, *find*, *kind*, *mind*, /ba:nd/, /fa:nd/, /ka:nd/, /ma:nd/, it may be that the significant factor was the preceding /l/. Whatever the explanation of Mn. /blint/ and /wint/, there is no spelling evidence in the MS. to suggest that /d/ was unvoiced in the environment /-iyn()/. In general it may be said that in those forms in which the lengthened nucleus was retained, /d/ also was retained; in those in which the nucleus became short, /d/ > /t/; and for some words and in some areas of the Northwest Midlands the structure /-VVr-l-nd/ alternated with the structure /-Vr-l-nt/.

The modern dialect shows evidence of unvoicing in disyllabic words in which primary stress falls on the second syllable; e.g. /biyont/ (Bolton), /biyond/ (Blackburn) 'beyond', but there is no graphic evidence in this MS. to indicate that the change had taken place by this date.

It is obviously impossible to determine from the relatively slight graphemic evidence in the text how extensively the unvoicing in question had been carried out. How one ought to transcribe, for instance the line, 'ſyn ȝe be loʀde of þe ȝonde londe þer j haf lent inne,' is questionable. That *loʀde* may be transcribed /lort/ is apparent from the alternate spelling *loʀt*, and that *ȝonde* and *londe* became in this dialect /yont/ and /lont/ is indicated by modern south Lancashire pronunciation. Considering the fact that the Gawain poet makes considerable use of the poetic device of skothending (internal rhyme of consonants with unlike vowels), the form *lent* adds some support to the interpretation of *loʀde*, *ȝonde*, and *londe* as /lort/, /yont/, and /lont/.

/d/ regularly became /t/ in the preterite and past participle of verbal stems ending in /l/, /ld/, /rd/, /m/, /n/, and /nd/ by analogy with verbal inflections in which /t/ was original, as in OE /ke:pɑn/, preterite /ke:pte/ 'kept'. (Wright, *EMEG* § 230). Thus, one finds the alternates *gyld* ~ *gilt*, *blende* ~ *blent*, *fonde* ~ *fonte*, *wende* ~ *went*, *dyd* ~ *dyt*. The conservatism of the spelling system prevents one from accurately defining the extent of the change. Although the past participle *gurde* ~ *gorde* is spelled only with *d* in the MS., consonantal rhyme may have been intended in the line 'gurde wyth a bront ful sure' (Gawain, 588), in which case *gurde* would be written phonemically /gurt/.

The alternates *founded* ~ *fondet*, *haled* ~ *halet*, *bluſched* ~ *bluſchet* illustrate the peculiarly West Midland unvoicing of the dental in the preterite and past participle following the reduction of stress in this morpheme. This change also took place in the northern dialects, at first under more limited conditions, namely, after /l/ and /r/. It was later extended to other environments and is still found in a number of Scottish counties.[12]

The alternates *comforte* ~ *coumforde* < OFr. /kownfort/, *pendauntes* ~ *pendaundes* < OFr. /pendant/, and the forms *marked* 'market' < Latin /merkatus/ (cf. OE /jarmɑrket/, *ioparde* < OFr. /ǰew parti/, and possibly *poyned* (?) may, theoretically, be interpreted in two ways. Without reference to the specific context in which the *d* spellings occur, one might assume a phonetic change of /t/ > /d/ in foreign loans following a shift in primary stress to an initial syllable (see Jordan, § 161). In the case of *ioparde*, in which /d/ is not morpheme-final, this seems to be the correct interpretation. In the other items, however, with the possible exception of *poyned*, *d* appears to be nothing more than a reverse spelling. *coumforde* rhymes with *lorde* : *remorde* : *myſerecorde* : *endorde* : *acorde* (Pearl, 361), and can perhaps be considered further evidence for the unvoicing of /d/ in this environment. *marked* is very likely a reverse spelling influenced by the spelling of the preterite morpheme {-ed} as in the preceding paragraph. Since *pendaundes* occurs under stress, 'ne þe ſaynt ne þe ſylk ne þe ſyde pendaundes' (Gawain, 2431), one suspects that *d* is a graphic change only.

The form *poyned* occurs in Pearl (217) in the following context:

pyȝt watȝ poyned and vche a hemme
at honde at ſydeȝ at ouerture
wyth whyte perle and non oþer gemme
and bornyſte quyte watȝ hyr ueſture.

[12] Jordan, § 200; Joseph Wright, *The English dialect grammar* § 304 (Oxford, 1905).

Gordon, following the syntax of the MS., takes *poyned* to be a noun in parallel structure with *hemme*, both modified by *pyȝt*, and derives it from OFr. /poynet/ 'wristband'. If this analysis is correct, the *d* is probably best considered to be a reverse spelling, although the OFr. /t/ may have been voiced following a shift in stress to the first syllable.

The variants *þat* ~ *þad* illustrate the assimilation of a final /t/ in weakly stressed syllables to initial voice in the following morpheme, as in 'þad daye' (Gawain, 686). This change is particularly noteworthy since graphic evidence of such assimilation is rare in ME (see Jordan, § 199).

<t> ~ <ø>. <t> is occasionally lost in the environment <-C()> : *ſayn* < OFr. /seynt/ 'girdle' (Gawain, 589), *ſayn* < OFr. /saynt/ 'saint' (Gawain, 1022), *myȝ* for *myȝt* (Gawain, 1858), *broȝ* for *broȝt* (Pearl, 286). It is possible that the omission of *t* in the first two forms represents a phonemic loss in the dialect of the poet or scribe. According to Miss Pope, examples of the loss of final 'unsupported' stops in pre-consonantal position begin to occur in the MSS. of the late twelfth century (§ 613). Since forms both with and without *t* occur in pre-consonantal position, and since none of these forms occurs in rhyme, it is difficult to know precisely what the phonological significance of the omission is. It may be an inconsistent attempt to represent a consistent phonological practice, it may represent the pronunciation of one or more of the scribes, but not all, or it may be the result simply of a spelling error, as the unique occurrences of *myȝ* and *broȝ* undoubtedly are.

The alternates *hes* ~ *heſt* < OE /hæ:s/ 'order', 'command' indicate the addition of an inorganic /t/, perhaps by analogy with other morphemes ending in /-est/ (so Jordan, § 199). One cannot be sure whether phonemic doublets, /hest/ ~ /hes/, occurred in the dialect at this relatively late ME date or not. The fact that there are six occurrences of *heſt* to one of *hes*, and the fact that /t/ had been added to the word as early as the beginning of the thirteenth century suggest that the spelling *hes* may be archaic. One notes, however, that *t*, and perhaps /t/, has not been added to *agaynȝ* ~ *agayneȝ* 'against' in this text although the form with /t/ was certainly, by this date, current in other parts of England. It may be that *hes* represents a common pronunciation in the Northwest Midland dialect.[13]

<t> ~ <þ>. The alternates *droȝt* ~ *droȝthe* and *heȝt* ~ *heȝþe* illustrate the fourteenth century dissimilation of OE /θ/ to /t/ following a spirant. Although spellings with *t* are much the more frequent in the MS., the fact that the modern dialect shows /t/ and /θ/ in this environment (as in /ðrowt/ and /ðrewθ/ suggests that <þ> was not simply an archaic spelling but that /t/ and /θ/ were actually neutralized in this position in the dialect of the MS.

Through French influence *t* frequently alternates with *th* especially in words of Greek origin; thus, *trone* ~ *throne*, *teme* ~ *theme* (see Jordan, § 262. Anm. 2). The alternation appears to be graphemic only. All *t* spellings in such words alliterate with /t/ in other words, while in the lines 'towarde þe throne þay trone a tras' (Pearl, 1113) and 'þe apoſtel in apocalyppce in theme con take' (Pearl, 944) both *throne* and *theme* seem clearly to alliterate with /t/.

<d> ~ <ø>. This alternation tends to occur in morpheme-final position following a consonant grapheme, especially <n>. In some cases, as in *hanſelle* ~ *hondeſelle*, it reflects the disappearance of an organic /d/ after /n/ analogous to the loss of /b/ after /m/ (see Jordan, § 200). In others, e.g. *mankyn* ~ *monkynd* < OE /mon + kyn/, *onende* < OE /on + emn/, the alternation reflects the addition of an inorganic *d* as a hyper-urbanized spelling; or, an inorganic /d/ may actually occur as the result of confusion with, or influence by, other morphemes. The reflex of OE /kyn/ may have been influenced by the reflex of OE /kynde/; that of OE /emn/ by the reflex of OE /ende/, etc. The inorganic /d/ in MnE *bound* 'setting out for' < ON /bu:n/ and *hind* 'servant' < OE /hi:gnɑ/ is not yet represented in the spelling system of this text. Pearl has, for instance, 'þat date of ȝere wel knawe þys hyne' (505), and Gawain, 'bot j am boun to þe bur barely to morne' (548).

<d> ~ <þ>. In a few forms in the MS. doublets occur as the

[13] Cf. also *myddes* 'midst'; *midst* seems not to have developed before the middle of the fifteenth century.

result of ON influence: *hondred* ~ *hundreth* < OE /hundred/ and ON /hundraθ/ respectively; *brayde* ~ *breyþed* < OE /brægd/ and ON /bregθa/. The variants of the intensive prefix *alder* ~ *alþer* < OE gen. plu. /ɑlrɑ/ are difficult to account for. An intrusive /d/ regularly developed in OE between /l/ and /r/, /n/ and /l/, and /n/ and /r/, as in *spindle* < OE /spinle/ and *þunder* < OE /θunre/. Now, whether the form *alþer* is a late fourteenth century instance of the regular fifteenth century change of /d/ to /ð/ before the syllabic allophones of /r/, as in /fader/ < /faðer/, /togeder/ < /togeðer/, whether it is a hyper-urbanized spelling influenced by the fact that /ðl/ and /ðr/ were already becoming /dl/ and /dr/, e.g. in *fyþel* < OE /fiθele/ 'fiddle' and *roþer* < OE /ro:θor/ 'rudder', or whether /ð/ reflects ON influence, is not clear. I suspect that it is the first; however, if it is, it is the only instance of such a change in the MS.

In the neighborhood of liquids the voiced allophone of OE /θ/ frequently became /d/. Throughout the ME period and into the MnE period /ð/ and /d/ appear to be neutralized in this environment until either the stop or the spirant is generalized in a given word. As a result, the standard dialect has, for instance, *afford*, *burden*, *murder* < OE /jeforθiɑn/, /byrθen/, /morθor/ beside *northern* and *worth* < OE /norθerne/, /wərθ/, while some non-standard dialects have *burthen*, *murther*, but *farding* < OE /fərθing/ (see Wright, *E.d.g.*). The spelling *forþe* beside *fordeȝ* < OE /ford/ seems to be a reverse spelling resulting from the fact that *þ* in this environment now represents /d/. If this is the case, one may assume that the spellings *burþen*, *fyþel*, and *roþer* (Purity, 1439, 1082, 419) are archaic and that the phonemic structure is /burden/, /fidel/, and /roder/. (The modern Lancashire dialect shows only /d/ in these forms and there is no evidence for a pronunciation */forð/ in the modern reflexes of the word). On the other hand, one can just as easily account for the spelling *forþe* by the assumption that /d/ and /ð/ had been neutralized in this environment.

<k> ~ <g> ~ <ȝ>. The phonemic significance of the graphic sequence *gh* in the alternates *ſtrenghþe* ~ *ſtrenkþe* and in *lenghe* (n.) beside *lenge* (v.) is not clear. In West Germanic the sound represented by *g* in the environment <-n()j/i-> was apparently a palatal allophone of /ɡ/ which became /ǰ/ in some dialects during the OE period. In final position after <n>, *g* represented a velar allophone of /ɡ/ which became /g/ in OE. All scholars do not agree that the palatal allophone of /ɡ/ became /ǰ/ in all dialects during the OE period, but some cite evidence to suggest that especially in the Northern, Midland, and Eastern counties the spirant was retained in OE and, with loss of OE contrast between /ɡ/ and /x/, was now a voiced allophone of /x/.

Knigge thinks that the spelling *gh* in *lenghe* represents /ǰ/ (68). This may be so; however, failure to find any reflexes of a LME */lenǰ/ or */strenǰ/ in the modern dialect together with the strong possibility that following the loss of inflections during the ME period the affricated stop would, in final position, have become /g/ by analogy with OE /strɑng/ and /lɑng/ leads me to suspect that the phoneme represented by both *g* and *gh* in this form is a stop. And further, that given the characteristic Northwest Midland unvoicing of stops in the environment /-n()/ the phoneme in question is /k/.[14] The spelling with *gh* may have been influenced by *ſtrenghþe* in which *gh* clearly seems to represent /k/.

In the environment /-n()C/ West Germanic /ɡ/ was not palatalized and became /g/ in OE. During the OE period the cluster /ng/ > /nk/ before voiceless consonants, but /g/ was frequently restored by analogy with forms in which /g/ regularly occurred in the environment /n()/. As a result, OE MSS. have /strenkθ/ beside /strengθ/ by analogy with /strɑng/, /lenkθ/ beside /lengθ/ by analogy with /lɑng/ (see Jordan, § 193). Whether this restoration was purely graphic, or whether it was actually phonemic cannot be determined. However this may be, one would expect that in this dialect and by the end of the fourteenth century the phoneme in question would be voiceless, just as it was voiceless in the environment /-n()/; for example in *ȝonge* ~ *ȝonke* < OE /jəng/, *þyng* ~ *þynk* < OE /θing/, and in *among* < OE /on + mong/ rhyming with *þonc* : *wlonc* : *bonc*. There seems little justification for

[14] See below, p. 133, for the argument that pre-consonantal reflexes of OE /x/ became allophones of /k/ in this dialect.

supposing that *gh* in the unique spelling *ſtrenghþe* represents anything but /k/. Its occurrence here may possibly be explained by the fact that after tense vowels + /r/ or /l/, the reflexes of OE /x/ tended to become allophones of /k/ in a number of areas during the ME period (see Jordan, § 197; cf. also the form *hawbrgh* < OFr. /hawberk/ in Gawain, 203). If this tendency were actually at work in the dialect in question, it may be that *ſtrenghþe* is a hyperurbanized spelling, *gh* occurring for *k* in a word in which *k* normally occurred.

<k> ~ <Ch>. For the most part, the alternation of these spellings occurs in the reflexes of Germanic forms which have undergone different developments in OE and ON, or in forms which have had variant developments in OE. *carle* /karl/ derives from the unpalatalized ON reflex of Germanic /k/, *choʀle* /čorl/ from the palatalized OE reflex. It is impossible to say to what extent the alternation of /k/ and /č/ in medial and final position is due to a double development of OE inflected and uninflected forms, and to what extent it is due to ON influence. OE /č/ > /k/ before consonants; thus, ME *much* < OE /mycel/, but ME *muckel* < OE /myklu/ (with syncopation of the unstressed vowel). Although *muckel* may have been reinforced in this dialect by ON /mikil/, there is no reason to suppose that it derives from it. Concerning the variants *woʀchen* (pres. plu.) ~ *wyrkeȝ* (imp. plu.), /k/ may have arisen from the OE syncopated form /wyrčeθ/ < /wyrčθ/ < /wyrkθ/, or it may have been the result of the influence of ON /yrkja/. In some instances, alternates may occur as the result of the influence of related words; e.g. *wrake* ~ *wrache* < OE /wrɑku/ 'vengeance' influenced by OE /wreččɑ/ 'wretch' and /wreččɑn/ 'to drive out', 'dispel'.

The alternates *rocheȝ* ~ *rokkeȝ* < AN /roke/, /roče/ appear to reflect the fact that in AN /k/ was retained in the dialects of Picardy and north Normandy, but elsewhere became /č/ (see Jordan, § 257; Wright, *EMEG* § 285; Pope, § 1320). If this is actually the case, it is likely that the two spellings represent distinct phonemes. However, it may be that the form *rocheȝ* is an archaic spelling reflecting an earlier AN scribal practice of using *ch* to represent /k/ before

/i/ and /e/ (see Pope, § 1209). It occurs only in the line, 'herneʒ & hauekeʒ to þe hyʒe rocheʒ' (Purity, 537), in which the phoneme /k/ is somewhat more stylistically desirable since it creates a consonance with the /k/ in *hauekeʒ*.

<k> ~ <kv>. See above, p. 90, for a discussion of the variants *koynt* ~ *quoynt* ~ *quaynt*.

There are two possible explanations of the alternates *venkkyſt* ~ *venquyſt*. Knigge points out that the form with *qu* derives from an OFr. perfect (114). A few OFr. verbs, among them /veyntre/ < Latin /vinkere/ with characteristic palatalization of /k/ and successive development to dental stop after /n/, formed weak perfects by adding inflections directly to the root; thus, /venkwi/, /venkwis/ (see Pope, § 1038).[15] Since in CF of the eleventh and twelfth centuries /w/ was lost in this position, but retained considerably longer in AN, the forms *venkkyſt* ~ *venquyſt* may represent phonemic doublets, the first from CF, the second from AN.

On the other hand, it is quite possible that the variants are merely graphic. In OFr., after the graphs *c* and *g* had come to represent /ts/ and /dz/ respectively, a number of various devices were used to represent /k/ and /g/. When initial /kw/ and /gw/ were simplified to /k/ and /g/, it then became possible for the sequences *gu* and *qu* to represent /g/ and /k/, especially before /i/ and /e/ (see Pope, § 701). It is conceivable, then, that the spelling *qu* in this word represents an archaic tradition. This interpretation receives some support from the occurrence of the variants *gere* ~ *guere* < ON /gervi/ where *guere* seems to be a hyper-urbanism reflecting an older scribal practice.[16] This spelling does not appear to be related to the later, and for the most part sixteenth century, re-spellings of OE and ON words by analogy with French loans, as in *guest*, *guess*, *guilt*, etc.

<k> ~ <ø>. The alternates *lenþe* ~ *lenkþe*, *ſtrenþe* ~ *ſtrenkþe* suggest an alveo-palatal [ñ] in noncontiguous partial assi-

[15] A new infinitive /veynkre/ ousted /veyntre/ as the result of the influence of the past participle /venku/ (see Pope, § 757).

[16] Jordan cites in this connection the spellings *guod* 'good', *biguynne* 'begin', *finguer* 'finger', *guyldhall* 'gildhall' (§ 185).

milation to /θ/, with consequent loss of /k/. Modern east middle, southeast, and northwest Lancashire generally have /lenθ/, although [n] and [ŋ] sometimes occur side by side within the same dialect area. In MnE, D21 has [leŋkθ], D22 and D31 have both [leŋkθ] and [lenθ]. The presumption is that doublets occurred in the dialect of the MSS.

In two verb forms internal sandhi occurs in which morpheme-final /k/ is replaced by /ø/ when followed by the preterite and past participle morphemes {-ed} and {-en}: *maked* ~ *made*, *taken* ~ *tan*. As the result of this replacement, a new present stem is formed: 1st and 2nd sg. *ma*, 3rd sg. *mas* ~ *mace* ~ *matʒ*, plu. *man; ta*, *tas*, *tan*. The latter forms are considered to have developed by analogy with the new formations of the former (so Wright, *EMEG* § 79 n. 2; Jordan, § 178.Anm. 4).

The pronunciation of the single occurrence of *ſclade* (Pearl, 1148) cannot be determined from the text; elsewhere only *ſlade* occurs. Knigge considers that the 'parasitic' *c* may be simply a diacritic marking a voiceless /l/ (60). Whatever the phonetic explanation, the scribal practice goes back at least to LOE where *c* is occasionally found inserted between *s* and a following *l*, *m*, or *n*.[17] It is quite possible, on the other hand, that the spelling with *c* is no more than a hyperurbanism influenced by the archaic spelling *ſcl* of an earlier OFr. cluster /skl/ in such ME forms as *ſclaunder* 'slander', *ſclavine* 'pilgrim's cloak', *ſclyſe* 'sluice', *ſclices* 'slices'. Whatever the history of the graphic cluster *ſcl* might have been, the fact that of the forms from OE and OFr. which one might expect to be so spelled only *ſclade* occurs suggests that the phonemic cluster is /sl/.[18]

<Ch> ~ <ø>. Final <Ch> in the derivational suffix {*-liCh*} tends to disappear under reduced stress: *luflych* ~ *lufly*, *frelich* ~ *frely*. There is no way to determine from the distribution of the

[17] See Eduard Sievers, *An Old English grammar*, trans. and ed. Albert S. Cook, 2nd. ed., § 210 (Boston, 1896).

[18] Jordan assumes that /k/ had disappeared between /s/ and /l/ before 1400 (§ 257. Anm. 2).

forms in the MS. whether the alternation is merely graphic or whether it reflects phonemic doublets.[19]

<g> ~ <i>. In EOFr. /ǰ/ was represented by *g* in all positions before /i/ and /e/, while before /a/, /o/, /u/ it was represented by *i*, later *j*: *gent*, *engin*, *iambe*, *ioie*, *donion*, *iuge*. Occasionally, however, this distribution was just reversed so that one finds *borieis*, *goie*, *dongon* (see Pope, § 699). It is as a result of this scribal confusion in OFr. that this text shows *gentyle* ~ *ientyle* ~ *jentyle*, and the forms *bougounȝ* (Purity, 1416) < OFr. /bowǰon/ 'a beating instrument' and *doungoun* (Purity, 158) < OFr. /donǰon/ 'dungeon'. From the latter part of the twelfth century, French scribes were able to maintain a graphic distinction between /g/ and /ǰ/ by using the sequence *gu* to represent /g/ after the loss of /w/ in this position. In AN, however, where /w/ persisted into the thirteenth and even fourteenth centuries, there must have been some confusion in the representation of /g/ and /ǰ/, especially in those instances in which *g* represented /ǰ/ before back vowels.

For several reasons, then, it is impossible to state in any useful way the distribution of the graphs which represent in this text the phonemes /g/ and /ǰ/. In the first place, *gu* spellings for OFr. /g/ do not occur in the MS.[20] Second, the distribution of the OFr. graphs *g* and *i* was, as we have noted, occasionally reversed, and frequently an original /i/ or /e/ ceased to be represented once the palatalization of the preceding consonant had taken place. Third, the AN scribes were obliged to adapt their graphemic system to an already established native tradition, and with the resultant system to represent three different and at times contradictory sets of phonological facts, those of AN, OE, and ON. It is only on etymological grounds that one can identify /ǰ/ in *gyngure* < OFr. /ǰinǰivre/, *gette* < OFr. /ǰet/, and /g/ in *gyng* < ON /gengi/, *gettes* < ON /geta/.

[19] It is perhaps worth noting that the suffix without <Ch> is sometimes reduplicated to emphasize an adverbial function as in *luflyly* (Gawain, 369; Purity, 163).

[20] The form *anguych* (Patience, 325) < EOFr. /angwise/ is a possible exception to this, though the /w/ is probably retained through AN.

In words of OE origin, <g> <gg> represent /ǰ/ in the environment <i/e()(e)> as in *bryg(g)e* 'bridge', *egge* 'edge', *heggeȝ* 'hedge', *rygge* 'ridge', and also in the environment <n()e> where *e* is a graphic reflex of an original /i/ as in *ſwangeande* 'swirling'. It should be noted, however, that in some areas of the North, East, and Midlands /ǰ/ was replaced by /g/ as a result of Scandinavian influence (see Wright, *EMEG* § 296). In MnE, therefore, D21 and D22 generally have /briǰ/, /riǰ/ 'bridge', 'ridge', but D31 has /brig/, /rig/. In words of ON origin, <g> ~ <gg> represent /g/ as in *big(g)e* 'settle', 'found', *leg(g)e* 'leg', *eggyng* 'instigation'. French loans occasionally have <gg> representing /ǰ/ as in *ſegge* 'siege', *legge* 'entitled to allegiance', *logge* 'lodge'.

<g> ~ <ȝ>. The spelling variants *foʀgat* ~ *foʀȝate*, *gef* ~ *ȝef*, *gate* ~ *ȝate*, *agayn* ~ *aȝayn* and the like represent phonemic doublets which reflect the divergent development of initial Germanic /ɡ/ in OE and ON. In ON, and in OE before back vowels, initial Germanic /ɡ/ > /g/; before palatal vowels this /ɡ/ remained a spirant, /j/, eventually becoming ME /y/, spelled <ȝ>. The extensive Scandinavian influence on this ME dialect is at least partially responsible for the phonemic alternation between /g/ and /y/ in initial position. However, some of these alternations undoubtedly arose in OE as the result of an alternation of the stem vowel in the paradigm; thus, ME *ȝate* /ya:t/ < OE nom. sg. *geat* /jat/, but *gate* < OE nom. plu. *gatu* /gɑtu/. The form *ȝaule* < ON /gawla/ appears to be anomalous. Alliteration with *ȝomerly* < OE /jə:mer + li:če/ and *ȝelle* < OE /jellɑn/ indicates that this is not simply a reverse spelling of *ȝ* for *g*. Presumably, EME /gawle/ and /yele/ existed side by side, but in LME /g/ was replaced by /y/ under the influence of the latter.

<g> ~ <gw> ~ <w>. That the alternates *gaynour* ~ *gwenoʀe* ~ *wenoʀe*, *gawayn* ~ *wawen* represent phonemic doublets is clear from the alliteration: 'there gode gawan watȝ grayþed gwenoʀe biſyde', 'and wener þen wenoʀe as þe wyȝe þoȝt', 'foʀ to haf greued gaynour and gart hir to dyȝe'. Both names are of Celtic origin and the alternates are the result of varying treatments of /gw/ and /w/ in Welsh, CF, and AN. In Welsh, initial /g/ tended to disappear in certain environments, one of which was before /w/. On the other hand, Celtic /w/ underwent the same change in CF as did Germanic /w/ in initial position and following /g/ or /k/; i.e. /gw/ > /g/, /kw/ > /k/, and /w/ > /gw/ > /g/. The forms *gwenore* and *wenore* may have existed in Welsh as phonemic doublets becoming *gaynour* in CF, or it may be that only the form *wenore* came early into OFr., was altered to *gwenore* > *gaynour* in CF, but was retained either as *wenore* or *gwenore* in AN.[21] In other words, *gwenore* ~ *wenore* < /gwen-/ may have come to the attention of the Gawain poet from either a Celtic or an AN source; *gaynour*, however, is clearly from a CF source.

A number of alternates occur in the text which reflect the CF treatment of Germanic /w/ in initial position: *wyle* ~ *gile*, *wyfe* ~ *gyfe*, *biwyled* ~ *bigyled*, etc. It is impossible to determine to what extent the forms with *w* have been directly inherited from OE, and to what extent they have been borrowed from or reinforced by ONFr.

<f> ~ <ʒ>. This alternation occurs only in the forms *þof* ~ *þoʒ* 'even though' < OE /θɑx/, ON /θox/ (Gawain, 624). In some parts of England, especially in the west, the development of OE /x/ in final position to /f/ took place early in the fourteenth century along with its alternate development to /w/, as in *innoghe* ~ *innoʒe* ~ *innowe* (see Jordan, § 197). H. C. Wyld, for instance, cites the rhyme *softe : dohter* in King Horn, MS. Harl. 2253, 391-2.[22] The phonological significance of this single occurrence of *f* for *ʒ* in the MS. may indeed be that the reflex of OE /x/ had become, or was in the process of becoming, /f/ in some forms. On the other hand, it is possible that the form *þof* was written by a scribe from a dialect area different from that of the poet; but if this were the case, it is surprising that no other examples of *f* for *ʒ* appear.

<f> ~ <ø>. The variants *joly* ~ *jolyf*, *haftyly* ~ *haftyfly* are the result of a morphophonemic change and a double stem formation which took place in OFr. Adjectives and nouns whose unin-

[21] On this point see J. R. R. Tolkien and E. V. Gordon, eds. *Sir Gawain and The Green Knight* 83.109 (Oxford, 1925).

[22] *A Short history of English*, 3rd ed. § 282 (London, 1927).

flected root ended in /f/ lost this phoneme before the nom. sg. inflectional morpheme {-s}: acc. sg. *jolif*, nom. sg. *jolifs* > *jolis* (see Pope, § 812). When final /s/ was lost along with other final consonants in OFr. and MFr. (beginning in about the latter twelfth century in preconsonantal position), a new stem was formed on the nom. sg., *joli*, which in the modern period has been generalized in all positions. Final /f/ was apparently retained considerably longer than final /s/, although it too began to disappear during the fourteenth and fifteenth centuries (see Pope, § 812). That it was pronounced in this MS. is evident from the rhyme *jolyf : wyf : ſtryf : fyf : þryf* (Pearl, 842-51). Presumably, beginning in EOFr., the development was something like this: nom. sg. /jolifs/ acc. sg. /jolif/ > nom. sg. /jolis/ acc. sg. /jolif/ > nom. sg. /jolis/ ~ /joli/ acc. sg. /jolif/ > nom. sg. /joli/ acc. sg. /jolif/. Since by the thirteenth century case affixes had lost their grammatical significance in ME, both /joli/ and /jolif/ occur as unaffixed stem variants; i.e. /ø/ is no longer significant here.

The form *mawgref* < OFr. /malgre/ is explained by Tolkien and Gordon as an alternation of *maugreþ* < OFr. /malgreθ/ influenced by the form *gref*. An alternative explanation might be that *mawgref* has simply been formed on analogy with such forms as *jolyf* and *haſtif*.

The alternates *haf* ~ *hafen* ~ *han* reflect both a phonemic and a morphemic change. In this MS., the 3rd plu. non-past allomorph /-en/ is in free variation with /-ø/: when /-en/ occurs, final /f/ of the stem is in free variation with /ø/.

<v> ~ <ø>. The variants *pouer* ~ *pore* < OFr. /povre/ illustrate the vocalization of pre-consonantal /v/ after lax vowels and before liquids, velar stops, and dentals, /n/ and /d/ (see Wright, *EMEG* § 242; Jordan, § 216). The nucleus in the latter form is /ow/, falling together with the reflex of OE /ɑ:/, MnE /u:/. Neither form occurs in rhyme, and it is not clear whether the variant spellings represent variant pronunciations in this text or not. The vocalization of pre-consonantal /v/ was a ME sound change which seems to have begun about the end of the thirteenth century (see Pope, § 1185). It is difficult to say how rapidly the new pronunciation ousted the old; however, the currency of spellings in which *u* represents /v/ throughout the fourteenth century suggests that /povre/ lingered, at least among the literary minded who knew French, until the end of the ME period.

It is frequently the case that /v/ becomes preconsonantal as the result of syncopation of a following vowel in unstressed syllables and is then vocalized; thus, *auenture* ~ *aunteres*, *nauel* ~ *naule*, *hauekeȝ* ~ *hawk*, *heued* ~ *hede*, *bihoues* next to the preterite *byhod*. In the dialect of this MS. it seems likely that the variant spellings, at least in some instances, represent different pronunciations. Pearl has only the form *auenture* which seems on metrical grounds to contain three syllables in the line 'in auenture þer meruayleȝ meuen' (64). Gawain has the spellings *auenture* ~ *a venture* ~ *a wenture* ~ *aunter*.[23] Purity has only *aunteres*. According to Tolkien and Gordon (Gawain, glossary), *aunter* is 'an older and more popular borrowing.' This statement is somewhat puzzling in the light of the fact that the word derives from OFr. *aventure*. Presumably what is meant is that *aventure* was borrowed before vocalization of preconsonantal /v/ occurred, and then /v/ in this word was vocalized along with /v/ in native words before the fourteenth century giving *aunter*. During the fourteenth century the word was again borrowed from French as *auenture* since /v/ was not vocalized on the Continent.

Evidence from the modern dialects indicates that *deuel* and *dele* 'devil' represented doublets since reflexes of both can be found (see Wright, *E.d.g.*). Before /l/ and /r/ one can expect to find varying treatments of /v/ depending upon whether the liquid involved is consonantal or vocalic. When /l/ or /r/ occur before the vowel of an inflectional syllable, for example, the preceding /v/ will be vocalized; when final, they become vocalic and the preceding /v/ will remain.

The form *mwe* alternating with *meue* < OFr. /moveyr/ may represent an extension of vocalized /v/ from an inflected dental preterite /me:ved/ > /me:vde/ > /mewde/ to the uninflected forms, or it may have been reformed on analogy with *remwe* < OFr. *remuer*.

23 For the spelling *a wenture* see below, p. 126.

<þ> ~ <ø>. The alternates *ſiþen* ~ *ſyn* indicate the fact that during the EME period [θ] and [ð] tended to be lost before [ṇ] and [ṛ] in unstressed syllables, and in morpheme-final position when that morpheme is the first element of a compound word and the second element begins with a consonant, as in *worſchyp* < OE /wərθ-šipe/.

<s> ~ <Ch> ~ <ſCh>. The alternates *ſchelde* ~ *cheldeȝ*, *ſchere* ~ *chere*, *freſche* ~ *frech*, *worſchyp* ~ *worchyp*, *cheriſch* ~ *cherych* ~ *cheryſen*, and the forms *englych*, *frenkyſch*, *deneȝ* 'Danish' represent two distinct phonological changes. During the course of the thirteenth century, LOFr. /č/ > /š/, /ǰ/ > /č/, /ts/ > /s/, /dz/ > /z/ (see Pope, § 194). However, in insular speech the change went forward much more slowly so that AN /č/ in *chere* appears beside CF /š/ in *ſchere*. It is not clear whether *ch* and *ſch* represent, in the forms in which they overlap, two phonemes or one. Doubtless French scribes continued to use the graph *ch* long after /č/ had become /š/, and that *ch* could represent /š/ in this MS. is clear from its use in native words: *cheldeȝ* ~ *ſcheldeȝ*, *worchyp* ~ *worſchyp*, etc. (One should not entirely rule out the possibility that some kind of dialectal variation existed even in native words). The variants *chere* ~ *ſchere* may reflect the fact that for this word there was both an insular and a continental pronunciation, and the line 'ſcho made hym ſo gret chere' (Gawain, 1259) argues for such an interpretation. On the other hand, it seems strange that of all the AN forms in this text this is the only one for which there is graphic evidence that it had followed the continental shift of /č/ to /š/. It is possible that *ſchere* represents a hypersophisticated pronunciation which the poet or scribe had picked up on his travels without realizing that it was indicative of a general sound shift on the continent. Alternatively, the form may simply be a reverse spelling; since *ch* could be used for *ſch* to represent /š/, *ſch* is here used for *ch* to represent /č/.

In Gallo-Roman, the Latin combinations /sk/ (especially in the inceptive infix before /i/ and /e/), /sty/, and /ks/ became /iš/ and then /is/ (Pope, § 880, § 325, § 315; Jordan, § 260): /angustia/ > /angustya/ > /angwiš/ > /angwis/, /finiski-/ > /finiš/ > /finis/ (cf.

Gawain, *fyniſment*, 499). In the northern areas, especially in Picardy and east Normandy, the development of /š/ to /s/ was retarded; as a result, this MS. shows reflexes of both the /š/ and /s/ stages: *cheryſen* and *cheryſch*, *venquyſt* and *venquyſche*. The occurrence of the /s/ forms in northern England, especially under English stress, may have reinforced, or been reinforced by, a LOE tendency to reduce the combination /sk/ in unstressed syllables to /s/. The forms *inglis*, *frenkis*, *denis*, *outlandis* are characteristic of the texts of northern England and Scotland (so Jordan, § 183). In this MS. only *deneȝ* occurs (Gawain, 2223); elsewhere only the spellings *ch* and *ſch* occur, as in *englych* (Gawain, 629) and *frenkyſch* (Gawain, 1116).

<sk> ~ <sCh>. The unique occurrence of the sequence *ſc* for *ſch* to represent /š/ in the alternates *ſchade* ~ *ſcade* suggests a northern scribal influence (cf. Cursor Mundi, Prologue, 'sumkins jestes for to scaw,' 115). That it represents a unit phoneme rather than a cluster is indicated by the alliteration in the line, 'and ſchrank þurȝ þe ſchyire grece and ſcade hit in twynne' (Gawain, 425).

<s> ~ <ø>. In OFr., pre-consonantal /s/ was voiced before voiced consonants and then, during the course of the eleventh, twelfth, and thirteenth centuries, was gradually lost, generally with compensatory lengthening of the preceding vowel. Although /s/ was lost, *s* was frequently retained by the scribes as a diacritic to mark length (cf. MnE standard *isle* /ayl/ < OFr. [izle] > [i:le]; see also Pope, § 377, 724-25, 1236; Jordan, § 261). The variants *diſmayd* (Gawain, 336) and *demay* (Gawain, 470) appear to reflect this situation; i.e. *diſmayd* derived from the earlier OFr. form, *demay* from the later. However, since /s/ was lost at a date considerably earlier than that of this MS., it is as likely that *diſmayd* represents a pronunciation with /s/ restored either as the result of spelling influence or by analogy with forms containing the prefix /dis-/ as in *diſceuer*, *diſcrye*, *diſpleſe*, *diſpoRt*, etc.

<n> ~ <m>. Complete progressive assimilation of /m/ to /n/ is illustrated by the alternates *blaunmer* ~ *blaunner* < OFr. /blank de mer/.

<n> ~ <ø>, <g> ~ <ø>. Since the variants *rengne* ~

regne and *bretaygne* ~ *bretayn* can be explained in terms of the same phonetic and scribal phenomena, they are considered together. Some time before the end of the twelfth century '*g* . . . was combined regularly with *n* and occasionally with *l* . . . to indicate the palatalization of these sounds; ordinarily it stood first, e.g. *segnour* for [seɲour], *viegn* for [vieɲ], but when the sound was final, and occasionally elsewhere, it was appended or written alone and thus [puɲ] might be written *puing* and *puig* as well as *puign* and [vieɲ], *vieng*, *vieg*, *viegn*.' (Pope, § 695). And again, 'In early Old French the nasalization of vowels was left unrecognised in spelling, but in the thirteenth century scribes began to mark the nasalization of the vowels that stood before intervocalic nasal consonants by the so-called tilde, a wavy line placed above the vowel: *fẽme*, *ãmer*, *sãine*, *ãime*, *plãine*, *siẽne*, *Bretãigne*, *ensẽigne*. Later on the tilde was often replaced by an additional nasal consonant: *femme*, *anmer* . . . *Bretaingne*, *enseingne*' (§ 715). In the course of OFr. a palatal glide developed before palatalized /n/ and /l/ which combined with the preceding vowel to form a complex nucleus with consequent depalatalization of the /n/ or /l/: thus, [bretañe] > [bretayñe] > [bretayne] > [bretayn]. From the rhyme schemes and spellings in this MS. it is apparent that the graphic combinations *ngn* and *gn*, used by French scribes to indicate palatalization of /n/ and nasalization of the preceding vowel, were archaic. The Pearl poet rhymes *vyne* < OFr. *vigne* : *declyne* < OFr. *decliner* : *hyne* < OE *higna* : *pyne* < EME *pine* (505-11). The AN palatalization and nasalization of the sounds in question were phenomena unfamiliar to native English ears; they were early modified in ME to conform to the sound system inherited from OE. OFr. *seignier* occurs in this MS. as *ſayned*, *bareigne* as *barayne*, *careigne* as *carrayne*, *compaignie* as *compaynye*, etc. Knigge notes that the scribe or scribes of the Cotton MS. Nero A.x. differ in their use of the archaic spellings from the scribe who copied St. Erkenwald (British Museum MS. Harleian 2250, Ff. 72b-75a) in that the first use the sequence *ngn* almost exclusively in such forms as *ſyngne*, *dingne*, *aſyngne*, *rengned*, while the second tends to be 'content' with *gn*. He wonders whether it may not be that the writer or writers of *ngn* were better phoneticians than the writer of *gn*, or whether they were simply following 'einem herkömmlichen Brauche' (115). Since both spellings were common in French scribal practice, and since there is no evidence that either palatalization or nasalization were represented by these spellings, any question of the phonetic competence of the scribes in question seems irrelevant.

<l> ~ <ø>. The alternates *colde* ~ *clolde*, *golde* ~ *glolde*, *glode* ~ *golde* are the result of scribal error. The forms *clolde* and *glolde* suggest the anticipation of a following graph, the form *glode* is a metathesis of *o* and *l*.

<wh> ~ <kw> ~ <wø>. Tolkien and Gordon explain this alternation thus: 'Original OE. *hw* usually appears as *wh* or *w* (*while*, *wyle; why*, *wy*), and OE. *cw* as *qu* (*quene*). Occasionally, however, northern spellings are used. In northern dialects OE. *cw* and *hw* had both become [xw] in sound, and by reason of this identity *qu* and *wh* were interchangeable in northern spelling. This northern confusion appears in Sir Gawain in forms like *quyle*, *quy;* and in *whene*, *whyssynes* for *quene*, *quyssynes*, although the alliteration shows that the author's dialect did not identify *qu* with *wh*' (124).[24] In the view of these editors, then, the northern spelling *qu* of reflexes of OE /xw/ was used in this MS. along with *wh* and *w* to represent the phoneme /w/. (Spelling and alliteration clearly indicate that the reflex of OE initial /x/ had been or was in the process of being lost in the environment /()w-/ by the end of the fourteenth century).

Noting that the spelling *qu* is generally accepted as a distinctively Northern feature pronounced [xw] or [kw], Whitehall goes on to cite evidence that there was in south Lancashire a spelling convention which regularly used *qu* for *w*, and that this spelling clearly represented the phoneme /w/. He concludes that it is not possible to use *qu* spellings as a Northern dialect feature since they may in fact be a Northwest Midland feature. Although he disagrees with

[24] On this point see also Karl Luick, *Historische Grammatik der Englischen Sprache* § 794 (Leipzig, 1921-40); Wright, *EMEG* § 303; Jordan, § 195; Harold Whitehall, A Note on a north-west midland spelling, *PQ* 9.1-6 (January, 1930).

Tolkien and Gordon on the provenience of the spelling tradition with *qu*, he agrees with their conclusion that *qu* represents /w/ in this dialect.

Jordan, on the other hand, seems to be of the opinion that *qu* spellings of etymological /xw/ in this dialect represent [xw] or [kw]: 'Auf *xw*- Aussprache (die *kw* nahekommt) deutet auch die umgekehrte Schreibung *whyssyn* für *cuissin* "Kissen" Gaw.' This position is difficult to maintain in view of the fact that *qu* spellings of etymological /xw/ can be shown to alliterate with etymological /w/. In its favor, however, is the fact that some lines occur in the MS. which suggest that *qu* spellings of etymological /xw/ alliterate with spellings of etymological /k/ and /kw/: 'quere ſo countenaunce is couþe quikly to clayme' (Gawain, 1490); 'Quat may þe cause be called bot foR hir clene hwes' (Purity, 1119); 'quen coRne is coRuen wyth crokes kene' (Pearl, 40); 'þe aȝtþe þe beryl cler and quyt' (Pearl, 1011); 'and couered many a cupboRde with cloþes ful quite' (Purity, 19440); 'loRde quo ſchal klymbe þy hyȝ hylle' (Pearl, 678). Examples of *wh* spellings of etymological /xw/ alliterating with /k/ or /kw/ are difficult to find; the line 'bot who ſo knew þe coſtes þat knit ar þerinne' (Gawain, 1849) may be one. It may be, of course, that the sounds in question are not intended to alliterate with /k/ and /kw/, but one cannot be absolutely sure of this.

Although the spellings *whene* and *whyſſynes* for *quene* and *quyſſynes* can be explained as the result of a general spelling confusion between *qu* and *wh*, such spellings would be more likely to occur if the writer were at least familiar with a dialect in which etymological /xw/, commonly spelled *wh* in this text, had remained /xw/, or had become /kw/. The only way that one can accommodate this notion to the fact that in the poems the reflex of etymological /xw/ can alliterate with etymological /w/ is to assume that one of the scribes, having lived in a border area, was equally at home in both the Northern dialect in which OE /xw/ > /kw/ and the Northwest Midland dialect in which OE /xw/ > /w/. (If he had been familiar with only the Northern pronunciation, one would have expected considerably more *wh* spellings for etymological /kw/). Even this, however, does not explain the possible alliteration noted above of etymological /xw/ with etymological /kw/ and /k/, for this must have been the work of the poet himself. If the examples are valid, one can only assume that the poet was familiar with both /w/ and /kw/ pronunciations of the reflex of OE /xw/ and used the one or the other depending upon which best served his stylistic purpose.

It must be admitted that evidence for a Northwest Midland pronunciation /kw/ of OE /xw/ is very slight indeed. If in fact it did exist, it must have been of extremely limited distribution, and soon ousted by the more general /w/ pronunciation.

<w> ~ <v>. Characteristic of northern England in general, but more particularly Scotland, was the use of *w* for *v* and *v* for *w;* thus in this MS., *a wenture* ~ *a venture*, *awyſe* ~ *auyſe*, *awowe* ~ *a vow*, *dewoyde* ~ *deuoyde*, *weng* ~ *venge*, *wowche* ~ *vouche*, *walour* < OFr. *valour*, *awayed* < OFr. *aveier*, *wyf* ~ *vyf* (see Wright, *EMEG* § 266; Jordan, § 163; Luick, § 761). It has been commonly held that this alternation indicates that in some Scottish and north English dialects ME /w/ > /v/, especially in view of the fact that etymological /v/ and /w/ are sometimes found to be linked by alliteration. Luick, for instance, believed in a native English sound change of /w/ to /v/ akin to that which took place in North Germanic; i.e. /w/ > /β/ > /v/. Bertil Sundby, however, thinks that there is little evidence in the living reflexes of these dialects to support such a theory, and suggests that the spellings in question indicate not a consistent phonemic change but rather occasional sound substitution as the result of Scandinavian influence. 'Substitution of [v] for [w] might be readily accounted for, since there was no distinctive opposition between initial ON [v] and ME (= OE) [w]: cf. *vel-wel*, *verk-werk- veykr-wa(i)k*, *viþ-wiþ* (etc.).' He conceives of three possible lines of development: '... in one Scottish (Northern) subdialect [v] was generalized, in a second [w], and in a third [v] and [w] were used indiscriminately. The third alternative would seem to represent a preliminary stage, since retention of both sounds would have served no useful, sc. distinctive, purpose. French words would naturally be affected by this phonemic instability, and it is by no means certain that *w* as rendering OF *v* is always an inverted spelling: [w] might be set down to the analogy of ON [v] in so far as that sound was levelled under ME *w*.'[25]

Evidence from this MS. and from its modern reflexes tends to support Sundby's interpretation of the *v* ~ *w* spellings. There is no hint of a systematic sound change in any of the modern dialect areas involved. In the MS. I have found only one sure instance of etymological /v/ alliterating with etymological /w/: 'þat wont watȝ whyle deuoyde my wrange' (Pearl, 15). *deuoyde*, elsewhere spelled *dewoyde*, may well represent a sound substitution resulting from the general confusion in this area between ON /v/ and OE /w/ as Sundby suggests. Knigge cites the form *ver*, in the line, 'þe ver by his uiſage verayly hit semes' (Gawain, 866), as an instance of *v* for *w* from OE /wer/ 'man'. (It is not clear from his notation whether he means a spelling substitution or a sound substitution or both). He also suggests *waſſayl* as an instance of *w* for *v* in the line, 'weȝe wyn in won waſſayl he cryes' (Purity, 1508). *ver*, as Tolkien and Gordon point out, is probably from Latin /ver/ 'springtime', rather than from OE /wer/. It is not my purpose to consider the stylistic merits of the poet here; however, it seems to me that the translation 'springtime' is, within the total context of the passage (and of the poem), considerably more appropriate than the translation 'man'. Knigge is surely mistaken in his interpretation of *waſſayl* as derived from OFr. *vassale*. The context of the line clearly suggests the OE etymon /wæs + hɑl/ 'your health', perhaps influenced by ON /ves + heyl/.

The alliterative pattern in the line 'j wowche hit ſaf fynly þaȝ feler hit were' (Gawain, 1391) is ambiguous since it is not clear whether one should consider the initial *w* of *wowche* to alliterate with *f* in *fynly* and *feler*, or with *w* in *were*. The most frequent alliterative pattern in the text is A A A B in which the first two alliterating sounds occur in the two primary stressed syllables of the first half-line, the third on the first primary stressed syllable of the second half-line: 'alle þat glydeȝ & gotȝ & goſt of lyf habbeȝ.'

[25] Middle English overlapping of *v* and *w* and its phonemic significance, *Anglia* 74.439 (1956).

INCLUSIVE alliteration, A B B A, is extremely rare in the poems; in his edition of Purity, R. J. Menner finds only three instances in a poem of 1811 lines. It does not seem unreasonable to assume that the more frequent type is the one represented in the preceding line from Gawain. If this is the case, *w* in *wowche* represents /v/, and the notion of a systematic sound change is easily dismissed. If it is not, and the line is an example of inclusive alliteration, the most that can be concluded is that *w* in this form is another example of sound substitution, /w/ for /v/, in some French words.

<h> ~ <ø>. The alternates *abraham* ~ *habraham, erne* ~ *herneȝ, aþel* ~ *haþel* raise the question of the phonemic status of ME [h]. According to Wright, the ME reflex of OE initial /x/ remained throughout the period before stressed vowels, although it tended to be lost before unstressed vowels. AN initial *h* was not pronounced, and as a result the graph *h* was in free variation with *ø* (§ 301-2). Jordan notes the 'isolated' occurrences of the omission of *h* in *alfpeny* and the addition of *h* in *hes* (< OE /æ:s/ 'corpse', 'carrion') in Ayenbite, 193.55. He goes on to say that 'Starke Schwankungen der *h*- Schreibung in betonter Silbe beruhen im allgemeinen auf französischem Einfluss ...' (§ 195). Wyld points out that '... a distinction must be made between words of pure English origin and those from French. It is doubtful whether the latter were originally pronounced with *h*-. Even in respect of genuine English words, a Norman, French-speaking scribe often omits initial *h*- in the M.E. period, but it would be rash to assume, on that account, that among English speakers the aspirate was already lost' (§ 284).

Before estimating the significance of *h* in the present MS., one should be aware of the following graphic and historical conditions which appear to obtain here. First, no English form which contained an original, pre-vocalic initial /x/ appears in the text without *h*. Second, words of French origin which in Late Latin contained an initial aspirate occur with or without *h* in the following alliterative patterns: (1) derivatives with *h* alliterate with native forms with *h*, 'ande honeſte in his houſholde and hagherlych ſerued'; (2) derivatives with *h* alliterate with native forms without *h*, 'boþe þat on and þat oþer myn honoured ladyeȝ'; (3) derivatives without *h* alliterate with native forms with *h*, 'þe abyt þat þou hatȝ vpon no halyday hit menſkeȝ'; (4) derivatives without *h* alliterate with native forms without *h*, 'and ete ay as a horce when erbes were fallen'; (5) such derivatives without *h* alliterate with other French forms which did not contain an original initial aspirate, 'I entered in þat erber grene.' Third, native forms with *h* alliterate with native forms without *h*, 'hit watȝ ennias þe athel and his highe kynde,' 'þer hales in at þe halle dor an aghlich mayſter,' 'þat aþel arthure þe hende haldeȝ hym one.' Fourth, there is some evidence of unetymological *h* ([h]?) being added to words, as *abıaham* ~ *habraham* in 'how miȝt j hyde myn hert fro habraham þe trwe' compared with 'abraham heldeȝ hem w^{t} hem to conveye'; and *erne* ~ *herneȝ* < OE /arn/ 'eagle' in 'herneȝ & haveкeȝ to þe hyȝe rocheȝ' compared with 'erne hwed he watȝ and al ouer-brawden'; also, *aþel* ~ *haþel* < OE /æθele/ 'noble', /æθelu/ 'noble nature'.[26] Fifth, the initial allophone [h] of OE /x/ has disappeared from the clusters /xl/, /xr/, /xn/, /xw/. Sixth, the phoneme /h/ does not occur in the modern dialects.

Clearly, the evidence for the loss of initial, pre-vocalic /h/ is not conclusive. Wyld's evidence, for the most part from more conservative dialects, indicates that the habit of 'dropping the h' and 'putting in an h' is clearly reflected in the writing system by the middle of the fifteenth century (§ 284-5). That [h] had ceased to function as a distinct phoneme before the end of the fourteenth century in the dialect of the Northwest Midlands is, I think, a reasonable conjecture.

<ȝ> ~ <w>, <ȝ> ~ <i>. <Ȝ> has been considered an archigrapheme representing in the environments *(-)a/o/u()(e)* and *(-)Vr/l()(-)* the neutralization of <ȝ> and <w>, and in the en-

26 This etymology for *herne* and *haþel* is not universally accepted. The NED derives the first from OFr. /hayron/ 'heron'; however, in his edition of Purity, Menner argues for OE /arn/ citing the occurrence of *hearnes* in Laȝamon's Brut, MS. B, next to *arnes* in MS. A (2.489, 25). Menner's reading seems to me more suited to the context of the line, at least from an ornithological point of view. The form *haþel* may, as most editors suggest, be derived from OE /hæleθ/ 'hero', with metathesis influenced by /æθelu/.

vironment *(-)e/i()(-)* the neutralization of <ʒ> and <i>. That <ʒ> represents a bi-labial postvocalic off-glide in the environment *(-)a/o/u()(e)* is clear from the alternate spellings *ſaʒe* ~ *ſawe*, *innoʒe* ~ *innowe*, and from such rhymes as *innoghe : alow* (< OFr. *alouer*). The spelling alternates *ſwey* ~ *ſweʒe*, *drye* ~ *dryʒe*, and the rhymes *hyʒe : byʒe : coRtayſye : byye* indicate that in the environment *(-)e/i()(-)* <ʒ> represents a palatal, post-vocalic off-glide.

In the environment *(-)Vr/l()-*, <ʒ> represents a bi-labial off-glide or on-glide, or both, depending upon its function in the syllable and the nature of the internal juncture about which very little can be known. That this is a likely interpretation is indicated by the spelling alternates *folʒande* ~ *folwande*, *ſoRʒe* ~ *ſoRewe* (by a corrector in Purity, 778). The reverse spelling *ʒolʒe* < OE /jəlu/ 'yellow' (Gawain, 951) supports the view that by the date of this MS. the reflex of OE final /x/ in this environment had either been labialized and vocalized itself, or had been supplanted by the labial glide of the oblique forms of the OE paradigm; e.g. OE n. sg. *horh* /xorx/ < gen. sg. *horwes* /xorwes/ (cf. Jordan, § 186; Wright, *EMEG* § 309). In the environment *(-)Vr/l()e*, <ʒ> will be interpreted to represent a vocalic allophone of /w/ by analogy with what appear to be the post-consonantal vocalic allophones of /r/ and /l/ as in the alternates *tytle* ~ *tytel*, *tryfle* ~ *tryfel*, *noble* ~ *nobele*, *entreʒ* ~ *enter*, et al.

It is quite likely that the form *folewande* beside *folwande* and *ſoRewe* beside *ſoRʒe* reflect a double stem development which took place at a much earlier date. In LOE, syncopation of the final vowel in some disyllabic stems of the structure /(-)V:CVC/ and /(-)V:CCVC/ before an inflectional morpheme of the structure /(-)V(C)/ resulted in the structures /(-)V:CCV(C)/ and /(-)V:CCCV(C)/: /mɑ:θum/, /mo:rxen/ next to /mɑ:θme(s)/, /mo:rxne(s)/ in the gen. and dat. sg. /x/ is then lost in the inflected forms: /mo:rxen/ > /mo:rxne/ > /mo:rne/. The forms *moRn(e)* ~ *moRoun* in Gawain (995, 1208) reflect this morphophonemic change: *moRne* < OE dat. sg. /mo:rxne/ > /mo:rne/ > /morn/; *moRoun* < OE uninflected /mo:rxen/ > /morwen/ > /morown/ (with development of an intrusive vowel making the glide vocalic).[27] The form *medoes* (Purity, 1761) < OE gen. sg. /mæ:dwe/ indicates the development of the intrusive vowel, perhaps through the stages /mæ:dəwe/ > /meduw/ (with shortening of stem vowel in trisyllabic forms before a single consonant) or /medow/. I would guess that the spelling *ſoʀewe* represents an intermediate stage in the development of this intrusive vowel; that the OE oblique form /sorxe/ > /sorwe/ > /sorəwe/ > /sorəw/ > /soruw/ or /sorow/ (cf. Wright, *EMEG* § 241). The development of an intrusive vowel before the reflex of OE /x/ took place after short accented vowels, principally in West Saxon after the tenth century; but beside those forms with intrusive vowels stand those without, especially in Anglian texts. The distribution of these forms in terms of their geographical boundaries is not, according to Luick, ascertainable.

The phonemic interpretation of the reflex of OE /x/ in the environment /(-)Vr/l()/ is difficult. ME handbooks and the editions of the poem in question assume the occurrence of a voiceless, palatal spirant in this position (see Wright, *EMEG* § 309; Jordan, § 197; Gordon, 92.ii). It is somewhat disturbing, however, to postulate a phoneme with such a limited and unique distribution. The question arises whether or not one can assign this reflex to some other phoneme. Since in the environment *(-)Vr/l()-* it has been assigned to /ow/ or /uw/, it would be expedient to make the same assignment when it occurs in final position.

There are some indications in the text, however, that such an interpretation would be wrong. In the first place, the two structures in question, *(-)Vr/l()-* and *(-)Vr/l()*, are not in free variations, but in partial complementation. The first occurs only in those syntactic positions in which one would expect the reflex of an OE oblique form, as in 'whyl j byde in yowre boʀʒe be bayn to ʒowre heſt' (Gawain, 1092). The second is not limited in its occurrences: 'þe boʀʒ brittened and brent to brondeʒ and askeʒ' (Gawain, 2), 'þenne þe beſt of þe burʒ boʒed togeder' (Gawain, 550), 'and enbelyſe his burʒ w^{t} his bele chere' (Gawain, 1034). Second, such

[27] Cf. Luick, *Historische Grammatik*, § 446.2.

lines as 'whyl j byde in yowre boʀʒe be bayn to ʒowre heſt' and 'to þe kyngeʒ burʒ buſkeʒ bolde' (Gawain, 2476) suggest that *ʒ* in *boʀʒe* and *burʒ* supports two different kinds of sound patterning. It is stylistically desirable, for instance, to re-write *boʀʒe* /borow/ in assonance with *yowre* and *ʒowre*, and to re-write *burʒ* with a final palatal, voiceless consonant in consonance with the /k/ of *kyngeʒ* and *buſkeʒ*. The unifying effect of the /k/ sounds in the lines

hir body watʒ ſchoʀt and þik
hir buttokeʒ balʒ and brode
moʀe lykkerwys on to lyk.
(Gawain, 966-8)

and in the line 'a balʒ berʒ bi a bonke þe brymme byſyde' (Gawain, 2172) seems to demand a similar sound in *balʒ* and *berʒ*.

The forms *ſtrenghþe* ∼ *ſtrenkþe* and *hawbrgh* < OFr. /hawberk/ have been noted above, together with Jordan's remarks that after tense vowels + /r/ or /l/ the reflex of OE /x/ tended to become /k/ in some ME dialects. The NED records the form *strenʒt*, and it is of some incidental interest that Spenser uses the archaic spelling *hawbergh* in the Fairy Queen. The form *meʒelmas* (Gawain, 532) may also have some bearing on the point at hand. According to Tolkien and Gordon, 'forms with *ch* [are] treated as spirant [sic], as OFr. *Mihiel*, used exclusively of the archangel' (175). Two comments suggest themselves. First, there is no particular reason to treat *ʒ* here as a spirant. According to the rules governing the distribution of <ʒ>, the phonemic form should be /meyelmas/ which is not much different from the sound structure indicated by the variant spellings *miel-*, *myel-*, *myhil-*, *myhell-*recorded by the NED. In the second place, it is not clear why 'forms with *ch*' should be treated as spirants. It is true that in the dialects of the North the graphic sequence *ch* was used to represent [x]; however, there is no evidence, so far as I know, that the *ch* in the OE form *michæles* necessarily represented a spirant. The spelling *ch* was used in Latin to represent Greek /kh/; according to Pope, however, '... the aspirated pronunciation of these sounds [Greek aspirates] was confined to the educated class and left no mark on later pronunciation . . .' (§ 629). The sound in Latin, and in later OFr., was /k/, and presumably remained so in OE. If *ȝ* in *meȝelmas* is not to be interpreted as representing an allophone of /y/, it is at least as reasonable to suppose that it represents an allophone of /k/ as that it represents a unique occurrence of a distinct phoneme /x/ in intervocalic position.

A reflex of OE /x/ represented by <ȝ> occurs in one additional environment, *(-)V()t*, as in *lyȝt*, *fyȝt*, *ſlaȝt*, etc. Since <ȝ> never alternates with <ø> in this position, and since Ellis records a Colne Valley pronunciation (D22) for 1840 containing a voiceless, palatal consonant in this environment, e.g. *thokht* 'thought', *nikjht* 'night', *rekjht* 'right', *bokht* 'bought', etc., it is assumed that such a consonant occurs in the ME MS. Whatever the phonetic nature of the sound might have been, we assign it to the /k/ phoneme since [k] from other sources does not occur in this position.

CHAPTER VI

THE GRAPHONEMIC SYSTEM

6.0. The following sections constitute a summary of the fit relationship between the graphemic system and the phonemic system of the MS.

6.1. Vocalic system.

6.11. Allographones.

ALLOGRAPHONES	ALLOGRAPHS	PHONEMES
<a>	*a, A*	/a/, /a:/
<a-e>	*a-e, A-e*	/a/, /a:/
<aa>	*aa*	/a:/
<ai>	*ai, ay*	/ay/, /ey/
<aw>	*aw*	/aw/
<av>	*au, av*	/aw/
<aȝ>	*aȝ, agh*	/aw/
<e>	*e, E*	/e/, /e:/, /i:/, /ay/, /a/, /ey/
<e-e>	*e-e, E-e*	/e/, /e:/, /i:/, /ey/
<ee>	*ee*	/i:/
<ei>	*ei, ey*	/i:/, /ay/, /ey/
<ew>	*ew*	/ew/, /iw/
<ev>	*eu*	/iw/, /i:/
<eȝ>	*eȝ, egh*	/i:/, /ey/, /ay/
<eav>	*eau*	/iw/, /ey + aw/
<i>	*i, j, I, y*	/i/, /i:/, /iy/
<i-e>	*i-e, y-e*	/iy/

<ii>	*ii, yy*	/iy/
<ie>	*ie, ye*	/i:/, /iy/, /iy + e/
<iȝ>	*iȝ, igh, yȝ, ygh*	/iy/
<v>	*u, v, V*	/u/, /uw/
<v-e>	*u-e, V-e, v-e*	/uw/, /iw/
<vv>	*uu*	/uw/
<vi>	*ui, uy*	/iy/, iw/
<vȝ>	*uȝ, ugh*	/uw/
<w>	*w*	/iw/
<o>	*o, O*	/o/, /u/, /o:/, /ow/, /u:/, /uw/
<o-e>	*o-e, O-e*	/o:/, /u:/, /ow/, /aw/
<oo>	*oo*	/u:/
<oi>	*oi, oy*	/oy/
<ow>	*ow*	/uw/, /aw/
<ov>	*ou, ov*	/u:/, /uw/
<oȝ>	*oȝ, ogh*	/uw/
<oe>	*oe*	/uw/, /iw/

6.12. Graphonemes.

GRAPHONEMES	ALLOGRAPHONES	PHONEMES
Simplex.		
/<a>/	<a>	/a/
/<e>/	<e>	/e/
/<o>/	<o>	/o/
Complex.		
/<a-e>/	<a-e>, <aa>	/a:/
/<i-e>/	<e-i>, <ii>, <iȝ>	/iy/
/<ov>/	<ov>, <oȝ>, <vv>, <vȝ>	/uw/
/<v-e>/	<v-e>, <w>, <ev>	/iw/
/<av>/	<av>, <aw>, <aȝ>	/aw/
/<oi>/	<oi>	/oy/

6.13. Graphonemic neutralization.

6.131.

ARCHIGRAPHONEMES	ALLOGRAPHONES	PHONEMES
Simplex.		
/<I>/	<i>	/i/
/<V>/	<v>	/u/
/<W>/	<w>	/iw/
Complex.		
/<E-E>/	<e-e>, <ee>	/e:/, /ey/, /i:/
/<EI>/	<ei>, <e>, <ai>	/ey/, /ay/
/<EW>/	<ew>	/ew/, /iw/
/<VI>/	<vi>	/iw/, /iy/
/<O-E>/	<o-e>, <oo>	/o:/, /ow/, /u:/
/<OE>/	<oe>	/uw/, /iw/
/<OW>/	<ow>	/uw/, /aw/

6.132. Heterographic neutralization.

/<a>/ ~ /<a e>/ as in *mad* ~ *made*, /ma:d/.
/<a>/ ~ /<EI>/ as in *gawan* ~ *gawayn*, /gawayn/.
/<a>/ ~ /<e>/ as in *arende* ~ *ernde*, /arnd/.
/<e>/ ~ /<E-E>/ as in *met* ~ *mete*, /me:t/; *ſtel* ~ *ſtele*, /sti:l/.
/<e>/ ~ /<EI>/ as in *reſoun* ~ *reyſoun* ~ *rayſoun*, /reyzuwn/.
/<I>/ ~ /<V>/ as in *byſily* ~ *buſily*, /bizili/.
/<I>/ ~ /<i-e>/ as in *fyr* ~ *fire*, /fiyr/.
/<V>/ ~ /<ov>/ as in *burne* ~ *buurne* ~ *bourne*, /buwrn/.
/<o>/ ~ /<V>/ as in *ſonne* ~ *ſunne*, /sun/.
/<o>/~/<O-E>/ as in *god*~*gode*, /gu:d/; *ſton*~*ſtone*, /stown/.
/<o>/ ~ /<ov>/ as in *floR* ~ *flour*, /fluwr/.
/<ou>/ ~ /<O-E>/ as in *goud* ~ *gode*, /gu:d/.
/<ov>/ ~ /<v-e>/ as in *aboute* ~ *abute*, /abuwt/.
/<v-e>/ ~ /<E-E>/ as in *leude* ~ *lude* ~ *lede*, /li:d/.
/<i-e>/ ~ /<E-E>/ as in *þyſe* ~ *þeſe*, /ði:z/ or /ðiyz/.
/<EI>/ ~ /<E-E>/ as in *maynteine* ~ *menteene*, /meynti:n/.
/<VI>/ ~ /<v-e>/ as in *fuyt* ~ *fute*, /fiwt/.
/<VI>/ ~ <i-e>/ as in *huyde* ~ *hide*, /hiyd/.

6.133.	HETEROGRAPHIC SEQUENCES	ALLOGRAPHONES	PHONEMES
	/<IE>/	<ie>	/i:/, /iy/, /iy + e/
	/<EAV>/	<eav>	/iw/, /ey+aw/

6.2. Consonantal system.

6.21. Allographones.

ALLOGRAPHONES	ALLOGRAPHS	PHONEMES
<p>	*p, P*	/p/
<pp>	*pp*	/p/
<t>	*t, T*	/t/
<tt>	*tt*	/t/
<Ch>	*ch, Ch*	/č/, /š/
<ChCh>	*chch*	/č/
<CCh>	*cch*	/č/
<Ck>	*ck*	/k/
<k>	*k, K*	/k/
<kk>	*kk*	/k/
<q>	*q, Q*	/k/, /w/
<C>	*c, C*	/k/, /s/
<b>	*b, B*	/b/, /p/, /ø/
<bb>	*bb*	/b/
<d>	*d, D*	/d/, /t/, /ø/
<dd>	*dd*	/d/
<i>	*i, I, j, y*	/y/, /ǰ/
<g>	*g, G*	/ǰ/, /g/, /k/
<gg>	*gg*	/ǰ/, /g/
<f>	*f, ff*	/f/, /v/
<ff>	*ff*	/f/
<ph>	*ph, Ph*	/f/
<þ>	*þ, Þ*	/θ/, /ð/
<þþ>	*þþ*	/θ/
<th>	*th, Th*	/θ/, /ð/

<thþ>	*thþ*	/θ/
<s>	*s, S, ſ*	/s/, /z/
<ss>	*ſſ*	/s/
<tʒ>	*tʒ*	/s/, /z/
<ʒ>	*ʒ, Ʒ*	/s/, /z/, /y/, /w/, /k/
<gh>	*gh*	/y/, /w/, /k/
<sC>	*ſc, Sc*	/š/, /sk/
<sCh>	*ſch, Sch*	/š/, /č/
<ssCh>	*ſſch*	/š/
<sChCh>	*ſchch*	/š/
<v>	*v, V, u*	/v/, /w/
<m>	*m, M*	/m/
<mm>	*mm*	/m/
<n>	*n, N*	/n/
<nn>	*nn*	/n/
<l>	*l, L*	/l/
<r>	*r, R,* ʀ	/r/
<rr>	*rr*	/r/
<w>	*w, W*	/w/, /v/
<ww>	*ww*	/w/
<wh>	*wh, Wh*	/w/, /kw/
<h>	*h, H*	[h], /ø/

6.22. Graphonemes.

GRAPHONEMES	ALLOGRAPHONES	PHONEMES
Simplex.		
/<p>/	<p>, <pp>	/p/
/<t>/	<t>, <tt>	/t/
/<k>/	<k>, <kk>, <Ck>	/k/
/<b>/	<b>, <bb>	/b/
/<d>/	<d>, <dd>	/d/
/<f>/	<f>, <ff>, <ph>	/f/
/<m>/	<m>, <mm>	/m/
/<n>/	<n>, <nn>	/n/
/<l>/	<l>, <ll>	/l/
/<r>/	<r>, <rr>	/r/
/<h>/	<h>	[h], [ø]

Complex.

/<Ch>/	<Ch>, <ChCh>, <CCh>	/č/
/<sCh>/	<sCh>, <ssCh>, <sChCh>	/š/

6.23. Graphonemic neutralization.

6.231.

ARCHIGRAPHONEMES	ALLOGRAPHONES	PHONEMES
/<Q>/	<q>	/k/, /w/
/<C>/	<C>	/k/, /s/
/<I>/	<i>	
	i, j, I	/ǰ/
	i, y	/y/
/<G>/	<g>, <gg>	/g/, /ǰ/
/<Þ>/	<þ>, <þþ>, <th> <thþ>	/θ/, /ð/
/<S>/	<s>, <ss>, <tȝ>	/s/, /z/
/<Ȝ>/	<ȝ>, <gh>	/y/, /w/, /k/
	ȝ	/s/, /z/
/<V>/	<v>	/v/, /w/
/<W>/	<w>, <ww>, <wh>	/w/, /v/

6.232. Heterographic neutralization.

/<Ch>/ ~ /<sCh>/ as in *worchyp* ~ *worſchyp*, /woršip/.
/<b>/ ~ /<p>/ as in *lombe* ~ *lomp*, /lomp/.
/<b>/ ~ /<ø>/ as in *klymbe* ~ *clym*, /klim/.
/<d>/ ~ /<t>/ as in *gyld* ~ *gilt*, /gilt/.
/<d>/ ~ /<ø>/ as in *hondeſelle* ~ *hanſelle*, /hansel/.
/<G>/ ~ /<k>/ as in *ȝonge* ~ *ȝonke*, /yonk/.
/<V>/ ~ /<f>/ as in *haue* ~ *hafe*, /ha:v/.
/<Ȝ>/ ~ /<k>/ as in *ſtrenghþe* ~ *ſtrenkþe*, /strenkθ/.
/<W>/ ~ /<Q>/ as in *whyle* ~ *quyle*, /wiyl/;
whene ~ *quene*, /kwi:n/.

/<I>/ ~ /<G>/ as in *ientyle ~ gentyle*, /ǰentiyl/, /ǰentil/; *ſeriauntes ~ ſergaunteʒ*, /serǰawnt/.
/<S>/ ~ /<Ʒ>/ as in *deſyre ~ deʒyre*, /deziyr/.
/<I>/ ~ /<Ʒ>/ as in *yowre ~ ʒowre*, /yuwr/.
/<Ʒ>/ ~ /<W>/ as in *ſaʒe ~ ſaghe ~ ſaweʒ*, /saw(ez/.
/<V>/ ~ /<W>/ as in *vyf ~ wyf*, /wif/; *deuoyde ~ dewoyde*, /dewoyd/.

6.233. Heterographic sequences.

/<SC>/ <sC> /sk/, /s/, /š/

APPENDIX A

OE AND MnE PHONEMIC SYSTEMS

A.1. The OE phonemic system assumed for this study is essentially that presented by Charles F. Hockett in The Stressed syllabics of Old English, *Language* 35.575-97 (1959), and by William G. Moulton, The Stops and spirants of Early Germanic, *Language* 30.1-42 (1954).

A.1.1. Vowels.

Simple.

/i/ <i>	/y/ <y>	/ɨ/ <io>	/u/ <u>
/e/ <e>		/ə/ <eo>	/o/ <o>
/æ/ <ae>, <æ>, <e>		/a/ <ea>, <æa>	/ɑ/ <a>

Complex.
Each of the simple nuclei plus a length phoneme, /:/.

A.1.2. Consonants.

/p/ <p>	/t/ <t>	/č/ <c>	/k/ <c>
/b/ <b>	/d/ <d>	/j/ <g>	/g/ <g>
/f/ <f>	/θ/ <þ>, <ð>	/s/ <s>	/x/ <h>, <g>[1]

[1] According to Moulton, the reflexes of Proto-Germanic [h] and [x] were phonemic in OE, distinguished by glottal articulation in the first instance and velar articulation in the second (26). Hockett accepts this view and includes both /h/ and /x/ in his phoneme inventory (576. fn. 4). Stockwell and Barritt, on the other hand, assuming phonetic similarity between syllable-initial [h] and post-vocalic [x], assign them to the same phoneme. Patterns of distribution and congruity within the system argue for the latter solution. [h] occurs only in syllable-initial position, [x] occurs elsewhere; further, if the two are to be

/m/ <m>	/n/ <n>	
	/l/ <l>	
	/r/ <r>	
/w/ <w>		/j/ <g>

---

considered separate phonemes, the limitations on their distribution is at least curious in view of the distribution of the other consonant phonemes in the system, none of which are so limited. The whole matter seems to me to be very much in doubt. Chomsky (review of Roman Jakobson and Morris Halle, *Fundamentals of Language* [The Hague, 1956], *IJAL* 23.234-42 [1957]) points out that the status and value of the principle of complementary distribution remain questionable; that such distribution is neither a necessary nor a sufficient condition for the identification of phonemes. At the same time, he makes it clear that one's application of the principles of phonetic similarity depends upon those features he chooses to regard as distinctive and those he chooses to regard as redundant within the system: '... two segments may be assigned to the same phoneme even if they are not phonetically similar in an absolute sense, and two closely matching segments may (in the case of partial overlapping) be assigned to different phonemes if they are identified in their respective oppositional sets by different feature indications. Similarly, two occurrences of the same phoneme may differ in redundant features' (239). I do not think we know that the glottal articulation of [h] and the velar articulation of [x] were not simply manifestations of a difference in redundant features. I have assigned [h] and [x] to the same phoneme partially because I do not believe the phonetic evidence is sufficient to warrant assignment to separate phonemes, partially on the basis of symmetry, and partially as a matter of convenience. According to Fred. W. Householder, Jr., review of C. F. Hockett, *A Course in Modern Linguistics* (New York, 1958), *Language* 35.515 (1959): 'The "principle of phonetic similarity" in phonemic analysis is too often put on the basis of comparison of individual sound-tokens (possibly in large numbers) without reference to system or patterns. Hockett (108-109) does somewhat better than this, by splitting his discussion between two "principles" (the other being "neatness of pattern"). It is not the similarity of one phone to another as such that is relevant ... but the similarity of the systematic differences of one phone from all the others in its paradigm ... to those of another phone from all those in its paradigm. Hockett seems to overlook this in his treatment of Old English (376), for instance, where he sets up a phoneme /h/ occurring only medial and final. Surely /h/ contrasts with initial /f/, /s/ and /θ/ in the same manner as /s/ does with the medial and final allophones of the same phonemes, regardless of the precise articulatory differences of [h] from [x] considered alone.'

As far as the rest of Hockett's system is concerned, I am quite well aware that it has not been wholly acceptable to all students of OE (see, for example, Sherman M. Kuhn, The Syllabic phonemes of Old English, *Language* 37.522-38 [1961] and Robert P. Stockwell and C. Westbrook Barritt, Scribal practice: some assumptions, *Language* 37.75-83 [1961]). It is not within the scope of this

A.2. The phonemic system assumed for the modern dialect areas of Lancashire, Northwest Derbyshire, and West Yorkshire is based partly on the phonetic transcriptions in Alexander J. Ellis' On Early English Pronunciation (*EETS*, Extra S. 56, pt. 5.D21-2, 31 [London, 1889]), partly on Joseph Wright's *The English dialect grammar* (Oxford, 1905), and partly on the educated Lancashire speech of Professor Harold Whitehall of Indiana University and Mr. J. A. Lavin of the State University of Iowa (formerly of Wigan, Lancashire).

A.2.1. Vowels.

Simple.

/i/		/u/
/e/		/o/
	/a/	

Complex.

/i:/ [iə], /iy/ [ii]		/u:/ [uə], /uw/ [uu]
/e:/ [ee], /ey/ [ei]		/oy/ [oi], /ow/ [oo], [ou]
	/a:/ [aa], [ai]	

A.2.2. Consonants.

/p/	/t/	/č/	/k/
/b/	/d/	/ǰ/	/g/
/f/	/θ/		
/v/	/ð/		
	/s/	/š/	
	/z/	/ž/	
/m/	/n/		
	/l/		
	/r/		
/w/		/y/	

present study to consider the nature of the controversies involved. With the exception noted above, the writer has found Hockett's formulations to be more congenial to his own notions of OE phonology than any other he has seen, and has therefore made use of them in the foregoing analysis.

APPENDIX B

SAMPLE TRANSCRIPTION

B.1. The following is a transcription of the first page of Pearl (f. 39a). Since it has not been the concern of this study to speculate on the nature of the suprasegmental system of the poet, the reader is obliged to impose his own stress, pitch, and juncture patterns on the selection.

Perle pleſaūte to prynces paye
/perl plezawnt tu: prinsez pay/
to clanly clos in golde ſo clere
/tu: klanliy klowz in gowld sow kleyr/
oute of ORyent j hardyly ſaye
/uwt ov oriyent iy ardiliy say/
ne proued j neu her precios pere
/ne: pru:ved iy never er presios peyr/
ſo roūde ſo reken in vche araye
/sow ruwnd sow reken in uč aray/
ſo ſmal ſo ſmoþe her ſydeʒ were
/sow smal sow smu:ð er siydez weyr/
quere ſo eu j jugged gēmeʒ gaye
/weyr sow ever iy ǰuǰed ǰemez gay/
j ſette hyr ſengeley ī ſynglure (-ere)
/iy set er singley in singleyr/
allas j leſte hyr ī on erbere
/alas iy lest er in on erbeyr/
þurʒ greſſe to groūde hit fro me yot
/θurk gres tu: gruwnd it from mi: yot/

j dewyne foʀ dolked of luf daungere
/iy dewiyn for dolked ov luf dawnǰeyr/
of þat pryuy perle wᵗ outen ſpot
/ov ðat priviy perl wiðuwten spot/

Syþen ī þat ſpote hit fro me ſprange
/siθen in ðat spot it frow mi: spranG/
ofte haf j wayted wyſchande þat wele
/oft (af) a:v iy wayted wišand ðat we:l/
þat wont watȝ whyle deuoyde my wrange
/ðat wont waz wiyl dewoyd miy wranG/
& heuen my happe & al my hele
/and even miy ap and al miy eyl/
þᵗ dotȝ bot þrych my hert þrange
/ðat doz bot θrič miy ert θranG/
my breſte in bale bot bolne & bele
/miy brest in ba:l bot boln and be:l/
ȝet þoȝt me neū ſo ſwete a ſange
/yet θokt mi: never sow swi:t a sanG/
as ſtylle ſtoūde let to me ſtele
/az stil stuwnd let tu: mi: ste:l/
foʀ ſoþe þ' fleten to me fele
/for su:θ ðeyr fli:ten tu: mi: fe:l/
to þenke hir coloʀ ſo clad ī clot
/tu: θink er koluwr sow klad in klot/
O moul þᵘ marreȝ a myry iuele
/o: muwl ðuw marez a miriy ǰuwe:l/
my pʳuy perle wᵗ outen ſpotte
/miy priviy perl wiðuwten spot/

þat ſpot of ſpyſeȝ mot nedeȝ ſprede
/ðat spot ov spiysez mot ni:dez spreyd/
þer ſuch rycheȝ to rot is rūnen (rune)
/ðeyr suč ričez to rot iz run/
blomeȝ blayke & blwe & rede
/blu:mez blayk and bliw and reyd/

þer ſchyneȝ ful ſchyr agayn þe ſūne
/ðeyr šiynez ful šiyr agayn ðe sun/
flor & fryte may not be fede
/fluwr and friwt may not bi: feyd/
þer hit doū drof ī moldeȝ dūne
/ðeyr it duwn drof (drowv/ in mowldez dun/
for vch greſſe mot grow of grayneȝ dede
/for uč gres mot grow ov graynez deyd/
no whete were elleȝ to woneȝ wōne
/now weyt weyr elez tu: wownez wun/
of goud vche goude is ay by gone
/ov gu:d uč gu:d iz ay bigun/
ſo ſemly a ſede moȝt fayly not
/sow si:mliy a si:d mokt fayliy not/
þᵀ ſprygande (ſpr̄ȳgande) ſpyceȝ up ne ſpōne
/ðat springand spiysez up nɛ: spun/
of þat pʾcios perle wyth outen ſpotte
/ov ðat presios perl wiðuwten spot/

APPENDIX C

INDEX OF CITATIONS FROM THE MANUSCRIPT

a – 80, 81, 82. Prl. 144, f. 40b.
aboute – 53, 103, 136. Prl. 75, f. 40a.
abowte – 103. Prl. 149, f. 41a.
abraham – 53, 128, 129. Pur. 601, f. 65a.
abute – 53, 91, 136. Pat. 290, f. 87a.
acoʀde – 108. Prl. 509, f. 46a.
Adam – 45. Prl. 656, f. 48a.
agayn – 54, 117. Prl. 1199, f. 55b.
agayneȝ – 109. Pur. 611, f. 65a.
agaynȝ – 109. Prl. 79, f. 40a.
ay – 80, 81, 82. Prl. 33, f. 39a.
ayþer – 80, 81, 82. Prl. 831, f. 50b.
alder – 54, 111. G. 1486, f. 110 b.
alow – 130. Prl. 634, f. 47b.
alþer – 54, 111. G. 1441, f. 110a.
among – 112. Prl. 470, f. 45b.
Ande – 46. Prl. 1212, f. 55b.
aquiloun – 44. Pat. 133, f. 84b.
aryȝt – 54. G. 1911, f. 116b.
arende – 54, 57, 136. Pat. 72, f. 84a.
aros – 72. Prl. 181, f. 41b.
aſyngnes – 123. G. 1971, f. 117a.
aþel – 128, 129. G. 2466, f. 124a.
aþer – 80, 81, 82. G. 1357, f. 109a.
auen – 68. Pur. 595, f. 65a.
auenture – 53, 120. Prl. 64, f. 39b.
auinant – 84. G. 806, f. 101b.
auyſe – 126. G. 45, f. 91b.
aune – 68. Pur. 11, f. 57a.
aunter – 53, 120. G. 27, f. 91b.
aunteres – 120. Pur. 1600, f. 79a.
aventure – 47, 120, 126. G. 2482, f. 124a.
avow – 126. Pur. 664, f. 66a.
avowes – 47, 55. Pat. 165, f. 85a.
awayed – 126. Prl. 710, f. 48b.
awen – 68. G. 836, f. 102a.
awenture – 120, 126. G. 29, f. 91b.
awyſe – 126. G. 1389, f. 109b.
awowe – 55, 126. Pat. 333, f. 87b.
aȝayn – 54, 117. G. 530, f. 98a.

babtem – 54, 104. Prl. 627, f. 47b.
balȝ – 132. G. 967, f. 104a.
banne – 59. Pur. 1361, f. 75b.
baptem – 54, 104. Prl. 653, f. 48a.
barayne – 123. G. 1320, f. 108b.
bare – 81. G. 207, f. 93b.
beaute – 53, 69. Prl. 749, f. 49a.
be – 79. Prl. 290, f. 43a.
bed – 94. G. 994, f. 104a.
begynes – 59. Pat. 76, f. 84a.
begynne – 54, 59. G. 495, f. 97b.
bene – 76. Prl. 198, f. 41b.
berȝ – 132. G. 2172, f. 120a.
bewte – 53, 69. Prl. 765, f. 49b.
byde – 87. Prl. 399, f. 44b.
bydene – 75. Prl. 196, f. 41b.
bye – 50, 57. Prl. 732, f. 49a.
bigged – 117. G. 20, f. 91a.
bigyled – 118. G. 2413, f. 123a.
bygynne – 54. Prl. 581, f. 47a.
byhod – 120. Prl. 928, f. 51b.
bihoues – 120. G. 1065, f. 105a.
byye – 50, 57, 130. Prl. 478, f. 45b.
bylde – 64. Prl. 123, f. 40b.
byled – 89, G. 2082, f. 118b.
bilyue – 99. G. 1128, f. 106a.
byrþe – 55, 62. Prl. 1041, f. 53a.
biſchop – 63. G. 112, f. 92b.

biʃy – 63. G. 89, f. 91b.
byʃily – 55, 57, 62, 63, 136. G. 1824, f. 115b.
biʃineʃʃe – 62, 63. G. 1840, f. 115b.
biwyled – 118. G. 2425, f. 123b.
byȝe – 130. Prl. 466, f. 45a.
blame – 67. Prl. 715, f. 48b.
blaunmer – 55, 122. G. 856, f. 102b.
blaunner – 55, 122. G. 155, f. 93a.
blende – 107. G. 1361, f. 109a.
blent – 107. G. 1610, f. 112b.
bleʃʃe – 56. Prl. 850, f. 50b.
blys – 29, 47. Prl. 123, f. 40b.
blyʃful – 29, 47. Prl. 409, f. 44b.
blyʃʃe – 99, 100. Prl. 372, f. 44a.
blober – 54. Pat. 266, f. 86b.
bloʃched – 54, 62. Pat. 343, f. 87b.
bloʃʃumeȝ – 57, 97. G. 512, f. 97b.
bluber – 54. Pat. 221, f. 86a.
bluʃched – 54, 62, 108. G. 793, f. 101b.
bluʃchet – 108. Pur. 982, f. 70b.
boerne – 53, 87. G. 1570, f. 112a.
boyled – 89. G. 2174, f. 120a.
bonc – 112. Prl. 90, f. 51b.
bone – 59. Prl. 912, f. 51b.
boRne – 53, 87. G. 731, f. 100b.
boRȝ – 54. G. 2, f. 91a.
boRȝe – 49, 132. G. 1092, f. 105b.
boʃum – 97. Pat. 107, f. 84b.
Bot – 46. Prl. 265, f. 42b.
bot – 46. Prl. 17, f. 39a.
bothe – 49. G. 1580, f. 112a.
boþe – 49. G. 111, f. 92b.
bougounȝ – 116. Pur. 1416, f. 76b.
bourne – 53, 54, 68, 87, 88, 136. Prl. 617, f. 47b.
brayde – 111. G. 440, f. 96b.
braunch – 84. G. 265, f. 94b.
bretaygne – 50, 123. G. 25, f. 91a.
bretayn – 50, 123. G. 20, f. 91a.
breyþed – 111. Pur. 1421, f. 76b.
bryd – 86. Prl. 769, f. 49b.
brygge – 62, 117. G. 821, f. 102a.
bryne – 55. G. 580, f. 98b.
bronch – 84, 85. Pur. 487, f. 63b.
bronde – 52, 106. G. 561, f. 98b.
bront – 52, 106. G. 588, f. 98b.
broȝ – 54, 109. Prl. 286, f. 42b.
broȝt – 54, 109. Prl. 286, f. 42b.
bruny – 55. G. 861, f. 102b.
brutage – 102. Pur. 1190, f. 73b.
buyrne – 53, 88. Pat. 340, f. 87b.
bult – 64. G. 25, f. 91a.
burde – 86. G. 613, f. 99a.
burghe – 49. Prl. 980, f. 52b.
burne – 53, 68, 87, 88, 136. Prl. 397, f. 44b.
burnyʃt – 49. G. 212, f. 93b.
burþe – 55, 62, 64. G. 922, f. 103a.
burþen – 111. Pur. 1439, f. 76b.
burȝ – 54, 132. G. 259, f. 94b.
buʃy – 63. G. 1066, f. 105a.
buʃyeȝ – 63. Prl. 268, f. 42b.
buʃily – 136. Pur. 1446, f. 77a.
buʃyly – 55, 57, 62, 63. G. 68, f. 92a.
buʃynes – 62, 63. G. 1986, f. 117b.
buʃkeȝ – 132. G. 1136, f. 106a.
buʃmar – 63. Pur. 653, f. 66a.
buurne – 49, 54, 68, 87, 88, 136. G. 825, f. 102a.

cayre – 81. Prl. 1031, f. 53a.
cambe – 58. Prl. 775, f. 49b.
carle – 54, 113. Pur. 876, f. 69a.
carrayne – 123. Pur. 459, f. 63a.
caʃt – 54, 58. G. 878, f. 102b.
cerue – 48. Pur. 1547, f. 78a.
ceuer – 48. Prl. 319, f. 43a.
chaffer – 94. G. 1647, f. 113a.
cheldeȝ – 121. G. 1611, f. 112b.
chere – 54, 121. G. 1759, f. 114b.
cherych – 54, 121. Pur. 1154, f. 73a.
cheriʃch – 54, 121, 122. Pur. 128, f. 58b.
cheryʃen – 121, 122. G. 2055, f. 118b.
ches – 47. Prl. 759, f. 49b.
cheʃe – 54, 85. Prl. 954, f. 52a.
cheuicaunce – 48. G. 1390, f. 109b.
cheuiʃaunce – 48. G. 1678, f. 113b.
chyde – 87. Prl. 403, f. 44b.
choRle – 54, 60, 113. G. 2107, f. 119a.
choʃe – 47, 54, 85. G. 863, f. 102b.
cience – 48. Pur. 1289, f. 74b.
clayme – 78. G. 1490, f. 111a.
clambe – 58. Prl. 773, f. 49b.
clem – 78. Prl. 826, f. 50a.
cleuen – 76. Prl. 66, f. 39b.

clyffe – 94, 95. Prl. 159, f. 41a.
clym – 50, 106, 139. Prl. 1072, f. 53b.
cloyſtoR – 91. Prl. 969, f. 52a.
clolde – 53, 124. Pat. 152, f. 85a.
clos – 50, 72, 100. Prl. 183, f. 41b.
cloſe – 50. Prl. 271, f. 42b.
cofer – 95, 102. Prl. 259, f. 42b.
colde – 53, 124. Prl. 50, f. 39b.
comfoRte – 108. Prl. 357, f. 43b.
compaynye – 123. G. 1011, f. 104b.
conquerour – 44. Pur. 1322, f. 75a.
contray – 79. G. 734, f. 100b.
coRbel – 75. G. 1355, f. 109a.
coRbyal – 75. Pur. 456, f. 63a.
coRt – 54, 91. G. 360, f. 95b.
coRtayſe – 46. Prl. 480, f. 45b.
coRtayſye – 130. Prl. 444, f. 45a.
coRtel – 54, 62. Prl. 203, f. 41b.
coRs – 91. G. 116, f. 92b.
couer – 102. Pur. 1440, f. 77a.
coumfoRde – 108. Prl. 369, f. 44a.
counſeyl – 78. G. 347, f. 95b.
counſel – 78. G. 682, f. 100a.
countre – 79. Prl. 297, f. 43a.
cource – 91. G. 135, f. 92b.
court – 54, 91. G. 43, f. 91b.
cubites – 54, 104. Pur. 405, f. 62b.
cupydeȝ – 54, 104. Pur. 315, f. 61a.
cuppe – 94. Pur. 1461, f. 77a.
curious – 88. G. 855, f. 102b.

daly – 82. G. 1253, f. 107b.
dame – 70. G. 470, f. 97a.
day – 67, 104. Prl. 486, f. 45b.
daylyeden – 82. G. 1114, f. 106a.
declyne – 123. Prl. 333, f. 43b.
ded – 68. G. 725, f. 100b.
dede – 95. Prl. 31, f. 39a.
dele – 120. G. 2188, f. 120a.
demay – 54, 122. G. 470, f. 97a.
deneȝ – 121, 122. G. 2223, f. 120b.
departed – 45. Prl. 378, f. 44a.
depres – 99. Prl. 778, f. 49b.
derk – 60. Prl. 629, f. 47b.
deſe – 99. Prl. 766, f. 49b.
deſyres – 55, 103, 140. G. 1257, f. 107b.
deueleȝ – 120. G. 2192, f. 120a.
deuiſe – 47, 99. G. 92, f. 92a.
deuys – 47. G. 617, f. 99a.
deuoyde – 55, 126, 127, 140. Prl. 15, f. 39a.
devaye – 47. G. 1497, f. 111a.
dewoyde – 55, 126, 127, 140. Pat. 284, f. 87a.
deȝyre – 55, 103, 140. Pur. 1648, f. 79b.
dyngne – 123. Pat. 119, f. 84b.
diſceuer – 54, 122. G. 1862, f. 116a.
diſcouer – 54. G. 418, f. 96b.
diſcrye – 76, 122. G. 81, f. 92a.
diſmayd – 54, 122. G. 336, f. 95b.
diſpleſe – 122. G. 1304, f. 108b.
diſpoRt – 122. G. 1292, f. 108a.
diſſtrye – 88. G. 2375, f. 122b.
dyd – 107. Prl. 306, f. 43a.
dyn – 57. G. 47, f. 91b.
dynt – 55, 62, 64. G. 2264, f. 121a.
dyſcreuen – 76. Prl. 68, f. 39b.
dyt – 107. Prl. 681, f. 48a.
dyȝe – 75. Prl. 306, f. 43a.
doggeȝ – 95. G. 1600, f. 112b.
doRſt – 54. Prl. 143, f. 40b.
dos – 49. G. 1308, f. 108b.
dotȝ – 49. Prl. 17, f. 39a.
doungoun – 116. Pur. 1224, f. 74a.
douſour – 91. Prl. 429, f. 44b.
dreȝ – 88. G. 1750, f. 114b.
dreȝe – 67. Pur. 1224, f. 74a.
dryf – 98. Prl. 777, f. 49b.
drye – 87, 88, 130. Pat. 338, f. 87b.
dryȝe – 67, 75, 87, 88, 130. G. 560, f. 98b.
droȝt – 110. G. 523, f. 98a.
droȝthe – 110. Pur. 524, f. 64a.
druye – 87, 88. Pur. 412, f. 62b.
Dubbed – 46. Prl. 73, f. 40a.
dubbet – 46. Prl. 97, f. 40a.
dunt – 45, 55, 62, 64. G. 452, f. 97a.
durſt – 54. G. 1575, f. 112a.
duſt – 57. G. 523, f. 98a.

egge – 95, 117. G. 212, f. 93b.
eggyng – 117. Pur. 241, f. 60b.
endeure – 53, 69. Prl. 1082, f. 54a.
endoRde – 108. Prl. 368, f. 44a.
endure – 69. Prl. 225, f. 42a.
endured – 53. G. 1517, f. 111a.

englych – 121, 122. G. 629, f. 99b.
ennourned – 91. G. 634, f. 99b.
ennurned – 91. G. 2027, f. 118a.
enpreſſe – 98. Prl. 1097, f. 54a.
enpryſe – 98. Prl. 1097, f. 54a.
enter – 130. Prl. 965, f. 52a.
entre – 130. Pat. 328, f. 87b.
Er – 46. Prl. 317, f. 46a.
er – 46. Prl. 372, f. 44a.
ernde – 54, 57, 136. G. 257, f. 94b.
erne – 53, 128, 129. Pur. 1698, f. 80b.
erraunt – 84. G. 810, f. 101b.
errour – 91. Prl. 422, f. 44b.
erþe – 54, 60. Prl. 840, f. 50b.
etayn – 79. G. 140, f. 93a.
euel – 62. Prl. 930, f. 51b.
euer – 45. Prl. 416, f. 44b.

face – 99, 100. Prl. 169, f. 41a.
fay – 68. Prl. 489, f. 45b.
fayn – 80. G. 840, f. 102a.
fayre – 81. Prl. 169, f. 41a.
falle – 103. G. 728, f. 100b.
fare – 95. G. 1973, f. 117b.
faſoʀ – 91. Prl. 431, f. 44b.
fauoʀ – 91. Prl. 968, f. 52a.
fauour – 91. Prl. 428, f. 44b.
fawre – 54. Pur. 938, f. 70a.
feerſly – 53, 60. G. 329, f. 95b.
feye – 68. G. 1067, f. 105a.
feler – 127. G. 1391, f. 109b.
ferſly – 53, 60. G. 832, f. 102a.
fewe – 69. Prl. 572, f. 46b.
ffoʀ – 46. G. 444, f. 97a.
fyf – 119. Prl. 849, f. 50b.
fyin – 102. Prl. 1204, f. 55b.
fyniſment – 122. G. 499, f. 97b.
fynly – 127. G. 1391, f. 109b.
fyr – 136. G. 1368, f. 109a.
fire – 136. G. 1925, f. 116b.
fiſſche – 95. Pat. 261, f. 86b.
fyſte – 55. Pur. 1723, f. 80b.
fyue – 92. G. 654, f. 99b.
fyþel – 111. Pur. 1082, f. 72a.
fyȝt – 133. G. 278, f. 94b.
flambe – 58. Prl. 769, f. 49b.
fle – 79. Prl. 294, f. 43a.
fleſch – 95. Prl. 306, f. 43a.
floʀ – 54, 68, 91, 136. Prl. 962, f. 52a.
flour – 54, 55, 68, 91, 136. Prl. 426, f. 44b.
flowreȝ – 55. G. 507, f. 97b.
fo – 57. Pur. 1219, f. 73b.
fole – 67. G. 173, f. 93a.
folewande – 130. Prl. 1040, f. 53a.
folwande – 52, 103, 130. Pur. 429, f. 62b.
folȝande – 52, 103, 130. G. 145, f. 93a.
fonde – 107. Prl. 283, f. 42b.
fondet – 53, 108. G. 2125, f. 119a.
fonte – 107. Prl. 327, f. 43b.
foo – 57. G. 716, f. 100b.
foʀ – 46, 103. Prl. 263, f. 42b.
foʀdeȝ – 54, 111. G. 699, f. 100a.
foʀgat – 54, 117. G. 2031, f. 118a.
foʀþe – 54, 111. G. 1617, f. 112b.
foʀȝate – 54, 117. G. 1472, f. 110b.
fote – 72. Prl. 970, f. 52a.
founded – 53, 108. G. 2130, f. 119b.
fowre – 54. Prl. 870, f. 51a.
frayn – 80. G. 489, f. 97b.
frech – 121. Prl. 87, f. 40a.
frely – 52, 115. Prl. 1155, f. 55a.
frelich – 52, 115. Prl. 1086, f. 54a.
frende – 56. Prl. 558, f. 46b.
frenkyſch – 121, 122. G. 1116, f. 106a.
freſche – 121. G. 122, f. 92b.
fryte – 88, 89. Prl. 29, f. 39a.
fruyt – 69, 89. Pur. 1468, f. 77a.
fuyt – 53, 89, 136. G. 1425, f. 110a.
ful – 57. G. 2005, f. 117b.
fuſt – 55, 57, 64. G. 391, f. 96a.
fute – 53, 89, 136. G. 1699, f. 113b.

gafe – 54. G. 1861, f. 116a.
gaynour – 55, 117, 118. G. 2460, f. 124a.
galle – 68. Pur. 1022, f. 71a.
gate – 54, 117. G. 778, f. 101b.
gaue – 54. Prl. 667, f. 48a.
gawayn – 53, 55, 79, 80, 117, 136. G. 838, f. 102a.
gawan – 53, 80, 136. G. 109, f. 92b.
gawen – 79. G. 463, f. 97a.
gawle – 68. Prl. 463, f. 45a.
gef – 54, 117. G. 370, f. 96a.
gent – 116. Prl. 1134, f. 54b.

gentyle – 54, 95, 116, 140. Prl. 632, f. 47b.
gerdeȝ – 54, 62. G. 777, f. 101b.
gere – 114. G. 569, f. 98b.
geſerne – 54, 60. G. 326, f. 95a.
gete – 116. G. 1871, f. 116a.
gette – 116. Pur. 1354, f. 75b.
gyld – 52, 107, 139. G. 569, f. 98b.
gile – 118. G. 1787, f. 115a.
gilt – 52, 107, 139. G. 2062, f. 118b.
gylt – 34, 55, 62, 64. Pur. 731, f. 67a.
gylteȝ – 64. Prl. 655, f. 48a.
gyltyf – 64. Prl. 669, f. 48a.
gyltleȝ – 64. Prl. 668, f. 48a.
gyng – 116. Prl. 455, f. 45a.
gyngure – 116. Prl. 43, f. 39b.
girdel – 54, 62. G. 1829, f. 115b.
gyrdeȝ – 54. G. 2160, f. 120a.
gyſe – 98, 118. Prl. 1099, f. 54a.
giſerne – 54, 60. G. 288, f. 94b.
glad – 95. G. 495, f. 97b.
glayre – 81. Prl. 1026, f. 53a.
glaſſe – 100. Prl. 1025, f. 53a.
glode – 124. Prl. 1111, f. 54a.
glolde – 53, 124. Pur. 1408, f. 76b.
god – 67, 136. Prl. 734, f. 49a.
gode – 67, 86, 136. G. 1148, f. 106b.
golde – 53, 124. Prl. 2, f. 39a.
good – 67. G. 129, f. 92b.
goʀde – 54, 62, 107. G. 1851, f. 115b.
goʀdel – 54, 62. G. 2035, f. 118a.
gos – 49. Prl. 521, f. 46a.
gotȝ – 49, 99, 100. Prl. 535, f. 46a.
goud – 67, 72, 136. Prl. 33, f. 39a.
gouernoʀes – 44. Pur. 1645, f. 79b.
gouernour – 44. G. 225, f. 94a.
grace – 45, 46, 99, 100. Prl. 436, f. 45a.
gray – 67. G. 82, f. 92a.
grame – 70. G. 2502, f. 124b.
grant – 52, 83. G. 1110, f. 1056.
graunte – 52, 83. G. 1841, f. 1156.
grece – 76. Prl. 231, f. 42a.
grene – 67. G. 451, f. 97a.
guere – 114. Pur. 1505, f. 77b.
gult – 34, 55, 62, 64. Pur. 690, f. 66b.
gulte – 64. Prl. 942, f. 52a.
gulty – 64. Pat. 210, f. 85b.
gurde – 54, 62, 107, 108. G. 588, f. 98b.
gurdel – 54, 62. G. 2395, f. 123a.
gwenoʀe – 55, 117, 118. G. 109, f. 92b.

habbes – 52. G. 327, f. 95a.
habbeȝ – 94. G. 452, f. 97a.
habraham – 53, 128, 129. Pur. 682, f. 66a.
hachche – 94. Pat. 179, f. 85b.
haf – 119. Prl. 194, f. 41b.
hafe – 99, 103, 139. G. 2135, f. 119b.
hayre – 79. Pur. 666, f. 66a.
haylſed – 80, 81. Prl. 238, f. 42a.
haled – 108. G. 788, f. 101b.
halet – 108. G. 1049, f. 105a.
halſed – 80, 81. Pur. 1621, f. 79b.
han – 52, 119. Prl. 373, f. 44a.
hanſelle – 50, 110, 139. G. 491, f. 97b.
harme – 56. G. 2511, f. 124b.
haſel – 102. G. 744, f. 101a.
haſtif – 119. Pat. 520, f. 90a.
haſtyfly – 53, 118. Pur. 200, f. 59b.
haſtily – 53. G. 605, f. 99a.
haſtyly – 118. G. 1135, f. 106a.
hatȝ – 49, 99. Prl. 291, f. 43a.
haþel – 128, 129. Prl. 676, f. 48a.
haue – 139. Prl. 132, f. 40b.
hauekeȝ – 114, 120. Pur. 537, f. 64a.
hauen – 52. Prl. 859, f. 50b.
hawbrgh – 104, 113, 132. G. 203, f. 93b.
hawk – 120. Prl. 184, f. 41b.
hede – 120. Prl. 1172, f. 55a.
hete – 73. Prl. 643, f. 47b.
heggeȝ – 117. G. 1708, f. 113b.
help – 104. G. 987, f. 104a.
hem – 45. Prl. 69, f. 39b.
hende – 60. Prl. 184, f. 41b.
here – 79. Pur. 52, f. 57b.
herneȝ – 53, 128, 129. Pur. 537, f. 64a.
hert – 60. Prl. 17, f. 39a.
hes – 54, 109, 110. G. 1090, f. 105b.
heſt – 54, 109. G. 1039, f. 105a.
heue – 73. Prl. 314, f. 43a.
heued – 120. Prl. 459, f. 45a.
heuen – 56. Prl. 473, f. 45b.
hewe – 53. G. 1471, f. 110b.
heȝe – 54, 75, 104. G. 281, f. 94b.
heȝt – 110. G. 788, f. 101b.
heȝþe – 110. Pur. 317, f. 61a.

hide – 87, 136. Pur. 1600, f. 79a.
hyde – 68, 87. Prl. 1136, f. 54b.
hyden – 87. G. 2511, f. 124b.
hille – 62, 64. G. 59, f. 91b.
hylle – 64. Prl. 678, f. 48a.
hynde – 60. Prl. 909, f. 51b.
hyne – 123. Prl. 505, f. 46a.
hyre – 87. Prl. 523, f. 46a.
hys – 99. Prl. 307, f. 43a.
hyſſe – 99, 100. Prl. 418, f. 44b.
Hit – 46. Prl. 1165, f. 55a.
hit – 46, 48. Prl. 10, f. 39a.
hyt – 47. Prl. 283, f. 42b.
hyure – 87. Pat. 56, f. 83b.
hiȝe – 54. Prl. 207, f. 41b.
hyȝe – 75, 130. Prl. 596, f. 47a.
ho – 50. Prl. 129, f. 40b.
hondele – 44. G. 289, f. 94b.
hondeſelle – 50, 110, 139. G. 66, f. 92a.
hondred – 111. G. 786, f. 49b.
honour – 91. Prl. 424, f. 44b.
hoo – 50. G. 2330, f. 122a.
hoʀſeluen – 91. G. 1394, f. 109b.
houreȝ – 53. Prl. 555, f. 46b.
hov – 47, 103. Pur. 140, f. 58b.
how – 103. Prl. 334, f. 43b.
huyde – 68, 87, 136. Pur. 915, f. 69b.
hult – 64, 65. G. 1594, f. 112a.
hundreth – 111. Prl. 1107, f. 54a.
hwe – 53. G. 147, f. 93a.

iche – 55. G. 126, f. 92b.
ientyle – 54, 116, 140. G. 542, f. 98a.
if – 54. G. 272, f. 94b.
iiſſe – 49. G. 732, f. 100b.
image – 47. Pur. 983, f. 70b.
ymage – 47. G. 649, f. 99b.
In – 46, 57. G. 22, f. 91a.
in – 45, 46, 48, 57. G. 645, f. 99b.
innoghe – 118, 130. G. 77, f. 92a.
innowe – 52, 118, 130. G. 1401, f. 109b.
innoȝe – 52, 118, 130. G. 514, f. 97b.
ioyleȝ – 47. G. 542, f. 98a.
ioly – 53. G. 86, f. 92a.
iolyf – 53. Pur. 864, f. 68b.
ionas – 47. Pat. 413, f. 88b.
ioparde – 108. G. 97, f. 92a.
is – 49. G. 33, f. 91b.

iugge – 47, 95. Pat. 224, f. 86a.
iwyſſe – 99. Prl. 151, f. 41a.
ywan – 80. G. 113, f. 92b.
yȝe – 67, 75. G. 198, f. 93b.
yȝen – 76. Prl. 200, f. 41b.

jn – 47, 57. Pat. 280, f. 86b.
john – 45. Prl. 836, f. 50b.
jonas – 47. Pat. 57, f. 83b.
joyleȝ – 47. Prl. 252, f. 42a.
jugge – 47. Pat. 224, f. 86a.
jentyle – 95, 116. Pat. 62, f. 83b.
joly – 118. Prl. 929, f. 51b.
jolyf – 118, 119. Prl. 842, f. 50b.
jeſus – 45. Prl. 711, f. 48b.
jeruſalem – 45. Prl. 804, f. 50a.

keſt – 54, 58. G. 228, f. 94a.
keſten – 46. Prl. 1122, f. 54b.
kynde – 62. Prl. 55, f. 39b.
kyngeȝ – 132. G. 2476, f. 124a.
kyrf – 62. G. 372, f. 96a.
kyryous – 88. Pur. 1109, f. 72a.
kyrtel – 54, 62. G. 1831, f. 115b.
kyſſe – 62. G. 1303, f. 108b.
kyth – 101. G. 460, f. 97a.
kyþe – 88, 101, 103. Prl. 356, f. 43b.
klyffe – 94. G. 1166, f. 106b.
klymbe – 50, 106, 139. Prl. 678, f. 48a.
kneȝ – 102. G. 577, f. 98b.
knyffe – 99. G. 2042, f. 118a.
knyt – 47. G. 1642, f. 113a.
knitte – 47. G. 1331, f. 108b.
knot – 50. Prl. 788, f. 49b.
knott – 50. G. 188, f. 93b.
koynt – 90, 114. G. 877, f. 102b.

lambe – 52, 58. Prl. 771, f. 49b.
laſt – 56. G. 1023, f. 104b.
laumpe – 84. G. 2010, f. 118a.
lawe – 68. G. 790, f. 101b.
le – 57. Pat. 277, f. 86b.
lede – 54, 85, 136. G. 833, f. 102a.
lee – 57. G. 1893, f. 116a.
legge – 117. G. 2228, f. 120b.
legge – 117. G. 346, f. 95b.
lenge – 111. G. 1672, f. 113b.
lenghe – 111, 112. Prl. 416, f. 44b.

lenkþe – 50, 114. G. 210, f. 93b.
lent – 107. G. 2440, f. 123b.
lenþe – 50, 114. G. 1627, f. 112b.
lette – 94. Prl. 1050, f. 53b.
leude – 54, 85, 86, 136. G. 1124, f. 106a.
leue – 73. Prl. 316, f. 43a.
leuen – 76, 103. Prl. 69, f. 39b.
lye – 52. G. 88, f. 92a.
lif – 47. G. 87, f. 92a.
lyf – 47, 98, 103. G. 98, f. 92a.
lyft – 62. G. 698, f. 100a.
lyttel – 62. Prl. 387, f. 44a.
lyſte – 64. G. 2133, f. 119b.
lyȝe – 52, 75. Prl. 304, f. 43a.
lyȝt – 84, 133. Prl. 1046, f. 53b.
lof – 98. Pur. 843, f. 68b.
logge – 117. Pur. 807, f. 68a.
lokeȝ – 49. Prl. 1134, f. 54b.
lokkeȝ – 49. G. 156, f. 93a.
lombe – 52, 84, 85, 104, 139. Prl. 1046, f. 53b.
lomp – 52, 104, 139. Prl. 815, f. 50a.
londe – 107. Prl. 937, f. 52a.
lone – 72. Prl. 1066, f. 53b.
loʀde – 46, 52, 106, 107, 108. Prl. 502, f. 45b.
Loʀde – 46. Prl. 108, f. 40a.
loʀt – 52, 106, 107. G. 849, f. 102a.
loue – 98. Prl. 285, f. 42b.
lowe – 68. G. 972, f. 104a.
lude – 53, 54, 85, 86, 136. G. 133, f. 92b.
lufly – 52, 115. Prl. 962, f. 52a.
luflych – 52, 115. G. 38, f. 91b.
lur – 64. G. 355, f. 95b.

ma – 115. Prl. 283, f. 42b.
mace – 115. G. 1885, f. 116a.
mad – 50, 136. Pur. 641, f. 65b.
madde – 49. Pur. 654, f. 66a.
made – 49, 50, 52, 115, 136. G. 687, f. 100a.
mayny – 54, 78. Pur. 514, f. 64a.
maynteine – 67, 136. G. 2053, f. 118b.
mayntyne – 67, 75. Pat. 523, f. 89a.
maked – 52, 115. G. 1152, f. 106a.
man – 34, 52. Prl. 386, f. 44a.
man – 115. Prl. 512, f. 46a.
manayre – 81. Prl. 1029, f. 53a.
mane – 67. G. 187, f. 93b.
mankyn – 50, 110. Prl. 637, f. 47b.
mare – 49. Prl. 145, f. 41a.
marked – 108. Prl. 513, f. 46a.
marre – 49. Pur. 279, f. 60b.
marreȝ – 103. Prl. 23, f. 39a.
mas – 49, 95, 115. G. 106, f. 92b.
maſkelles – 46. Prl. 744, f. 49a.
Maſkelles – 46. Prl. 781, f. 49b.
maſkelleȝ – 99. Prl. 756, f. 49a.
matȝ – 49, 115. Prl. 610, f. 47a.
maugre – 53. Pat. 44, f. 83b.
maugref – 53. Pat. 54, f. 83b.
mawgref – 119. G. 1565, f. 112a.
medoes – 131. Pur. 1761, f. 81a.
meyny – 53, 54, 78. Prl. 542, f. 46b.
mele – 49. Pur. 736, f. 67a.
melle – 49. Prl. 797, f. 50a.
mene – 61, 68. G. 233, f. 94a.
meny – 53, 78. G. 101, f. 92a.
menteene – 67, 75, 136. Prl. 783, f. 49b.
mercy – 48. Prl. 356, f. 43b.
mery – 59. G. 497, f. 97b.
meryly – 54. G. 740, f. 101a.
merſy – 48. Prl. 383, f. 44a.
merþe – 52, 54, 59, 103. G. 541, f. 98a.
metail – 80. G. 169, f. 93a.
metalle – 80. Pur. 1513, f. 78a.
mete – 49, 67, 73, 136. G. 45, f. 91b.
mette – 49. G. 1370, f. 109a.
meue – 120. G. 985, f. 104a.
meȝelmas – 132, 133. G. 532, f. 98a.
mych – 62. G. 1281, f. 108a.
myyn – 68. G. 1067, f. 105a.
miyry – 53. G. 1447, f. 110a.
myn – 68. G. 257, f. 94b.
mynde – 45. Prl. 156, f. 41a.
myne – 68. G. 342, f. 95b.
mynt – 62, 64. G. 2345, f. 122a.
miry – 53, 59. G. 1691, f. 113b.
mirþe – 52, 54, 59. G. 45, f. 91b.
myſerecoʀde – 108. Prl. 366, f. 44a.
myſſe – 95, 99. Prl. 329, f. 43b.
myþe – 88. Prl. 359, f. 43b.
myȝ – 54, 109. G. 1858, f. 115b.
myȝt – 54, 109. Prl. 765, f. 49b.
mokke – 94. Prl. 905, f. 51b.
mon – 52. G. 57, f. 91b.

mon – 49. Prl. 374, f. 44a.
mone – 72. Prl. 1068, f. 53b.
monkynde – 50, 110. Pur. 564, f. 64b.
moon – 49. Pur. 377, f. 62a.
moRe – 72. Prl. 234, f. 42a.
moRne – 130. G. 740, f. 101a.
moRoun – 130. G. 1208, f. 107a.
mote – 72. Prl. 972, f. 52a.
mourneʒ – 44. Pat. 508, f. 89a.
mouthe – 53. G. 1447, f. 110a.
much – 113. Prl. 244, f. 42a.
muche – 62, 64. G. 1992, f. 117b.
muckel – 94, 113. G. 142, f. 93a.
mulne – 64. G. 2203, f. 120b.
munt – 62, 64. G. 2350, f. 122b.
muryly – 54. G. 2295, f. 121b.
muthe – 53, 68, 91. G. 447, f. 97a.
mwe – 120. G. 1565, f. 112a.

nauel – 120. Pat. 278, f. 86b.
naule – 68, 120. Prl. 459, f. 45a.
ne – 50. Prl. 65, f. 39b.
nece – 76, 102. Prl. 233, f. 42a.
nee – 50. Prl. 262, f. 42b.
neghe – 104. G. 697, f. 100a.
neuer – 103. Prl. 913, f. 51b.
new – 53, 69. G. 1075, f. 105b.
neʒ – 53. G. 929, f. 103b.
nye – 52, 54, 68, 88, 89. G. 2141, f. 119b.
nieʒ – 53. G. 1922, f. 116b.
niyʒt – 53. G. 929, f. 103b.
nyʒe – 52, 68. G. 2002, f. 117b.
nyʒt – 53, 104. G. 751, f. 101a.
nobele – 130. G. 1264, f. 108a.
noble – 130. G. 623, f. 99a.
noye – 54, 89. Pur. 1236, f. 74a.
noyſe – 69. G. 118, f. 92b.
nov – 47. Pur. 64, f. 57b.
Now – 46. Prl. 397, f. 44b.
now – 46. G. 10, f. 91a.
nuyeʒ – 54, 55, 89. Pur. 578, f. 65a.
nw – 53, 69. Prl. 527, f. 46a.
nwy – 55, 89. Pur. 301, f. 61a.

Of – 46. Prl. 457, f. 45a.
of – 46. Prl. 31, f. 39a.
offred – 95, 97. G. 593, f. 99a.
onende – 110. Prl. 186, f. 41b.
onlyue – 98. G. 385, f. 96a.
oRyʒt – 54. G. 40, f. 91b.
ouer – 97. Prl. 454, f. 45a.
oure – 53. Prl. 551, f. 46b.
owen – 68. G. 408, f. 96b.

pacience – 46. Pat. 531, f. 90a.
Pacience – 46. Pat. 1, f. 83a.
paſſe – 100. Prl. 1110, f. 54a.
pece – 67. Pur. 1348, f. 75b.
pendaundes – 108. G. 2431, f. 123b.
pendauntes – 108. G. 168, f. 93a.
pene – 54, 61. Prl. 510, f. 46a.
peny – 54, 61. Prl. 546, f. 46b.
peril – 45. Pur. 856, f. 68b.
pes – 99. Prl. 742, f. 49a.
pyeſe – 67. Pur. 1124, f. 72b.
pyne – 123. Prl. 330, f. 43b.
pipe – 94. G. 118, f. 92b.
pyſe – 67, 76. Prl. 229, f. 42a.
play – 67. G. 1014, f. 104b.
pleſaunt – 84. G. 808, f. 101b.
poyned – 108, 109. Prl. 217, f. 42a.
poynt – 69, 90. Prl. 309, f. 43a.
poRe – 54, 119. Prl. 573, f. 46b.
poRpos – 100. Prl. 508, f. 46a.
pouer – 54, 119. Prl. 1075, f. 53b.
precios – 44. Prl. 4, f. 39a.
pres – 99. Prl. 1114, f. 54a.
preſented – 45. Pur. 1217, f. 73b.
pretermynable – 45. Prl. 596, f. 47a.
pryde – 87. G. 587, f. 98b.
pryncece – 102. G. 1770, f. 114b.
prynceʒ – 102. Prl. 1164, f. 55a.
pryſe – 99. Prl. 1131, f. 54b.
prophete – 44, 95. Prl. 831, f. 50b.

quaynt – 54, 90, 114. G. 999, f. 104b.
quel – 60. G. 822, f. 102a.
quen – 55. Prl. 79, f. 40a.
quene – 55, 67, 75, 94, 124, 125, 139. G. 647, f. 99b.
quy – 55, 124. Prl. 561, f. 46b.
quyl – 60. G. 1035, f. 104b.
quyle – 55, 124, 139. G. 814, f. 102a.
quod – 45. Prl. 241, f. 42a.
quoynt – 54, 90, 114. Prl. 889, f. 51a.

quoyntyſe – 90. Pat. 39, f. 83b.

raas – 67. Prl. 1167, f. 55a.
rayſoun – 54, 68, 78, 136. Prl. 268, f. 42b.
rande – 56. G. 1710, f. 114a.
regne – 52, 123. Prl. 501, f. 45b.
reyſoun – 53, 54, 68, 78, 136. Pur. 328, f. 61b.
reme – 93. Prl. 448, f. 45a.
remoRde – 108. G. 2434, f. 123b.
remwe – 120. G. 1475, f. 110b.
rengne – 52, 122. Prl. 692, f. 48b.
rengned – 123. Pur. 1321, f. 74b.
reniſchche – 55. Pur. 96, f. 58a.
renk – 52, 60. G. 303, f. 95a.
rent – 56. G. 1332, f. 108b.
repayre – 81. Prl. 1028, f. 53a.
reſoun 53, 78, 136. Prl. 52, f. 39b.
rybe – 55, 88. Prl. 1007, f. 52b.
ricchis – 94. G. 8, f. 91a.
richche – 49, 65. G. 1898, f. 116b.
riche – 49. Prl. 993, f. 52b.
ryf – 98. Prl. 770, f. 49b.
rygge – 62, 117. G. 1344, f. 109a.
rynk – 52, 60. Pat. 216, f. 86a.
rys – 98. Prl. 1093, f. 54a.
ryſe – 92, 98. G. 1001, f. 105b.
ryue – 98, 99. G. 2046, f. 118a.
Ryȝt – 46. Prl. 673, f. 48a.
ryȝt – 46. G. 373, f. 96a.
robbed – 49. Pur. 1156, f. 73a.
robe – 49. Pur. 144, f. 58b.
rocheȝ – 54, 113. Pur. 537, f. 64a.
rogh – 50. G. 1432, f. 110a.
rok – 54. Pur. 446, f. 63a.
rokkeȝ – 113. Prl. 68, f. 39b.
ronk – 57. Prl. 844, f. 50b.
ros – 100. Prl. 437, f. 45a.
rot – 103. Prl. 26, f. 39a.
roþer – 111. Pur. 419, f. 62b.
rowwe – 103. Pat. 216, f. 86a.
roȝ – 49, 68. G. 2198, f. 120b.
roȝe – 68. G. 745, f. 101a.
rubies – 88. Pur. 1471, f. 77a.
ruchched – 65. G. 367, f. 96a.
ruchen – 65. Pat. 101, f. 84a.
runiſch – 54. G. 457, f. 97a.
ruȝe – 68. G. 2166, f. 120a.

ſade – 80, 81. Prl. 532, f. 46a.
ſaghe – 103, 140. Prl. 226, f. 42a.
ſayde – 80, 81. Prl. 289, f. 43a.
ſayn – 54, 109. G. 1022, f. 104b.
ſayn – 109. G. 589, f. 98b.
ſayned – 123. G. 761, f. 101a.
ſaynt – 54, 80, 81, 82. Prl. 457, f. 45a.
ſays – 49, 53, 103. Prl. 295, f. 43a.
ſaytȝ – 49, 53, 99, 100, 103. Prl. 501, f. 45b.
ſayȝ – 100. Prl. 615, f. 47b.
ſame – 70. Prl. 1099, f. 54a.
ſancta ſanctoRum – 45. Pur. 1491, f. 77b.
ſange – 58. Prl. 19, f. 39a.
ſant – 53, 80, 81, 82. Prl. 788, f. 49b.
ſatȝ – 81. Prl. 677, f. 48a.
ſaue – 99. G. 2139, f. 119b.
ſawe – 52, 130. Pur. 109, f. 58b.
ſaweȝ – 103, 140. Prl. 278, f. 42b.
ſaȝ – 53, 100. Prl. 689, f. 48b.
ſaȝe – 52, 130, 140. Pur. 1670, f. 80a.
ſcade – 53, 95, 122. G. 425, f. 96b.
ſcelt – 48. Pur. 827, f. 68a.
ſchade – 54, 122. Pur. 1690, f. 80a.
ſchame – 70, 72. G. 2504, f. 124b.
ſchawe – 54, 93. G. 27, f. 91a.
ſchelde – 121. G. 205, f. 93b.
ſcheldeȝ – 121. G. 1456, f. 110b.
ſchene – 76. Prl. 203, f. 41b.
ſchere – 54, 121, G. 334, f. 95b.
ſchewe – 54, 93. G. 420, f. 96b.
ſchome – 72. G. 2372, f. 122b.
ſchoRe – 72. G. 2161, f. 120a.
ſclade – 53, 115. Prl. 1148, f. 54b.
ſclaȝte – 53. Pur. 56, f. 57b.
ſe – 67, 79. Prl. 296, f. 43a.
ſeche – 54, 62. G. 1543, f. 111b.
ſeete – 49. Pur. 92, f. 58a.
ſegge – 117. G. 115, f. 92b.
ſene – 75. Prl. 194, f. 41b.
ſergaunteȝ – 54, 140. Pur. 109, f. 58b.
ſeriauntes – 54, 140. Pat. 385, f. 88b.
ſeſoun – 78. G. 501, f. 97b.
ſet – 49. Prl. 545, f. 46b.
ſeuen – 60, 102. Prl. 838, f. 50b.

ſyde – 88. Prl. 975, f. 52b.
ſyence – 48. Pur. 1454, f. 77a.
ſyn – 54, 121. G. 919, f. 103a.
ſyngne – 123. G. 625, f. 99a.
ſynne – 62. Prl. 610, f. 47a.
ſyre – 45. G. 685, f. 100a.
ſiſter – 55. G. 11, f. 92b.
ſiþen – 95, 121. G. 6, f. 91a.
ſyþen – 54, 97. G. 43, f. 91b.
ſyþeʒ – 92. G. 656, f. 99b.
ſyʒe – 75. G. 83, f. 92a.
ſlade – 53, 115. Prl. 141, f. 40b.
ſlaʒt – 54, 133. Prl. 801, f. 50a.
ſlepe – 95. Prl. 115, f. 40b.
ſlomeryng – 106. G. 1182, f. 106b.
ſloumbe – 106. Pat. 186, f. 85b.
ſmyle – 64. G. 1789, f. 115a.
ſnaw – 68. G. 2088, f. 119a.
So – 46. Prl. 97, f. 40a.
ſo – 46, 68. G. 2140, f. 119b.
ſoghe – 44. Pat. 67, f. 84a.
ſolemne – 52, 104, 105. Pur. 1171, f. 73a.
ſolemnete – 105. Pur. 1313, f. 75a.
ſolempne – 52, 104, 105. Pur. 1447, f. 77a.
ſolempnete – 105. Pur. 1757, f. 81a.
ſonge – 58. Prl. 891, f. 51a.
ſonne – 55, 57, 136. Prl. 530, f. 46a.
ſoʀewe – 53, 130, 131. Pur. 778, f. 67b.
ſoʀʒe – 53, 130. Prl. 352, f. 43b.
ſoth – 50. Prl. 482, f. 45b.
ſoþ – 50. G. 348, f. 95b.
ſpace – 99, 100. G. 1418, f. 110a.
ſpyce – 76. Prl. 235, f. 42a.
ſprange – 58. Prl. 13, f. 39a.
ſtayre – 81. Prl. 1022, f. 53a.
ſtayred – 82. Pur. 1396, f. 76a.
ſtaue – 99. G. 2137, f. 119b.
ſted – 54. G. 2213, f. 120b.
ſtel – 136. G. 426, f. 96b.
ſtele – 136. G. 211, f. 93b.
ſtewarde – 69. Pur. 90, f. 58a.
ſtyf – 98. Prl. 779, f. 49b.
ſton – 68, 136. Prl. 380, f. 44a.
ſtone – 68, 136. G. 2230, f. 120b.
ſtrenghþe – 54, 111, 112, 113, 132, 139. Prl. 128, f. 40b.
ſtrenkþe – 52, 54, 111, 114, 132, 139. G. 1496, f. 111a.
ſtrenþe – 52, 114. Pur. 1155, f. 73a.
ſtryf – 98, 119. Prl. 776, f. 49b.
ſtud – 54. Pur. 389, f. 62a.
ſture – 64. G. 331, f. 95b.
ſturne – 64. G. 334, f. 95b.
ſuche – 54, 62, 64. Prl. 58, f. 39b.
ſum – 103. G. 93, f. 92a.
ſumme – 103. G. 28, f. 91b.
ſunne – 54, 57, 103, 136. Prl. 28, f. 39a.
ſuſter – 55. G. 2464, f. 124a.
ſwangeande – 95, 117. Prl. 111, f. 40b.
ſware – 81. Prl. 1023, f. 53a.
ſwefte – 53, 60. Prl. 354, f. 43b.
ſwey – 52, 67, 130. Pur. 788, 67b.
ſweʒe – 52, 68, 130. G. 1796, f. 115a.
ſwyfte – 53, 60. G. 1825, f. 115b.
ſwyþe – 88. Prl. 354, f. 43b.

ta – 115. G. 413, f. 96b.
take – 67. G. 682, f. 100a.
taken – 52, 115. G. 2448, f. 123b.
tan – 52, 115. G. 1396, f. 109b.
tas – 49, 115. G. 2305, f. 121b.
taſſel – 102. G. 219, f. 94a.
tatʒ – 49. Pur. 735, f. 67a.
telle – 94. G. 26, f. 91a.
teme – 53, 110. Pat. 358, f. 88a.
that – 45, 101. Prl. 253, f. 42b.
Thaʒ – 101, 102. Pat. 285, f. 87a.
The – 101, Prl. 85, f. 40a.
theme – 53, 110. Prl. 944, f. 52a.
Then – 101, 103. Prl. 589, f. 47a.
Thys – 47, 49, 101. Prl. 841, f. 50b.
Thow – 101. Prl. 337, f. 43b.
throne – 53, 110. Prl. 1113, f. 54a.
Thus – 101. Pur. 161, f. 59a.
tyde – 87. G. 585, f. 98b.
tytel – 130. G. 480, f. 97b.
tytle – 130. G. 626, f. 99a.
toʀ – 91. Prl. 966, f. 52a.
toʀ – 50. G. 165, f. 93a.
toʀe – 50. G. 719, f. 100b.
totʒ – 100. Prl. 513, f. 46a.
trawe – 69. G. 70, f. 92a.
tryfel – 130. G. 547, f. 98a.
tryfle – 130. G. 1301, f. 108b.

trone – 53, 110. Prl. 1055, f. 53b.
trowe – 68, 69. G. 2238, f. 121a.
true – 45. Prl. 311, f. 43a.
truly – 55. G. 380, f. 96a.
trwly – 55. G. 2348, f. 122b.

þad – 109. G. 686, f. 100a.
þare – 81. Prl. 1021, f. 53a.
þat – 45, 101, 109. G. 1775, f. 114b.
þaȝ – 101. G. 350, f. 95b.
Þe – 47. Prl. 785, f. 49b.
þe – 47, 101. Prl. 28, f. 39a.
þef – 54. G. 1725, f. 114a.
þenk – 60. Prl. 1151, f. 54b.
þenne – 101. Prl. 326, f. 43b.
þer – 45. Prl. 21, f. 39a.
þeſe – 54, 92, 136. Prl. 551, f. 46b.
þewes – 54. Pur. 1142, f. 72b.
þider – 95. G. 1424, f. 110a.
þinges – 44. Pur. 5, f. 57a.
þyng – 52, 112. Prl. 771, f. 49b.
þink – 52. Pur. 1359, f. 75b.
þynk – 112. Pur. 819, f. 68a.
þynk – 60. Pur. 749, f. 67a.
þys – 49, 101. Prl. 250, f. 42a.
þiſe – 54. Prl. 287, f. 42b.
þyſe – 92, 136. Prl. 555, f. 46b.
þyſſe – 99, 100. Prl. 370, f. 44a.
þof – 54, 118. G. 624, f. 99a.
þonc – 112. Prl. 901, f. 51a.
þos – 100. Prl. 515, f. 46a.
þou – 45, 101. Prl. 23, f. 39a.
þow – 45. Prl. 411, f. 44b.
þoȝ – 54, 118. G. 69, f. 92a.
þrange – 58. Prl. 17, f. 39a.
þre – 79. Prl. 292, f. 43a.
þryf – 119. Prl. 851, f. 50b.
þurled – 64. G. 1356, f. 109a.
þus – 101. G. 733, f. 100b.

ueſture – 47. Prl. 220, f. 42a.
uyne – 47. Prl. 502, f. 45b.
uoched – 47. Prl. 1121, f. 54b.

Vche – 47. G. 1888, f. 116a.
vche – 47, 55. Prl. 5, f. 39a.
venge – 126. Pat. 71, f. 84a.
venkkyſt – 49, 114. Pur. 1071, f. 71b.
venkquyſt – 49. Pur. 544, f. 64b.
venquyſt – 114, 122. G. 2482, f. 124a.
ver – 127. G. 866, f. 102b.
vertu – 57. Pat. 284, f. 87a.
vertuus – 44, 57. G. 2027, f. 118a.
veſture – 47. G. 161, f. 93a.
vyf – 55, 98, 126, 140. Prl. 772, f. 49b.
vygour – 91. Prl. 971, f. 52a.
vilanye – 53, 80. G. 345, f. 95b.
vylaynye – 53, 80. Pur. 863, f. 68b.
vyne – 47, 102, 103, 123. Prl. 504, f. 45b.
vyſayge – 82. Prl. 178, f. 41a.
vnhyde – 87. Prl. 973, f. 52b.
vouche – 55, 126. Pur. 1358, f. 75b.
vp – 57. G. 369, f. 96a.
vrþe – 54, 60. Prl. 442, f. 45a.

wace – 99, 100. Prl. 65, f. 39b.
waye – 104. G. 1077, f. 105b.
walour – 126. G. 1518, f. 111a.
wame – 106. Pat. 300, f. 87a.
ware – 81. Prl. 1027, f. 53a.
warp – 54, 57. G. 2253, f. 121a.
was – 49. G. 169, f. 93a.
waſchen – 54, 58. G. 72, f. 92a.
waſſayl – 127. Pur. 1508, f. 77b.
waſſe – 100. Prl. 1112, f. 54a.
watȝ – 50, 99, 100. Prl. 45, f. 39b.
wawen – 55, 117. G. 1010, f. 104b.
wedde – 95. Prl. 772, f. 49b.
wende – 107. G. 900, f. 103a.
wene – 76. Prl. 201, f. 41b.
weng – 126. Pur. 201, f. 59b.
wenoʀe – 55, 117, 118. G. 945, f. 103b.
went – 107. G. 688, f. 100a.
were – 127. G. 1391, f. 109b.
werk – 60, 126. G. 494, f. 97b.
werp – 54, 57. Pur. 284, f. 60b.
wertes – 54, 62. Pat. 478, f. 89b.
weſche – 54, 58. G. 887, f. 103a.
When – 47. G. 590, f. 99a.
when – 47, 55. Prl. 332, f. 43b.
whene – 55, 124, 125, 139. G. 2492, f. 124a.
why – 50, 55, 124. Prl. 329, f. 43b.
while – 55, 124. G. 1852, f. 115b.
whyle – 139. G. 1469, f. 110b.

whyſſynes – 124, 125. G. 878, f. 102b.
wy – 52, 55, 124. Prl. 290, f. 43a.
wyf – 55, 119, 126, 140. G. 2404, f. 123a.
wyghe – 49. G. 1487, f. 111a.
wyle – 55, 124. G. 60, f. 91b.
wyle – 118, G. 1728, f. 114a.
wyrkeʒ – 62, 113. Prl. 536, f. 46a.
wynne – 62. Prl. 154, f. 41a.
wyſchande – 62. Prl. 14, f. 39a.
wyſe – 98, 99, 118. G. 185, f. 93b.
wyte – 103. Pur. 76, f. 58a.
with – 45. G. 38, f. 91b.
wyth – 45. G. 364, f. 95b.
wyþer – 97. Prl. 230, f. 42a.
wyþerly – 97. Pat. 74, f. 84a.
wyʒe – 50. G. 249, f. 94a.
wlonc – 112. Prl. 903, f. 51b.
wlonk – 103. Prl. 122, f. 40b.
wombe – 106. G. 144, f. 93a.
woʀch – 54, 62. G. 1039, f. 105a.
woʀchen – 113. Prl. 511, f. 46a.
woʀchyp – 121, 139. G. 1267, f. 108a.
woʀchip – 54, 95. G. 1521, f. 111b.
woʀk – 55. Pur. 663, f. 66a.
woʀſchyp – 54, 121, 139. G. 2441, f. 123b.
woʀt – 54, 62. G. 518, f. 98a.
woʀþe – 60. Prl. 451, f. 45a.
wowche – 55, 126, 127, 128. G. 1391, f. 109b.
wrache – 113. Pat. 185, f. 85b.
wrake – 103, 113. G. 16, f. 91a.
wrange – 58. Prl. 488, f. 45b.
wrathþe – 95. Prl. 362, f. 44a.
wruxeled – 65, 66. Pur. 1381, f. 76a.
wruxled – 65, 66. G. 2191, f. 120a.

ʒaule – 117. G. 1453, f. 110b.
ʒate – 54, 117. G. 820, f. 102a.
ʒed – 103. G. 1595, f. 112a.
ʒede – 85, 86. G. 1122, f. 106a.
ʒef – 54, 103, 117. G. 1964, f. 117a.
ʒeferus – 102, 103. G. 517, f. 98a.
ʒelle – 117. G. 1453, f. 110b.
ʒender – 54, 60. Pur. 1617, f. 79a.
ʒerne – 60. G. 1478, f. 110b.
ʒet – 47. G. 1122, f. 106a.
Ʒet – 47. G. 536, f. 98a.
ʒif – 54. G. 406, f. 96b.
ʒirneʒ – 60. G. 529, f. 98a.
ʒod – 85, 86. G. 1146, f. 106a.
ʒolʒe – 130. G. 950, f. 103b.
ʒomerly – 117. G. 1453, f. 110b.
ʒonde – 107. G. 2440, f. 123b.
ʒonder – 54, 60. G. 678, f. 100a.
ʒonge – 112, 139. G. 89, f. 92a.
ʒonke – 112, 139. G. 1526, f. 111b.
ʒoʀ – 91. Prl. 761, f. 49b.
ʒowre – 103, 132, 140. G. 1065, f. 105a.
yowre – 104, 132, 140. G. 836, f. 102a.

LIST OF WORKS CITED

A Middle English Dictionary, ed. Francis Henry Stratman, rev. Henry Bradley (Oxford, 1891).

A New English Dictionary on Historical Principles, eds. Sir James A. H. Murray, Henry Bradley, W. A. Craigie, C. T. Onions (Oxford, 1888-1928).

Abercrombie, David, What is a Letter? *Lingua* 2.15-20 (August, 1949).

Bateson, H., ed., *Patience* (Manchester, 1912).

Bazell, C. E., Review of R. P. Stockwell and C. W. Barritt, *Some Old English graphemic-phonemic correspondences*, *SIL*, Occasional Papers 4 (Norman, 1951), *Litera* 1.75-7 (1954).

—, The Grapheme, *Litera* 3.43-6 (1956).

—, The Phonemic interpretation of the Old English diphthongs, *Litera* 3.115-20 (1956).

—, Three conceptions of phonological neutralization, *For Roman Jakobson*, ed. Morris Halle a.o., 25-30 (The Hague, 1956).

Bazire, Joyce, ME ē and ę̄ in the rhymes of Sir Gawain and The Green Knight, *JEGP* 51.234-5 (1952).

Bloch, Bernard, A Set of postulates for phonemic analysis, *Language* 24.3-46 (1948).

Bloomfield, Leonard, *Language* (New York, 1933).

—, Linguistic aspects of science, *International encyclopedia of unified science*, I, No. 4 (Chicago, 1939).

Bolinger, Dwight L., Intonation levels versus configuration, *Word* 7.199-210 (1951).

—, Visual Morphemes, *Language* 22.333-40 (1946).

Borgström, C. H., The Technique of linguistic descriptions, *Acta linguistica* 5.1-14 (1945-9).

Brown, Carleton F., The Author of the Pearl, considered in the light of theological opinions, *PMLA* 19.115-53 (1904).

Brunner, K., The Old English vowel phonemes, *English studies* 34.247-51 (1953).

Cargill, O. and M. Schlauch, The Pearl and its Jeweller, *PMLA* 43.105-23 (1928).

Chapman, C. O., Authorship of The Pearl, *PMLA* 47.346-53 (1932).

Chomsky, Noam, Review of C. F. Hockett, *A Manual of phonology* (1955), *IJAL* 23.223-34 (1957).

—, Review of Roman Jakobson and Morris Halle, *Fundamentals of Language* (The Hague, 1956), *IJAL* 23.234-42 (1957).

—, Morris Halle, and Fred Lukoff, On accent and juncture in English, *For Roman Jakobson*, ed. Morris Halle a.o., 65-80 (The Hague, 1956).

Coulton, G. G., In defense of 'Pearl', *MLR* 2.39-43 (1906).

Crossland, R. A., Graphic linguistics and its terminology, *Proceedings of the University of Durham Philosophical Society*, ser. B, 1.13-6 (1957).

Daunt, Marjorie, Some notes on Old English phonology, *Transactions of the Philological Society* 1952. 48-54 (London, 1953).

Edgerton, W. F., Ideograms in English writing, *Language* 17.148-9 (1941).

Ellis, Alexander J., On Early English Pronunciation, *EETS*, Extra S. 56, pt. 5 (London, 1889).

Facsimile Reproduction of Cotton MS. Nero A.x., introd. Sir Israel Gollancz, *EETS* 162 (London, 1923; repr. 1931).

Francis, W. Nelson, *The Structure of American English* (New York, 1958).

Gleason, H. A., *An Introduction to descriptive linguistics* (New York, 1955).

Gollancz, Sir Israel, ed., *Pearl* (London, 1891).

Gordon, E. V., ed., *Pearl* (Oxford, 1953).

Greg, W. W., A Bibliographical paradox, *The Library*, 4th ser., 13.188-91 (1933).

Guest, Edwin, *History of English rhythms*, ed. W. W. Skeat (London, 1882).

Hall, Robert, *A Theory of graphemics*, unpubl. paper (Ithaca, 1957).

Haugen, Einar and W. F. Twaddell, Facts and phonemics, *Language* 18.228-37 (1942).

Hockett, C. F., *A Course in modern linguistics* (New York, 1958).

—, *A Manual of phonology*, Indiana University Publications in Anthropology and Linguistics, Memoir 11, *IJAL* 21. no. 4 (October, 1955).

—, Review of John De Francis, *Nationalism and language reform in China* (Princeton, 1950), *Language* 27.439-45 (1951).

—, The Stressed syllabics of Old English, *Language* 35.575-97 (1959).

Horn, W., *Untersuchungen zur neuenglischen Lautgeschichte* (Strassburg, 1905).

Householder, Fred W. Jr., Accent, juncture, intonation and my grandfather's reader, *Word* 13.234-45 (1957).

—, Review of C. F. Hockett, *A Course in modern linguistics* (New York, 1958), *Language* 35.503-27 (1959).

Hulbert, J. R., The "West-Midland" of the Romances, *MP* 19.1-16 (August, 1921).

Jordan, Richard, *Handbuch der mittelenglischen Grammatik*, rev. H. Ch. Matthes (Heidelberg, 1934).

Kaiser, Rolf, Zur Geographie des mittelenglischen Wortschatzes, *Palaestra*, no. 205 (Berlin, 1937).

Kelley, Gerald, *Graphemic theory and its application to a Middle English text: Sir Gawain and the Green Knight*, unpubl. diss. (University of Wisconsin, 1956).

Knigge, Friederich, *Die Sprache des Dichters von Sir Gawain and the Green Knight, der sogenannten Early English Alliterative Poems und De Erkenwalde* (Marburg, 1886).

Kuhn, Sherman M. and Randolph Quirk, Some recent interpretations of Old English digraph spellings, *Language* 29.143-56 (1953).

—, The Old English digraphs: a reply, *Language* 31.390-401 (1955).

Kurath, Hans, The Binary interpretation of English vowels: a critique, *Language* 33.111-22 (1957).
—, The Loss of long consonants and the rise of voiced fricatives in Middle English, *Language* 32.435-45 (1956).
Luick, Karl, *Historische Grammatik der Englischen Sprache*, 2 vols. (I, 1921; II, 1940) (Leipzig, 1921-40).
—, *Untersuchungen zur englischen Lautgeschichte* (Strassburg, 1896).
Madden, Sir Frederick, ed., *Syr Gawayn and the Grene Knyȝt* (London, 1839).
Martinet, A., Neutralisation et archiphonème, *TCLP* 6.46-57 (1936).
McDavid, Raven I., Review of George L. Trager and Henry Lee Smith, *An Outline of English structure* (Norman, 1951), *JEGP* 52.387-91 (1953).
McIntosh, Angus, The Analysis of written Middle English, *Transactions of the Philological Society* 1956. 26-55.
Menner, R. J., ed., *Purity* (New Haven, 1920).
—, Sir Gawayn and the Green Knight and the West Midland, *PMLA* 37.503-26 (1922).
Middle English Dictionary, ed. Hans Kurath and Sherman M. Kuhn (E-F, 1952-5; A-C, 1956-9) (Ann Arbor, 1952-9).
Morris, Richard, ed., Early English alliterative poems, in the West-Midland dialect of the fourteenth century, *EETS* 1 (London, 1864).
—, ed., Sir Gawayne and the Green Knight: An Alliterative Romance-Poem, *EETS* 4 (London, 1864).
Mossé, Fernand, *Manuel de l'anglais du moyen âge des origines au XIVe siècle*, 2 vols (Paris, 1949).
Moulton, William G., The Stops and spirants of Early Germanic, *Language* 30.1-42 (1954).
Neilson, George, '*Huchown of the Awle Ryale*,' *The Alliterative poet. A Historical criticism of the fourteenth century poems ascribed to Sir Hew of Eglintoun* (Glasgow, 1902).
Oakden, J. P., *Alliterative poetry in Middle English, the dialectal and metrical survey* (Manchester, 1930).
—, The Scribal errors of the MS. Cotton Nero A.x., *The Library*, 4th ser., 14.356-8 (1933-4).
Orton, Harold, The Isolative treatment in living North-Midland dialects of OE *e* lengthened in open syllables in Middle English, *Leeds studies in English and kindred languages*, nos. 7-8.97-128 (1952).
Osgood, C. G., ed., *Pearl* (Boston, 1906).
Pike, Kenneth L., On the phonemic status of English diphthongs, *Language* 23.151-9 (1947).
Pope, M. K., *From Latin to modern French with especial consideration of Anglo-Norman* (Manchester, 1934).
Pulgram, Ernst, Phoneme and grapheme: a parallel, *Word* 7.15-20 (1951).
Samuels, M. L., The Study of Old English phonology, *Transactions of the Philological Society* 1952. 15-47 (London, 1953).
Saporta, Sol, Morph, morpheme, archimorpheme, *Word* 12.9-14 (1956).
Savage, W. L., *The Gawain poet* (Chapel Hill, 1956).
Schofield, W. H., Nature and fabric of The Pearl, *PMLA* 19.154-215 (1904).
Serjeantson, M. S., The Dialect of the West Midlands, *RES* 3.319-31 (July, 1927).

Sievers, Eduard, *An Old English grammar*, trans. and ed. Albert S. Cook, 2nd ed. (Boston, 1896).

Sledd, James, Review of George L. Trager and Henry Lee Smith, *An Outline of English structure* (Norman, 1951), *Language* 31.312-35 (1955).

Stetson, R. H., The Phoneme and the Grapheme, *Mélanges de Linguistique et de Philologie offerts à Jacq. van Ginneken*, 353-6 (Paris, 1937).

Stockwell, Robert P., *Chaucerian graphemics and phonemics: A study in historical methodology*, unpubl. diss. (University of Virginia, 1952).

—, The ME 'long close' and 'long open' vowels, *Texas studies in literature and language* 4.530-8 (1961).

Sundby, Bertil, Middle English overlapping of *v* and *w* and its phonemic significance, *Anglia* 74.438-44 (1956).

Swadesh, Morris, On the analysis of English syllabics, *Language* 23.137-50 (1947).

Tannenbaum, Samuel A., *The Handwriting of the Renaissance* (New York, 1930).

Ten Brink, B., *History of English literature*, 2 vols. in 3 (New York, 1889).

Thomas, M. C., *Gawain and The Green Knight* (Zürich, 1883).

Tolkien, J. R. R. and E. V. Gordon, eds., *Sir Gawain and The Green Knight* (Oxford, 1925).

Trager, George L. and Henry Lee Smith, Jr., *An Outline of English structure*, *SIL*, Occasional Papers 3 (Norman, 1951).

Trautmann, M., *Über Verfasser und Entstehungszeit einiger alliterierender Gedichte des Altenglischen* (Halle, 1876).

Uldall, H. J., Speech and writing, *Acta linguistica* 4.11-6 (1944).

Vachek, Josef, Some remarks on writing and phonetic transcription, *Acta linguistica* 5.86-93 (1945-9).

Whitehall, Harold, A Note on a north-west midland spelling, *PQ* 9.1-6 (1930).

Wright, Joseph, *The English dialect grammar* (Oxford, 1905).

—, and Elizabeth Mary Wright, *An Elementary historical new English grammar* (Oxford, 1924).

—, and Elizabeth Mary Wright, *An Elementary Middle English grammar*, 2nd ed. (Oxford, 1928).

Wyld, H. C., *A Short history of English*, 3rd ed. (London, 1927).

—, The Treatment of OE. $\bar{\breve{y}}$ in the dialects of the Midland and South Eastern counties in Middle English, *Englische Studien* 47.1-58 (1914).

Zachrisson, R. E., *Pronunciation of English vowels 1400-1700* (Göteborg, 1913).